YOGA

A Synthesis of Psychology and Metaphysics

YOGA

A Synthesis of Psychology and Metaphysics

SWAMI RAJARSHI MUNI

MOTILAL BANARSIDASS PUBLISHERS
PRIVATE LIMITED • DELHI

First Indian Edition: Delhi, 2006
Reprinted from "Yoga: The Ultimate Spiritual Path"
*Previously titled as **Awakening the Life Force***
Published by Llewellyn Publications St. Paul,
MN 55107 USA www.llewellyn.com

ISBN: 81-208-3098-9

MOTILAL BANARSIDASS
41 U.A. Bungalow Road, Jawahar Nagar, Delhi 110 007
8 Mahalaxmi Chamber, 22 Bhulabhai Desai Road, Mumbai 400 026
203 Royapettah High Road Mylapore, Chennai 600 004
236, 9th Main III Block, Jayanagar, Bangalore 560 011
Sanas Plaza, 1302 Baji Rao Road, Pune 411 002
8 Camac Street, Kolkata 700 017
Ashok Rajpath, Patna 800 004
Chowk, Varanasi 221 001

Printed in India
BY JAINENDRA PRAKASH JAIN AT SHRI JAINENDRA PRESS,
A-45 NARAINA, PHASE-I, NEW DELHI 110 028
AND PUBLISHED BY NARENDRA PRAKASH JAIN FOR
MOTILAL BANARSIDASS PUBLISHERS PRIVATE LIMITED,
BUNGALOW ROAD, DELHI 110 007

To the memory of my guru,
His Holiness Yogacharya Swami Shri Kripalvanand

Contents

Foreword

In the Western world, we are familiar with writings that document human history. Beneath human events, however, lies a silent, inscrutable history that often goes unheeded. It is the history of the soul's journey, the unfolding of consciousness manifesting its uniquely divine potential.

It is my special privilege to introduce Swami Shri Rajarshi Muni's *Yoga: The Ultimate Spiritual Path*, which offers a holistic picture of the soul's journey, a portrayal of the map and milestones leading to enlightenment. This work discusses the various systems of Indian philosophy and their cosmology, giving insight into the doctrine of karma, which is the cause of suffering and liberation, and describing the metaphysics of yoga with its varied states of consciousness.

In addition, the book contains appendices that describe in practical terms the stages of spiritual growth in which the physical, subtle, and causal levels of a yogi are progressively purified. Thus, *Yoga: The Ultimate Spiritual Path* provides a comprehensive overview of traditional yoga philosophy for the Western reader and at the same time creates a context that helps us place ourselves on the spiritual pathway, so that we may understand the deeper purpose for our existence.

This is no ordinary book of philosophy. It is not only the expression of direct realizations of spiritual principles by the ancient sages who practiced and lived them, but also a transmission from one who himself has spent years perfecting his spiritual practice. With more than twenty-five years of one-pointed practice of kundalini yoga and meditation, Rajarshi Muni has surrendered his life to that calling, writing and teaching from the depths of his inner wisdom.

Rajarshi Muni, my "Guru brother," studied and received instruction from Swami Shri Kripalvanandji, or Bapuji, as we lovingly referred to our guru and teacher, who was himself an accomplished master of yoga. Rajarshi Muni's years of practice and contemplation lend integrity to this systematic approach, which is based on the revelations arising out of his direct contact with yogic experience.

The beauty of *Yoga: The Ultimate Spiritual Path* is that the teaching is not a relic of the past; neither is it unattainable. A series of timeless universal truths are presented, accessible to anyone willing to enter the rigors of practice. Rajarshi Muni provides a bridge between East and West, defining the stages of the yogi's journey and depicting the systems of Indian thought that arose as a product of meditative experience. Unlike historical events or philosophies, universal truth never grows old or dies; it lies within us as potential, to be discovered through concentrated practice and experience.

This work provides a great service to everyone; I am privileged to recommend *Yoga: The Ultimate Spiritual Path*, which sets the stage for the entire cosmology and practice of yoga to emerge. Swami Shri Rajarshi Muni helps restore yoga to a place of prominence, reminding us, through his careful and articulate map of consciousness, of the need for a spiritual approach to the causes of human suffering.

Yogi Amrit Desai

[Both Swami Rajarshi Muni and Yogi Amrit Desai are disciples of the same guru, the late Swami Kripalvanand. Swami Rajarshi Muni stayed in India devoting his life to the persistent practice of yoga. Yogi Amrit Desai chose to move to the United States in 1960 and has taught kripalu yoga to innumerable students, conducting lectures, workshops, and retreats in the United States, Canada, Europe, and several other countries. Kripalu yoga is a unique approach to hatha yoga developed to suit westerners. It is a systematic means of integrating body, mind, and emotions through gentle yoga postures and dynamic meditative practice. It offers a new approach to the art of healthy and harmonious living in tune with one's true inner nature. Yogi Amrit Desai is the founder of the Kripalu Ashram near Philadelphia (1970) and Kripalu Center, Lennox, Massachusetts (1982). Both institutions offer year-round programs related to yoga and also services for holistic living and medical as well as psychological consultations.]

Preface

The value of any spiritual discipline can be measured by the degree to which it is capable of transforming not only one's way of life but also one's personality. In the current century humanity pursues the physical sciences so as to master matter, but only the future will reveal whether we become matter's master or slaves to technological convenience. Perhaps we will end up becoming more technologically sophisticated, but lack the personal inner resources necessary to actualize our inherent divinity.

Today, as much as ever, we stand in need of a spiritual discipline that enables us to understand and harmoniously master the workings of the human psyche. Yoga is such a system. Developed by the ancient sages, even today it provides a cogent means for sincere spiritual seekers to transcend all temporal limitations and become established in our own blissful inner nature.

In the present day nearly everyone, in the West as well as in the East, is familiar at least with the word *yoga* if not with its meaning. Despite the fact that the world market is flooded with works on the subject, with new books coming out every year, there are very few contemporary authors who have explained the term as it really is.

The tragicomic result of this trend is the prevalent popular misconception of yoga as consisting only of physical exercises, mental concentration techniques, energy mastery exercises, and other similar methods. Such techniques are effective in their own way for promoting physical, mental, and emotional well-being, but they are not the yoga referred to in the classical texts; only preliminary preparations for the practice of yoga.

Part of the problem is that modern authors are writing for readers who are scientifically oriented, with logical parameters for the understanding and acceptance of new ideas and concepts. They require proof or evidence and seek the "whys and wherefores" of any concept before considering its viability.

Such an attitude is both laudable and intellectually healthy. But when carried to the extreme, it often entails a dogmatic rejection out of hand of any evidence not quantifiable by modern empirical methods.

Contemporary authors are thus overly sensitive to the possibility of negative reactions from their readers and limit themselves to presenting only those truths that are palatable to modern understanding. In so doing they not only misrepresent yoga, but starve their readers of real spiritual knowledge. A genuine author need not "sugarcoat" or dilute the truths narrated by the ancient sages. Nor need the author assume the onus of needing to prove to modern minds concepts not yet quantifiable by modern science.

Despite the strides made in experimental psychology, neurology, artificial intelligence, and related disciplines in the last three decades, the functioning and properties of the human psyche still remain a largely grey area about which relatively little is really known. For this reason the bulk of the concepts and dynamics contained within yogic philosophy remain as yet unquantifiable by current empirical methods.

As any author who is also a practicing yogi will know, most yogic experiences can at present only be quantified by special corroborative techniques that have been a part of yoga practice for millennia. So an author who has personally experienced the power and profundity of the truths expounded by the ancient sages need not be shy in presenting these same truths to contemporary audiences. Of course they should be presented in a way most suitable to modern understanding, but without sacrificing an iota of truth.

At present, the only way of proving or disproving the statements made by sages and yogis of yore is to experiment with the methods they taught for realizing those self-same statements. Any genuine seeker who does so will realize through inner experience the validity of experiments initially verified thousands of years ago and minutely described in the ancient texts by the classical sage-scientists.

In this book I have tried to present without distortion the philosophy and metaphysics of yoga as taught by the ancient sages. The intention here is to provide a work of straightforward truth on the subject for the benefit of sincere spiritual seekers who have had to make do with the vast body of obscure literature that is at present the only available source of information on this illuminating science.

It must be kept in mind throughout that this work primarily addresses the philosophy and metaphysics of yoga, and, as such, is not a guide to applied yoga. Furthermore, the usefulness and utility of any work on applied yoga is severely curtailed by the traditional stricture that certain basic techniques in yogic practice are closely guarded secrets that can only be verbally transmitted by an experienced guru (preceptor) to an aspirant who has reached the stage where the student can make use of them.

Let it suffice to say that the nature of yogic practice is such that any genuine aspirant desirous of attaining the higher levels of consciousness described in the text should proceed only under the guidance of an experienced guru if he or she wishes to surmount the obstacles present in the early stages of yogic practice.

Rajarshi Muni

Acknowledgments

I offer my gratitude to almighty God for providing me with this opportunity and with the understanding necessary to present this work for the benefit of aspiring seekers.

I wish to thank all those who have offered their help in the creation of this book: Yogi Amrit Desai, for writing the foreword; Mr. Nanubhai Amin for his introduction; Kimberly Nightingale (repackaging editor at Llewellyn Publications) for putting in a lot of energy, spirit, and intelligence in editing and designing this second edition afresh; Shivananda (Thomas Amelio) for his editing help with the appendices; and finally Mr. Fateh Singh Jasol and Mrs. Sita Jasol for responding to all queries from the publisher and providing their services for proofreading. May God bless all of them.

Rajarshi Muni

Introduction

Rarely, very rarely, will you find someone like Rajarshi Muni who can match a remarkably prodigious, long-term practice of the highest yoga with equally accomplished scholarship. With that unique blend of time-tested experience, intelligence, and skill, he has produced this masterful work.

Above all else, he is a yogi. After seventeen years of exceptional practice of the willful disciplines of yoga, he embarked on the "spontaneous" path of yoga, as described in this book. He has continued for twenty-five years, eight to ten hours a day: In this *sadhana,* or spiritual practice, the body and mind are fully surrendered to the awakened vital force. This sadhana is intense, fascinating, blissful, and sometimes painful. It is to this highest spiritual purification process that the sages are referring when they speak of yoga in the ancient scriptures of India.

To come across anyone doing this sadhana regularly is highly unusual. To meet someone who practices it with such singular dedication, for such long hours daily, and over a span of a quarter century, is quite awesome! He is still going strong. As a result of this practice, Rajarshi Muni has reached certain yogic stages described in the ancient scriptures. They are unmistakably happening within his body and mind. When normal scholars come across such descriptions, they are often dismissed as symbolic or, if the scholar is more objective, incomprehensible.

When a yogi discovers that certain changes in his body, perceptions, and mind are described in a scripture, in often minute detail and even in the same sequence as in his personal experience, his faith in the truth of the entire scripture deepens greatly. Also, it is not surprising that in a yogi as experienced as Rajarshi Muni, there is an awakened inner sight that enables him intuitively to understand abstruse scriptural truths incomprehensible to most. It is a great blessing that this book, which clearly presents the highest yoga as taught by the ancient scriptures, is now being offered by one as supremely qualified as Rajarshi Muni.

Shri Yashavantsinh D. Jadeja, later to be known as Rajarshi Muni, was born February 11, 1931, in Porbandar, India. Throughout his school and college days he was a bright and active student as well as a prize-winning athlete in several sports. He received his B.A. with honors from Bombay University, and his M.A. in Sociology from Poona University.

He served in the government of India between 1954 and 1970. In the beginning he became an executive officer, and for much of the above period he was deputy director in charge of training executive officers in four states of western India. In addition to his other duties, he also established a fine reputation as a top researcher. His research papers in sociology, education, public administration, social work, and other areas were published in many professional journals of repute. In 1969, he became deputy director of research under the eminent Indian sociologist, Dr. I. P. Desai.

From a young age, Yashavantsinh had strong spiritual inclinations. In 1951, during his college days, he began faithfully practicing yoga postures and breathing exercises for hours, twice daily. With unfailing diligence, he never missed even one session in the next seventeen years. His intense practice and study of yoga disciplines continued, and in 1969 he met his guru, Swami Shri Kripalvanandji, also known as Kripalu. The swami helped his young disciple understand the mysteries and knowledge of yoga.

Kripalu wrote many books on yoga before leaving his mortal frame in 1981. His remarkable life story will be related in an upcoming book by Rajarshi Muni. It was Swami Kripalu who initiated Yashavantsinh into certain secrets of "spontaneous" yoga sadhana that must be passed on directly from guru to disciple. In order to give his entire life and full-time energy to the pursuit of the highest liberation, Yashavantsinh renounced all worldly responsibilities and became a *sannyasi,* or renunciate, on February 19, 1971. At that time he received the monastic name Rajarshi Muni, which means "Royal Sage."

Rajarshi Muni has written several books, mostly in Gujarati, that succinctly express and explain the philosophy of yoga as revealed by the ancient scriptures and his own intensive yoga sadhana. In these works, he vividly describes yoga exercises and experiences in a scientific manner. They are also used as guides in the training seminars conducted at Shri Lakulish Yoga Institute in Kayavarohan, India. Rajarshi

Muni has designed the syllabus for the courses offered there.

Despite his great yogic attainments, Rajarshi Muni humbly describes himself as a "practitioner," or *sadhak,* until he reaches, in this life or another, final liberation, which manifests as the immortal, unlimited divine body described in this book. While humble, he is also confident about what his experience, research, and insight communicate to him as the truth. Though possessed of a highly scientific mind, he is not interested in watering down or softening the higher truths of yoga because they might be hard to swallow or do not necessarily meet the empirical requirements of modern physical sciences.

Most spiritual systems teach that this physical world is created and sustained by a higher, subtler, nonphysical consciousness. The sages taught that, just as the physical world has its own structure, constituents, scientific laws, and principles, so also does the subtle cosmos, which is normally unperceived by most of humanity.

Scientific knowledge of the physical world is discovered through the means of the mind, five senses, and manufactured instruments. The fully liberated sages, or *siddhas,* who composed the ancient scriptures, possessed supersensory powers that enabled them to perceive the workings of both the physical and nonphysical worlds, and beyond. (These abilities are described in Section III of Patanjali's Yoga Sutras.)

For a seeker, it is not enough just to practice the disciplines of yoga; philosophical understanding is necessary. It is important that we start with at least an intellectual comprehensive overview of what the physical and subtle cosmos is: its nature, origin, and laws. We can then understand more easily where we fit in, how we came to be where we are, and how we can, if we are so moved, achieve truly unlimited freedom that includes not only the soul, but the body as well.

By understanding the wisdom of those who have successfully treaded the path before us, a genuine seeker can save much precious time and energy by avoiding fruitless or frustrating detours. In this regard, Rajarshi Muni has done a great service to seekers by synthesizing truths from the greatest yogic scriptures through his personal experiences attained by very rigorous yoga sadhana.

This treatise brings out yoga in its pristine form. The constant endeavor of spiritual seekers is to achieve the final stage of perfection in which the individual self merges into the universal self through the process of yoga, or union. The author clearly maps out this process of growing, unfolding, and purifying, which culminates in the seeker becoming a perfect being with an eternal divine body, free from disease or decay, and a cosmically vast consciousness free from the bondage of time and space.

This book traces the origin and history of yoga philosophy and its significance as a unifying link among the six principal philosophical systems of India. It clearly describes the metaphysics of yoga, bondage in the form of afflictions, *karma*, and the resultant cycles of birth and rebirth. The nature of time and space is also explained. It establishes yoga as both a philosophy and science with its precepts and practical stages of attaining liberation.

As a unified discipline, yoga aims at physical, mental, and spiritual development step by step. It improves physical health and resilience, harmonizes thought and emotion, and awakens supersensory abilities. Yoga purifies each level of the whole being—physical, mental, and subtle—systematically. Thus the seeker is prepared for eventual liberation, the final state of eternal, unlimited freedom, and immortal physical perfection.

This work, I am sure, will serve as a guiding light for genuine sadhaks, whatever goal they set forth on the path of self-realization.

Nanubhai Amin

[Nanubhai Amin was a renowned Indian scientist and industrialist who received awards in the United States and India for his scientific and humanitarian achievements. Nanubhai Amin graduated in electrical engineering from the Massachusetts Institute of Technology in 1942. He did his postgraduate studies in electrical engineering at Cornell University in 1943. In 1985 he was given the Energy for Mankind Award by the Global Energy Society for Eradication of Poverty and Hunger. Nanubhai Amin had a deep abiding interest in the development of renewable sources of energy, technical education, and the preservation of wildlife and the environment. His advice was sought by several governments and national bodies in these areas. He was also a yoga sadhak and scriptural scholar. He served as President of Life Mission, a public charitable trust set up by the author to serve the community and spread the message of yoga and abiding moral and spiritual values. Nanubhai Amin passed away in March 1999 after a lifetime of outstanding accomplishment and service to the community.]

chapter one

General Concept of Yoga

The word *yoga* derives from the Sanskrit root *yuj* meaning to unite, to join, to harness, to yoke, to contact, or to connect. Yoga means union, joining, harnessing, yoking, contact, or connection. It is the union between the individual self and the universal self. It is the joining of a healthy body and a disciplined mind for spiritual development. It is the harnessing of one's own underlying nature as well as wider natural forces from which one has emerged. It is the yoking together of the body, mind, and spirit through self-discipline. It is the contact with the element that is higher than the highest of the known elements, through the process of absorption or dissolution. It is establishing oneness between the finite and the infinite, between the microcosm and the macrocosm, between the inner being and the supreme being. Such union or oneness is experienced only when a higher state of consciousness is reached through the spiritual effort of yoga. When the duality of matter and mind is totally dissolved into the original source, spirit, the supreme goal of yoga, is achieved. In order to experience eternal bliss, the conscious self should merge into the divine superconscious self which gives rise to it. That transcendent self is beyond all forms and names, beyond the cycles of births and deaths, beyond the notions of bondage and release, and beyond even the concepts of time and space. There is *Brahman* (ultimate reality), which is *advaita* (nondual), *eka* (one-without-a-second), *sanatana* or *nitya* (eternal), *avikari* (changeless), *sarvagata* (all-pervading), *achala* (unshakable), *sthanu* (stable), *gunatita* (transcendental), and *ananta* (infinite).

Yoga Is a Gift from the Sages

In India from time immemorial, many great sages devoted their entire lives to studying the secrets of human nature and existence. They pursued this search with indefatigable striving and iron endurance. They completely withdrew themselves from the commotions of the world and concentrated all their efforts solely upon this pursuit. Ultimately, their dedicated efforts bore fruit. They discovered the deepest secrets of life and the mysteries of being. They discovered a hiddenmost path leading upward to freedom and emancipation. Collectively they named it yoga.

Subsequently, out of pity for suffering humankind, they systematized this yoga in the form of a discipline with definite techniques. Whosoever applies them properly and in earnest can enter bliss and reach the goal of liberation. This great gift of the ancient Indian sages, yoga, is passed on to society in continuous traditional succession so that everyone may benefit.

The great Indian sages of the past dedicated their lives in search of the truth. Incidentally, they tried to save the world from misery, apart from reaching perfection themselves. Just as a person with sight can lead a blind person along the proper path, in the same way, a realized yogi can lead other human beings along the right spiritual path. In the Bhagavad Gita, Lord Krishna enjoins Arjuna to practice yoga not only for the sake of his own spiritual uplift but also out of consideration for the world order and *loka sangraha* (conservation of society). He says, "Whatever is done by a great person, the very same is followed by the ordinary ones. Whatever standards are set up by him, the common people adhere to them." (III:21) The great sages worked out the system of yoga in order to make it possible for every person with genuine aspiration to attain the self-appointed goal of liberation.

Yoga Is Both Philosophy and Science

Yoga is the greatest philosophy of India. It deals with the mysteries of life as well as of the universe. It deals especially with those aspects of life and universe that are beyond the comprehension of normal human intellect. Its doctrines are based on spiritual experiences, and so they appeal more to intuitive discrimination rather than to intellectual understanding.

These doctrines are of a profound nature since they deal with a very wide range of transcendental experiences. They have stood the test of time, since they have proven to be in conformity with the facts of experience. These doctrines are not mere dogmas but are scientific truths and those who have experimented with them have invariably borne witness to their practicability.

Yoga is not a mere theoretical philosophy but a practical discipline based on personal spiritual experiences. It is the most ancient science of spiritual self-development, based on the laws governing the natural forces and the higher life. It is a science that is as perfect as it is exact in its methods and techniques. It not only lays down the philosophical precepts, but also teaches the practical means by which a human being can attain salvation. It is a profound system of spiritual efforts that can be practiced through definite procedures of physical and mental mortifications with positive results at each stage. Yoga is at once a unified philosophy and science.

Yoga Is Not a Religion

Yoga is neither a religion by itself nor part of any other religious system. In fact, it is around the practice of yoga that the great religions of the world have developed, be it Hinduism, Buddhism, Jainism, Christianity, Muslim, Zoroastrianism, Confucianism, Taoism, or any other religion. Great persons of all these religions (call them yogis, mystics, sufis, or saints) have obtained glimpses of spiritual experiences through arduous training and discipline that basically resembles yoga. That is why the basis of all religious faiths of the world is common. All religious teachers have expressed in their own language and words that the soul is immortal and it emerges from some source higher and greater than itself. We may call this divine source to be Brahman, Ishvara, God, Allah, supreme being, universal spirit, divine principle, ultimate reality, highest truth, or give it any other name. But all religions believe that the individual soul belongs to this divine source that can be realized by the former, and that such realization can bring eternal bliss and emancipation. What such realized souls speak arises from that divine source that is beyond the intellectual comprehension of ordinary human beings. Their words are uttered by the divine source itself. They become the driving forces of nations. The knowledge revealed by them is yoga of one sort or the other. All teachings of the great masters of different religions are esoterically similar, leading toward one and the same truth.

Yoga is universal and a yogi is not necessarily bound to any particular religious faith. The yogi may belong to any religion if he or she so chooses or the yogi may not accept any religious faith at all. The science of yoga is much older and higher than any religion. No religious philosophy or dogma can give to the human being knowledge about his or her true self or offer salvation. That can be provided only by a practical and higher spiritual discipline like yoga.

It is true that India has been the home of yoga, but that does not mean that yogic practice is the monopoly of Indians only. Anyone belonging to any other nation or race and following any religion has a right to practice it, because yoga has a much broader appeal than nationality, race, or religion. It does not bind a person to specific dogmas or notions leading to prejudices but guides a person to follow an independent, individualized path to self-discovery. It permits an individual to establish a relationship with the divine in his or her own chosen manner. That yoga discipline, even today, provides practical as well as sublime teachings to people of all religions and cultures throughout the world is itself the greatest proof of its broad appeal and universality.

Emphasis of Yoga

Indian yogis, since early history, have discovered the Brahman (ultimate reality) and its independent entity, *atman* (individual spirit), both of them being identical, eternal, imperishable, changeless, beyond time and space, and also beyond the veiling net of causality and the dominion of the physical eyes. Yogis have mainly explored not the visible world, which belongs to the sphere of time, space, and change, but to the hidden forces of life underlying the conscious human personality and the physical frame. Yoga philosophy has always provided information about metaphysical principles, ethical values, and moral standards, but its primary goal is to bring about a complete transformation of human nature in a spiritual manner. Its chief aim has been not merely a renovation of intellectual understanding, but also a radical change of heart at the core of human existence. Its emphasis has been not on the outer and tangible spheres leading to bondage and limitation but on the inner and intangible spheres leading to freedom and perfection. Yoga envisages a sort of alchemical transformation or a total conversion of the bound soul into the released self, bringing an end to the soul's rounds of births and deaths.

Yoga philosophy propounds that the bound human soul is reflected as an animating principle in the gross human physique. In the same manner, the veiled divine spirit is reflected in the entire universe. A human being can transcend the gross body and realize the true nature of self through the techniques of yoga. Similarly, one can also transcend gross creation and realize God or Brahman through yoga. As the human body is the vehicle or instrument for self-realization, so also creation is the instrument for God-realization. Yoga is the ladder through which a person reaches God.

Approach of Yoga

Yoga philosophy views an individual person as a whole being that includes his or her physical, mental, intellectual, emotional, and spiritual nature. Its view of a human being is much grander than that of any other philosophy since it tries to see a person beyond the limits of time and space. It views the entire being and not just a few of his or her aspects. The final conception is that of a perfect being with perfect manifestation in the body, a divine human. Yoga is a process of growing, unfolding, and becoming aware or conscious as a whole, and not partially, so as to reach perfection: the psychological interpretation embraces the intermediary objective, while the spiritual interpretation formulates the lofty objective of liberation, which is the final goal of yoga.

Yogic discipline works up gradually through its various techniques to unfold and develop all the forces that are existent in a human being. Such growth begins at the gross level or the physical plane and then proceeds slowly toward the subtler levels, finally ending in the spiritual plane. Of course, such transformation occurs very slowly and usually continues for many years before one realizes his or her inner self.

The achievement of the final stage of perfection in which an individual self merges into or becomes one with the universal self is extremely difficult. It remains beyond the reach of even many advanced yogis. Very few can reach the final stage of perfection after passing through the various planes below that highest level. Only a few exceptional yogis, worthy by their own merits, can attain such a level of perfection. For most ordinary human beings it remains beyond conception, let alone an attainable experience.

The approach of yoga is to unfold the real nature of the self by bringing out all the best from within and to lead a finite human being toward the infinity. Yogic discipline enables one to differentiate between the ego and the true self through proper discrimination and right knowledge. Such discrimination and knowledge spontaneously dawn upon a person through the practice of yoga. They are born out of actual spiritual experiences.

On the other hand, the knowledge acquired by reading books or hearing discourses is dry understanding derived through the psychomental intellect. It is devoid of experience and is likely to be wrong at times. Moreover, such acquired knowledge depends upon one's memory and is often forgotten after a lapse of time and certainly lost after death. Contrary to this, real knowledge born out of yogic experiences is always true, and being transcendent (beyond the scope of intellect and memory), it can never be forgotten. Even the catastrophe of death cannot destroy it. Once it dawns upon a soul, it becomes eternally enjoined with that soul even if there is a rebirth.

The chief approach of yoga is that it envisages the fuller exploitation of one's entire inner resources. As such, yogic discipline is an inward journey not dependent on any kind of outer aid. Its external techniques (only so-called) are fully concerned with the body and partly with the mind, while its internal techniques are concerned partly with the mind and fully with the spirit. These external and internal techniques together constitute the scientific system of yoga, which is designed to bring about a complete and harmonious development of the three-fold aspects of a human being—matter, mind, and spirit. Yoga does not recognize the body, mind, and spirit as separate entities but as a trinity that covers all areas of human existence under a single fold. It approaches each unrealized area of human nature and expands human consciousness beyond the gross plane of experience. It makes one fully aware and inwardly conscious about one's whole being through experiences on the spiritual plane.

Yoga should not be misunderstood only as a physical discipline or merely as a mental discipline, or even as a purely spiritual discipline. It is a unified system of all three. Beginning with physical prowess at the gross level, a student of yoga progresses toward the subtler phases of mental and spiritual development. Because of such a unified approach, yoga is frequently described as a process of harmonizing the body, mind, and spirit.

Objectives of Yoga

The objectives of yoga can be interpreted in physical, psychological, as well as spiritual ways because it deals with body, mind, and spirit. The physical interpretation is connected with the preliminary objective of yoga, the psychological interpretation embraces the intermediary objective, while the spiritual interpretation formulates the highest objective.

There are several levels of development along the path of yoga. An aspirant has to attain these levels in turn and step by step. Starting from the lowest level, he or she has to proceed gradually, mastering the preliminary and intermediate levels and finally reaching the highest one. As a person masters one level, he or she shifts goals to the next level. Moreover, as the aspirant approaches a particular level, he or she also finds the necessary means to cover the distance to the next higher level.

During such step-by-step advancement, a person goes on fixing higher and higher objectives for him or herself, from the preliminary to the intermediary, and from the intermediary to the final objective. In this manner, he or she goes on shifting objectives, each time focusing on a different but quite modest objective that may remain within grasp. One does not suddenly jump to a lofty objective that may be beyond reach for the time being. One proceeds gradually, level by level, until finally the distant goal of liberation is reached.

The preliminary objective of yoga is to improve body health and physical abilities. It is through physical soundness and stability that mental prowess can be achieved. Thereafter, the intermediary objective of yoga is to bring a greater degree of harmony between one's thoughts, emotions, desires, aims, motives, reasoning, etc. Through that coalescence it is possible to discover the hidden potentials of the mind. It is by way of unfolding potential mental powers that one can become aware of the inner spirit.

To whatever degree one may develop physical abilities and mental powers, one remains incomplete without spiritual growth. It is through spiritual development that a person realizes one's whole being and becomes perfect. Such spiritual growth is the ultimate objective of yoga. In order to attain the final goal of yoga, one first has to realize the inner spirit and then to merge the atman (individual spirit) with the Brahman (universal spirit), while still in this body. Thus it can be said that the overall objective of yoga is to aid and guide a person to transcend one's temporal limitations and to break the barriers that separate one's individual self from the universal self.

Access to Yoga

We have seen that the preliminary objective of yoga is the purification of the body and the intermediate objective is the purging of mental impurities. When both the body and the mind are freed from defilements, consciousness becomes clear and pure. The inner spirit is reflected without any distortion. It means that the highest objective of self-realization is facilitated by the external as well as internal purity attained during the preliminary and the intermediate stages.

But it is by no means easy to attain this. One may succeed in arriving at it after many lives. One has to go through spiritual mortifications in many previous lives as prior preparation for the final birth. In Bhagavad Gita, Lord Krishna says, "After journeying through many cycles of birth, the enlightened one reaches me with the conviction that everything is *vasudeva* (myself), but it is exceedingly rare to find such an exalted person." (VII:19) It may take thousands of years and may require many births to attain perfect evolution of the soul and to reach the final goal of yoga.

One has to strive hard and pay a very high price for attaining that lofty objective. One must undergo arduous asceticism for many years, living a life of renunciation, practicing celibacy and moderation in diet, observing silence and residing in seclusion. Such a difficult path obviously cannot be within the reach of every person. It certainly is not for an average person. Only those who are above average stand a chance of getting access to the path of yoga. And it will really be a great fortune for any of them to attain the final goal of yoga. Of those who strive for the final target, only a few fortunate ones succeed. In Bhagavad Gita, Lord Krishna also says, "Among thousands of persons, hardly one strives to achieve the goal of perfection; and even of those who strive, one hardly knows me in reality." (VII:3)

The final objective of yoga or liberation is not such an ordinary thing for which everyone can aspire. Thousands of aspirants grope along to cross the ocean of existence, yet scarcely anyone succeeds in reaching the other shore. Of those aspirants who take to the practice of yoga in the present times, hardly anyone truly learns to live by the arduous rules and discipline.

Aspirants of Yoga

It is no doubt true that the path of yoga is very difficult. None is barred, however, from practicing it. One should only be careful in fixing the goal to be achieved. An aspirant should recognize his or her own shortcomings and limitations, but with sincerity of effort, should strive persistently to achieve a modest goal. He or she should choose a goal that is really attainable. It may be a preliminary or intermediary goal; it does not matter so far as even these lead to physical health and the development of mental abilities.

Those aspirants who have not yet overcome the appetites, passions, vanity, arrogance, selfishness, greed, cravings, etc., are not fit to receive higher spiritual experiences. They should not fix higher spiritual goals for themselves. They should be modest in fixing their goal and at the same time should sincerely try to avoid their shortcomings if they genuinely intend to go further along the path of yoga.

A true aspirant has to conform strictly with all the rules set down by yoga discipline. The student should have *shraddha,* full faith that the truth can be discovered through the techniques of yoga. The aspirant should have *mumukshutva,* earnest longing for attaining freedom from the bondage of worldly existence. He or she should have *viveka,* discriminating insight to differentiate between what is permanent and real and what is transient and illusory. The pupil should have *vairagya,* readiness to renounce the worldly way of life, or say, indifference to worldly enjoyments. The aspirant should possess *shat-sampatti* (treasure of six precious virtues), *shama* (pacification of mind and passions), *dama* (self-restraint or subjugation of senses), *uparati* (withdrawal from the outer world), *titiksa* (endurance), *shraddha* (perfect faith), and *samadhana* (composure of mind). Such an aspirant is truly qualified to tread upon the higher spiritual path of yoga.

Guidance and Self-effort in Yoga

The path of yoga is rigorous, but there are experienced yogis or gurus who have achieved higher spiritual levels and can guide others. Such gurus have themselves learned yoga through hard training and arduous discipline. A real guru (preceptor) is one who has experienced the real nature of his or her own self and attuned him or herself with God or universal self. Such a person always experiences oneness with all and loves all without discrimination. He or she abides serene in the uninterrupted stillness and superconsciousness. This person has achieved the highest goal of yoga.

According to ancient tradition, and even today in India, the knowledge of yoga is passed on from a guru to a disciple. But in ancient times, this sacred knowledge was never revealed to an undeserving person. Moreover, the teaching of yoga was never made a business. Yoga was not a commodity for sale as it is at present. In ancient times a guru gave this knowledge only to a worthy disciple as a sacred gift, expecting nothing in return. The guru also sincerely wished that the disciple would excel the guru in prowess. Such was the nobility and goodness on the part of a guru in ancient times. The disciple also revered the guru sincerely and intensely. The aspirant received the sacred knowledge of yoga from the guru as a great blessing. Then the student regularly applied the practice of yoga. The aspirant always remained vigilant and practiced without any lapse or laziness, surrendering everything, including the aspirant's own self, at the holy feet of the guru without reservation. Such model relationships existed between guru and *shishya* (disciple). But this also is a rare thing in present times.

The basic tenet of yoga discipline is that every individual is responsible for his or her own liberation. One has to climb the ladder of yoga step by step reaching each successive level by one's own efforts. In the Bhagavad Gita, Lord Krishna also says, "One should raise himself by his own self; he should not cause his self to degrade. For, the self alone is the benefactor of the self and the self is the enemy of the self." (VI:5)

Though in the initial stages one has the need for a guru to show the ladder of yoga and the technique of climbing it, the role of self-effort cannot be underrated. The guidance from a guru, in subsequent stages, makes the progress smooth and easy and also saves time and energy, no doubt; but it is entirely left to the pupil to make efforts to attain the goal. One can help a child practice walking by providing support, but it should be left entirely to the child's own effort to learn walking. In the same manner, a guru can set the truth before a pupil and also give directions on how to reach it, but it remains entirely the student's responsibility to strive and train in conformity with the guru's teachings.

A guru may inspire a pupil to know the truth and guide the pupil toward the path of yoga, but the guru cannot compel the aspirant to walk or to walk on the right track. If the pupil falls short in self-efforts or loses interest halfway or even goes astray, the student will suffer and the guru should not be blamed for that. On the other hand, if the pupil is completely receptive and possesses a genuine desire to know the truth, then the pupil is bound to make efforts with all his heart to reach the set goal. Such a pupil is a true seeker who will succeed.

chapter two

Yoga in the Context of Time and Space

In Indian philosophy it is said that none can meddle with *daiva* (fate or destiny) except a yogi. All ordinary beings must accept daiva and its unalterable decree. No one is strong enough to defend against it. Often it is considered to be an arm of divinity since it controls all beings and events. It cannot be brought down to the scale of ordinary human understanding or imagination.

This daiva is closely related to the other two determinative forces of the universe, *desha* or *sthala* (space) and *kala* (time). The mysterious force of daiva (destiny) drives forward the evolutionary process, working out changes in the mundane world that is engulfed in the immense space and struggle for existence through the tides of time. A human being is but an infinitesimal creature against the vast and mighty background of the stellar universe. He or she is sometimes tossed to shoot up like a rocket and at other times is pulled down to fall like a meteor through the ceaseless play of daiva. With a single stroke of daiva, a prince may become a pauper and vice-versa. Daiva operates in cycles of ups and downs, expansions and contractions.

But this daiva is neither divine nor devilish in itself. It is designed by human beings themselves by way of their desires and deeds in former existences. A person mixes up the ingredients to prepare his or her own future. That is why a person becomes helpless against daiva when it begins to operate in accordance with the metaphysical laws of nature upon which it is based. Daiva is not a pessimistic or fatalistic concept evolved out of despair, but is based on the subtle laws of cause and effect operating on the metaphysical level. Ordinary human beings with awareness of only the physical plane cannot grasp the functioning of daiva. It can be understood only by spiritually advanced persons. In the transcendent state of a perfected yogi, predetermined destiny begins to recede and finally a yogi is lifted beyond the force of daiva. For the yogi, all differentiations of time and space vanish; time is not finite and space is not reality. The only reality for the yogi is transcendent essence, or Brahman.

Since yoga is the discipline leading to the realization of the eternal and the transcendental Brahman, it should be viewed with the background of eternal time and transcendent existence. The divisions of time into past, present, and future are only transitory and not permanent. They only indicate the processes of becoming and vanishing. They exclude and contradict each other. They are secondary characters as compared to eternal time. Similarly, all space-locations belong to the phenomenal sphere and the realm of subjective experience. They manifest out of the interplay of the *gunas* (constituent qualities) of *prakriti* (nature), resulting in the pairing of opposites that are transient in nature. Phenomenology and space-locations also are secondary characters as compared to transcendent existence. Yoga should be viewed beyond the limits of past, present, and future and the finiteness of phenomenality and space-locations. It should be understood against the infinite background of eternal time and transcendent existence.

Yet in order to comprehend the true nature of eternal transcendent essence, it is first necessary for our clouded minds to know the illusory nature of time divisions and space-locations and shatter our existing concepts of time and space experiences. Unless we do this, they will prove to be impediments in comprehending the eternal and transcendent essence. First, one must try to understand the measure and process of time and then proceed to study the cosmological evolution as described in ancient Indian scripture.

Measures of Cosmic Time

According to the ancient Indian *Puranas* (ancient classical works),.cosmic time is measured in terms of either *yugas* (aeons or ages) or *manvantaras* (periods of *manu*). Manu is the first human, or the progenitor of the human race. The yugas are of four types, each of a different duration. They are, as follows:

1. *Krita* or *satya yuga* 1,728,000 years
2. *Treta yuga* 1,296,000 years
3. *Dvapara yuga* 864,000 years
4. *Kali yuga* 432,000 years

The duration of dvapara is twice that of kali yuga. The durations of treta and satya yugas are three and four times that of kali yuga, respectively. Along with the regularly decreasing period of these yugas, there is supposed to be a corresponding physical and moral deterioration of the people living during each of them. Satya yuga is thus considered to be the "golden age," treta as the "silver age," Dvapara as the "copper age," and kali (our present yuga) as the "iron age."

One complete cycle of these four yugas constitutes one *mahayuga* or *paryaya* having the duration of 4.32 million years. One thousand such mahayugas equals a single day of *Brahma* (Lord, the creator), whose night is also equally as long. According to manvantara calculation, fourteen periods of manu comprise one day of Brahma. Each period of manu consists of nearly seventy-one mahayugas or paryayas, or 306.72 million years. Between two periods of manu , and at the beginning as well as the end of Brahma's day, there is supposed to be a joining interval of 1,728,000 years each. Thus the duration of Brahma's day is 4,320 million years, which is also called *kalpa.*

Methods of Calculating Time

In Indian Puranic literature, one encounters three different methods of calculating time. The first is based on the calculations of yugas (aeons), the second is based on the calculations of manvantaras (periods of manu s), and the third is based on changes in the position of the stellar constellation known as Saptarshi (Great Bear). The table of calculations on page 14 is used to calculate time from a fraction of a second to years, aeons, and a Brahma's day.

Yuga System Timetable

1	*Nimesa,* or blink	=		0.088 seconds
18	Nimeshas	=	1	Kashtha (1.6 seconds)
2.5	*Kashthas*	=	1	Shvasa or breath (4 seconds)
6	*Shvasas*	=	1	Pala (24 seconds)
2	*Palas*	=	1	Kala (48 seconds)
30	Kalas	=	1	Ghati (24 minutes)
2	*Ghatis*	=	1	Muhurta (48 minutes)
30	Muhurtas	=	1	full day (24 hours)
15	full days	=	1	Paksha or fortnight
2	*Pakshas*	=	1	Masa or month
6	Masas	=	1	Ayana or solstice (summer solstice is divine day and winter solstice is divine night)
2	*Ayanas*	=	1	*Varsha* (year)
30	years	=	1	*Divya Masa* or divine month
360	years	=	1	Divya Varsha or divine year
3030	years	=	1	Saptarshi year or Great Bear year
9090	years	=	1	*Dhruva* year or polar year
432,000	years	=	1	Kali yuga or iron age
864,000	years	=	1	Dvapara yuga or copper age
1,296,000	years	=	1	Treta yuga or silver age
1,728,000	years	=	1	Satya yuga or golden age
4,320,000	years	=	1	Paryaya or Mahayuga or great age
306,720,000 or 71	years Mahayugas	=	1	Manvantara or period of manu
1000 or 4,320,000,000	Mahayugas years	=	1	day of Brahma or kalpa (One night of Brahma is equally long)

Brahma and His Lifespan

Brahma (the creator) is one of the sacred trinity of godheads, the other two being *Vishnu* (the preserver) and *Maheshvara* (the dissolver). According to the Purana scriptures of India, Brahma was born out of a fully blossomed lotus springing forth from the navel of Vishnu. Vishnu entrusted the work of creating the worlds to Brahma. There is also another account about Brahma's incarnation. According to Manu Smriti, in the beginning there was no universe and nothing existed except the unmanifest Brahman, or the self-existent overlord. Everything was enveloped in darkness and engulfed in a void for a very long period. Subsequently, in order to dispel the gloom, the overlord manifested into something new: first creating the waters, and then depositing a seed in them. When that seed developed into a golden cosmic egg, the overlord entered into it as a supreme soul and remained in that embryonic state for one hundred years. Finally, the overlord was born as Brahma, the creator of all manifest worlds and all the different kinds of lives therein. As Brahma emerged out of the egg, it was divided into two parts, the upper and the lower. Brahma held these halves of the cosmic egg and through extraordinary mental powers created Heaven out of the upper portion and the Earth from the lower one. Brahma later created ten mind-born sons called *prajapatis* (prime progenitors) who completed the task of further creation of the universe.

We have already observed that one kalpa or a day of Brahma comprises 4,320 million years. Equally long is Brahma's night. Hence, 8,640 million years make one full day of Brahma or one cosmic day. Three hundred and sixty such cosmic days make one year of Brahma or one cosmic year. One hundred such cosmic years (311.04 billion earthly years) is said to be the lifespan of a Brahma. At the end of such a fantastically long life, even Brahma merges again into the unmanifest Brahman or the self-existent overlord.

Pralaya or Partial Deluge

At the end of a kalpa or Brahma day, all kinds of life on Earth is destroyed through devastating floods that submerge the whole earth under water. This is known as *pralaya* (deluge). Of course, certain prior indications are observed before the occurrence of the actual deluge. Indian scriptures point out that long before the occurrence of a deluge there are untimely rains, frequent floods, earthquakes, tempests, droughts, and such other vagaries of nature. A long period of all such natural calamities is followed by a complete drought for several years in succession. Most living creatures die in the scorching heat of the sun. This period of great drought is followed by very heavy and continuous rainfall for a period of twelve years. During this period of rain, the whole earth is submerged under the waters of the floods and everything is completely destroyed, including all plant life. Not even microscopic life survives. Thus ends a day of Brahma with the destruction of all life on Earth.

Then begins the night of Brahma that is as long as Brahma's day, 4,320 million years. During this kalpa or a night of Brahma, there is no life on Earth, and Earth remains submerged under water. Again, at the end of Brahma's night, Brahma's new day dawns and gradually different kinds of life begin to appear on the surface of the earth. This is no doubt a very slow process and it takes many years for all the different species of life known to us at present to evolve. A multitude of life in the form of innumerable species appears, revolves into innumerable life cycles, and again gets helplessly annihilated by way of a deluge. This, however, is only a small or partial deluge. There is still another kind of deluge that is great or total deluge known as *maha pralaya.*

Cosmogonic Cycle of Creation and Dissolution

The duration of the universe is considered to be one full lifespan of a Brahma, or 311.04 billion years. At the end of that period, all creation is dissolved through maha pralaya (great deluge) for an equally long period, known as the night of the overlord or Brahman. Such is the cycle of creation and dissolution of the universe.

According to the atomistic doctrine of Indian philosophy, individual souls combine with various atoms during the cosmogonic cycle beginning a new creation and day of Brahman or overlord. Souls are eternal substances not bound to time and space. Another eternal substance is the atom. This eternal atom has no dimension and is invisible; yet in combination with other atoms it becomes extensive and visible. So, when these atoms are not in combination, there is no creation or visible world. That is the period of maha pralaya, total dissolution or Brahman's night. When the movement of atoms is renewed, the souls unite with various atoms and the process of creation sets in.

Though the atoms are eternal, they are bound to time and space, unlike souls. These atoms act as intermediaries between the soul and the senses. Whenever the soul desires to perceive or act, the atoms form themselves to that sense.

The atoms are bound by time and space, so they prevent the soul from exercising unlimited perceptive powers or actions. If the soul can transcend the atom through yoga techniques, it can realize its true nature of omniscience, omnipotence, and omnipresence. It can thus be liberated even before the end of creation, or Brahman's day.

Those souls that are not liberated, however, undergo continuous cycles of births and deaths. This continuous wandering, activity, and suffering in the manifest world tire out souls. Ultimately, when the combinations of all the atoms dissolve, the visible world disappears and Brahman's night begins. During this period of dissolution of the world or Brahman's night, the fatigued souls rest, retaining all their merits and demerits acquired during the journey through Brahman's day. Again, at the beginning of the new cycle of creation, they unite with atoms. The cycle of creation and dissolution goes on continuously and eternally. The purpose of human life is to escape this cycle through the practice of yoga to attain liberation forever.

For the benefit of souls, the Lord teaches yoga to the first human or manu, who in turn passes on this knowledge to future progeny. This knowledge is subsequently preserved and passed on in the lineage from guru (master) to disciple. If and when, during the long course of a Brahma day this knowledge is distorted or forgotten, the Lord appears as an incarnation upon the earth and renews the forgotten knowledge by teaching it directly to the most deserving person. This is how yoga is preserved as an eternal knowledge. That is why ancient Indian religion is called *sanatana dharma* (eternal religion). This sanatana dharma has its basis in yoga. It shows the way to eternity through yoga practice. Different religions may come and go, but yoga exists forever. Any religion based on the discipline of yoga is likely to sustain much longer than other religions.

Lifespan of Other Godheads

We have already observed that Brahma (the creator) has a fantastically long life. But that is not the ultimate limit of the lifespan. Brahma is not the blessed incarnation of the overlord. Even 311.04 billion years of Brahma's life is but a trifle measure of time compared to the lifespan of Vishnu (the preserver). Lifespans of a thousand Brahmas taken together are equivalent to only one ghati (24 minutes) of Vishnu's life. The period of a thousand Vishnus equals only one pala (244 seconds) of the lifespan of Maheshvara (the dissolver). Further, the period of a thousand Maheshvaras is but a trifle half a pala (12 seconds) for the supreme Lord or the supreme Brahman, whose existence is beyond time-measure and endless. The supreme Brahman is eternity.

One may be astounded to know that incarnate divine beings with such vast lifespans may exist and wield the responsibilities of creation, maintenance, and dissolution of the universe and other lives ranging from the amoeba to human beings, and from demons to demigods. All this may sound irrelevant to us from the point of view of the extremely limited span of our human life. It does have relevance with yoga, however, which offers not only freedom from bondage but also immortality and eternity.

Yogi Can Transcend Time

A yogi reaching the highest level in yoga attains a divine body filled with nectar. The yogi virtually transcends time and space and becomes omniscient and immortal. His or her divine body has a miraculous beauty and fine fragrance. It is pure and without bad odors of flesh, perspiration, or breath. It is free from hunger, thirst, fatigue, and sleep. It is unaffected by heat and cold, and is not subject to disease, old age, and death. It is purged of biological physicality and looks similar to the bodies of the *devas* (lesser gods).

Classical texts of yoga declare that a perfected yogi who has attained such a divine body does not die even through the lifespans of a hundred Brahmas. Not only that, but the yogi counts the period of a hundred Brahmas as only seconds. The yogi is not destroyed even by the great deluge that occurs at the end of the lifespan of each Brahma. He or she faces it cheerfully and survives through it. The yogi enjoys all worlds, having obtained immortality and true liberation. Anyone who has not attained such a divine body is not a perfected yogi.

Our Place in Cosmic Time

According to Indian scriptures half of the lifespan of the present Brahma has already passed. That means the present Brahma is fifty cosmic years old. The universe has just entered the fifty-first cosmic year and this is its first cosmic day, or kalpa. This kalpa is named *shweta varaha kalpa.* As we now know, there are fourteen periods of manu (progenitor) in each kalpa. In the present shweta varaha kalpa, six manu s have already passed. At present, the period of the seventh manu, named *shraddhadeva* or *Vaivasvat Manu,* is going on. We also know that the period of each manu is equivalent to seventy-one mahayugas. Twenty-seven mahayugas in the present period of manu have already passed. At present, we are living through the fourth or kali yuga of the twenty-eighth mahayuga. This current kali yuga (or iron age) is believed to have started February 13, 3102 B.C. This is where we presently stand in the context of cosmic time. We shall remain bound by time, undergoing continuous cycles of births and deaths, until, in one lifetime we obtain liberation through the practice of yoga.

ॐ

chapter three

Origin and History of Yoga

Yoga originated in India. It is impossible to say anything authoritatively with regard to its time of origin, but it certainly is of a great age. It can be called ageless since it is believed to have been taught initially by the Lord. Both Lord Krishna (divine incarnation of Lord Vishnu) and Lord *Shiva* are known as the originators of yoga. In the Bhagavad Gita (chapter IV), Lord Krishna tells Arjuna that he preached this timeless knowledge of yoga first to *Vivasvat* (Sun) many ages ago. Vivasvat then preached it to his son Vaivasvat Manu (the first man of the present human race). Manu gave that knowledge to his son, King *Ikshavaku,* and from Ikshavaku the knowledge of yoga was passed on to many *rajarshis* (royal sages) in traditional succession. But after a long lapse of time, the true knowledge of yoga disappeared and none could master it. So, once again, Lord Krishna revealed the true knowledge of that very same ancient yoga to his beloved friend and devotee Arjuna on the battlefield of the great Mahabharata war.

Manu is regarded as the progenitor of the human race for the period of nearly 306.72 million years. Vaivasvat Manu, referred to above, is considered to be the progenitor of the present race of human beings. Out of 306.72 million years (that is the lifespan of the present manu), 120.53 million years have already passed. We are at present living in the twenty-eighth kali yuga, which is supposed to have begun February 13, 3102 B.C. That means Vaivasvat Manu received the knowledge of yoga from his father Vivasvat nearly 120.53 million years ago, but Vivasvat received it from the Lord even earlier than that. This indicates the timelessness of yoga.

The Mahabharata War, during which Lord Krishna revived the knowledge of yoga by preaching it to Arjuna, was fought toward the end of the third yuga of the present cycle. That means Arjuna received yoga from Lord Krishna at least 5,100 years ago, which is just before the period of the current kali yuga. Lord Krishna cautioned Arjuna to keep this knowledge secret and not to divulge it to those who are unfit to practice it. Thus, yoga was taught only verbally by a guru (preceptor) to a few deserving disciples. So the secret of yoga, even today, is transmitted orally by the teacher to the pupil.

Historical Trace of Yoga

The oldest scripture that refers to yoga in its content is Rig-Veda, dating around 3000 B.C. It is a compilation of sacred mantras and hymns with mystical meanings and effects. It is with the Rig-Veda that knowledge of yoga, which was traditionally transmitted orally through the ages, found its place into written Sanskrit. Later on, three more Vedic scriptures presented the philosophic contents of yoga along with the mantras, hymns, and liturgies. This Vedic collection of four books was completed by 1200 B.C.

Between 1200 B.C. and 800 B.C. the Brahmana caste established itself as the priesthood in India. Only the caste's members knew reading and writing. They alone could carry out the immense range of elaborate and indispensable rites prescribed by the Vedas. During this sacerdotal period the Brahmana scholars produced voluminous literature consisting of directions for carrying out elaborate rituals and for performing mystic sacrificial rites. This literature is known as Brahmanas. They are prose compositions appended to the four Vedas. Aitareya and Kaushitaki Brahmanas belong to the Rig-Veda, Shatpatha and Taitareya Brahmanas to Yajurveda, and Gopatha Brahmana to the Atharvaveda. The Samaveda has eight other Brahmanas of which the best known are Panchavimsha and Shadvimsha Brahmanas. Vedic mantras and hymns have esoteric meanings and the sacrificial rituals are subtle yogic processes bestowing superhuman powers and the final beatitude. But the Vedic writings are too mystical to be easily understood. The Brahmanas contain detailed explanations of what is mentioned in the Vedas. They discuss the elements and the connotations of the Vedic rites and lay down the rules and elaborate directions for carrying out the sacrificial rituals. Yet the real esoteric meaning of sacrificial rites remained a mystery to most people, except to Brahmana philosophers.

The period of the Brahmanas was followed by that of the Upanishads from 800 B.C. to 500 B.C. This was the golden age of Indian theology and philosophy. The philosophy of ancient India is completely set forth in a remarkable series of sacred books called Upanishads. The word *Upanishad* has two different meanings. One is "to sit at the feet of the realized preceptor to gain knowledge" and another meaning is "to set the ignorance of the pupil at rest by revealing the knowledge of the supreme spirit." As indicated by these meanings, the Upanishads are the philosophical dialogues between the highly enlightened preceptors or the ancient *rishis* (sages) and their deserving disciples. Many Upanishads are attached to different Brahmana literature. Their chief aim is to ascertain and assimilate the mystical meanings of the Vedas. Their emphasis is on rediscovery of the self.

The number of Upanishads was considered to be one hundred and eight in the beginning, but later on many more were added to the list, raising the total to over two hundred. A remarkable group of yogis who lived as hermits in the forest composed a series of philosophical treatises as Upanishads. They developed and systematized certain basic doctrines that can be summarized as follows:

1. Brahman is the ultimate reality that is unchanging, eternal, and stable. It forms the substratum of the outward phenomenal world that constantly changes and passes. It constitutes the innermost being of a person and lies beyond the changing world of senses.

2. The inner being, the basic self of a person or the individual self is atman, which is identical with Brahman. As the air in a jar, though enclosed, is one with the air outside, atman is one with Brahman that pervades the universe.

3. The phenomenal world is mere illusion or *maya.* It is in reality nonexistent. It appears to exist only because the external objects are related in the self behind the mind. It is nothing but a mere illusory projection of the atman.

These basic doctrines expound the principle of advaita (nonduality) that unites apparent opposites. The Upanishads revealed the esoteric meanings of the Vedic hymns and the brahmanical sacrificial rites with greater clarity. They explain that what is being searched in the macrocosm can be found in the microcosm. What was sought through the performance of the external sacrificial rites could be realized within one's own self through yoga techniques. This indicates a critical shift of philosophical thought from the outer universe to the tangible spheres of the body. All attention is turned inward in order to attain self-realization through the systematic and stern disciplines of yoga.

The period of Upanishads was succeeded by the period of early heroic epics (600 B.C. to 400 B.C.). But during this period, everything was not rendered into writing. Knowledge was generally preserved orally. This was more applicable when the composition was meant for the masses rather than for scholars. Heroic epics belong to this kind of knowledge that includes heroic and religious tales, moralizing, as well as miscellaneous folklore. This knowledge was intended for popular learning and not for propounding special philosophical doctrines. As they were not committed to writing, with the passage of time, they became nonexistent, either totally or in part. Some special schools of rememberers, however, preserved some epics in fragments and on the basis of those remains, developed a vast body of literature in the subsequent period (400 B.C to A.D. 500). This voluminous literature marks the creativity of that period and includes two great epics called *Ramayana* and *Mahabharata* and twenty *Puranas.* The celebrated Bhagavad Gita forms a part of the *Mahabharata* epic and the most popular among the *Puranas* is *Shrimad Bhagavata,* which mainly depicts the life of Lord Krishna as the divine incarnation. The epics and *Puranas* do possess all the major principles of the ancient yogic compositions mingled with oceans of other data.

Systematization of Yoga

Around the third century B.C., a great sage named Patanjali composed his celebrated Yoga Sutras (yoga aphorisms). Though the knowledge of yoga existed thousands of years before him, Patanjali is considered to be the first author who systematized the theme of yoga and set down clear-cut methods or techniques for attaining it. His work is considered to be the greatest classic on the subject. Though yoga is not his discovery but a discipline of great antiquity, Patanjali has certainly rendered a great service in presenting the traditional doctrine of yoga in Yoga Sutra. He dealt with the highly intricate subject of yoga with utmost brevity. In spite of being excessively abbreviated, these aphorisms are extraordinarily effective in expressing a subject of the most profound nature. This masterpiece has stood the test of time and experience, and has served as the most authoritative and practical handbook to those who have taken to deeper and systematic practices of yoga. The treatment of the subject is a very systematic and rational condensation of yoga even though it is only 196 *sutras* (aphorisms), most of which even lack the form of a sentence. Yet they are not simply loosely collected words. The aphorisms are written by a master mind and give all the essential information about yoga that comes within the range of spiritual experience.

Patanjali set himself to the task of collecting and systematically classifying all the yogic techniques that were already validated by the long-existing classic tradition in practice. He established yoga as a practical discipline emphasizing its eight important limbs or aspects, *yama, niyama, asana, pranayama, pratyahara, dharana, dhyana,* and *samadhi.* This resulted in removing the element of mysticism that had so far prevailed as an essential characteristic of yoga. The credit of lifting classical yoga out of a mystical tradition and advancing it to a level of practical discipline, no doubt, goes to Patanjali. After a long journey through the innumerable currents of metaphysical thoughts and mystic movements in India, at last a classical system of yoga was established.

Almost all spiritual movements that sprang up in India have since incorporated the techniques of this classical yoga as expounded by Patanjali. Many sects came into existence during the later periods in India. Some of them did develop their own approaches to yoga and preached accordingly. In general, however, almost all followed the broad framework of practice laid down by Patanjali. Various authors have subsequently written many classical texts on yoga. All of them have more or less followed the system formulated by Patanjali. Such is the origin and history of the profound spiritual discipline known as yoga. The very fact that yoga has existed for thousands of years is proof of its veracity and usefulness to humankind. Even now it attracts people as much as it did in past aeons.

A Long Search for the Truth

The chief motivation of Indian philosophy has always been the search for a hidden, supreme power that serves as a source and basis for the unity underlying the manifold and diversified phenomenal world. From the beginning of historic time, the Vedic period, Indian thought was centered around the goal of finding out that hidden power. It was a long search for the power that is the source behind all. This inquiry into the secret power existing in all aspects of the universe evolved in stages.

During the Vedic period the inquiry was conducted with an approach based on archaic natural science. It was discovered that all diverse natural phenomena stemmed from the same root. This was revealed through intuitive insight as well as through the comparison and identification of the continuous processes of metamorphoses. This search led to the mystery of a ubiquitous power that worked like a supreme faculty of self-transmutation. It was called maya. It was then understood as a supernatural, magical force with the power to change form and appear under innumerable deceiving masks producing illusory effects,

During the period of Brahmanas, the task of fathoming this mysterious maya was approached through pictographic reasoning of mythology and theology. Superhuman gods and demons were believed to be wielding this magical power and directing the world. Soon, the whole series of masks that could possibly be assumed by this magical force was identified and comprehended and a vast pantheon of gods emerged. These gods were given different names and were labeled with appropriate functions depicting various cosmic phenomena. These gods were considered to be superhuman, and endowed with cosmic powers, but it was not considered impossible to communicate with them. They could be invited as guests through invocation and could be propitiated through sacrifices and oblations. They could be flattered and harnessed for various projects of concern to human beings. With this inquiry, the function of brahmanical theology became that of laying down sacrificial codes, invocations, litanies, and the proper way to communicate with each of those gods. The brahmanical inquiry resulted in the knowledge of the principal manifestations of forces and their identification in the macrocosm and the microcosm. The forces and elements of macrocosm (such as *agni* or fire, *anna* or food, *maruta* or wind, etc.) were identified with various faculties, organs, and limbs of the human microcosm, and were further identified with the details of the sacrificial rituals. These rituals were the instruments for contacting and harnessing the macrocosmic forces to serve the needs and desires of microcosmic human beings.

With the advent of the Upanishadic period, however, the abstract devices of metaphysics superseded the applied technology of practical magic or ritualistic activity. The inquiry became disengaged from ritualistic magic and the symbolic guardians of the natural world and social orders. Instead, attention was turned inward and the inquiry became extraordinarily speculative research. Deeper studies about the identity between the specific forces of macrocosm and corresponding faculties and forces of human microcosm were carried out. The results established equations and correlations between the cosmic and personal elements. These concepts and ideas, however, being circumscribed by the intellect, were regarded as merely helpful indications for recognizing something higher than the power of the mind.

The real quest was not for merely setting up equations between the constituents of macrocosm and microcosm, but for discovering the ultimate power in the universe that transcended both. The researchers were not satisfied with the personal identity of the temporal masks of phenomenal manifestation. The researchers knew that they could not be released from their doom by establishing personal identification with what is itself perishable. They appreciated and sought metaphysical knowledge only in as much and so far as it could lead them toward the knowledge of the ultimate reality, which alone could procure salvation from all sufferings and provide everlasting peace and bliss.

They wanted to identify themselves with something everlasting and all-pervading, because the release from doom consisted in feeling identical not with the masks but with the imperishable essence, wherefrom everything proceeds.

Through the yogic practice of withdrawal and meditation, the researchers transformed metaphysical knowledge into the inner spiritual experience of the real spirit. They looked upon the mystery of the oneness of all things in a single divine power and called it Brahman, which was the core of all existences. They further identified atman (individual self) with this Brahman (cosmic self). This Brahman/atman identity cannot be achieved by means of logic. The mind itself being the created substance is inadequate for the task of comprehending what is transcendent.

This identity was sought by the ancient philosopher/researchers by turning inward and practicing the spiritual path of yoga. The mystery of the absolutely transcendent principle, Brahman, from which the dynamism of the phenomenal spectacle of the world originates, can only be experienced through the techniques of yoga. The discovery of life's inexhaustible and imperishable power, Brahman or atman, was at last won by the creative, free-thinking, intellectual philosopher/researchers of that grand age of the Upanishad. The knowledge derived during the period of the Upanishads provided the basis for the development of *shad darshanas* (six philosophical systems) that formulate a unique orthodox tradition of Indian philosophy.

chapter four

Yoga in Indian Philosophy

Orthodox Indian philosophy is presented in shad darshanas (six classical systems), one of which is the doctrine of yoga. These systems of philosophical thought were developed as a result of knowledge filtered down after long philosophical inquiries by sages through the Vedic, Brahmanic, Upanishadic, and Puranic periods of Indian history as discussed earlier. Ancient sages of India, out of their higher spiritual realizations and contemplative visions, originated these systems.

The word *darshana* means direct perception, contemplative vision, or spiritual revelation. It also indicates knowledge or insight. When used in the philosophical sense, darshanas means knowledge about *tattva,* the real essence, or the ultimate principle underlying the whole phenomenal creation. And the sage who is the seer or perceiver of the tattva (reality essence principle) is known as *tattvadarshin* (one to whom the truth has been revealed). Darshanas, as a philosophical system, constitutes the store of knowledge about the tattva derived by a seer or sage through direct spiritual revelation or vision.

The six systems of Indian philosophical thought have been founded by different sages who perceived the same truth, but from different angles and to varying depths. None of them can singly and exclusively represent Indian orthodox philosophy as a collective doctrine based on all the six darshanas (systems). Such coordination, however, of the six systems into a single, classical, orthodox philosophy was attempted much later, around A.D. 800. Until then, each darshana (system) existed as a separate school of philosophy. Amalgamation of all the six darshanas into a joint school was realized during A.D. 900 or A.D. 1000.

The names of these six classical systems of Indian philosophy, along with the names of their founders, are as follows:

1. *Sankhya* system: founded by sage Kapila.
2. *Yoga* system: founded by sage Patanjali.
3. *Mimamsa (purva)* system: founded by sage Jaimini.
4. *Vedanta* system: founded by sage Vyasa.
5. *Vaisheshika* system: founded by sage Kanada.
6. *Nyaya* system: founded by sage Gautama.

There is no definite information concerning the period during which the founding sages of these six systems lived. It is certain, however, that they are all ancient, legendary figures and existed many centuries before the classic texts of the systems founded by them were formalized. The texts of most of these systems are considered to have been arranged in their present form somewhere between 200 B.C. and A.D. 450.

These six philosophical systems initially analyze the constituent elements of human existence and experience. Subsequently, they try to understand the relationship between the fundamental tattvas (spirit and nature). Ultimately, they aim to comprehend the spirit sufficiently and truly, because the only way to salvation is through its realization. Apart from presenting philosophy, the six systems also detail methods for achieving actual spiritual experiences. Thus, they not only provide philosophical understanding but also impart real awakening and practical directions for the application of theory. Their scope is not limited to mere intellectual activity, but extends to the wider spheres of contemplation and enlightenment. They are at once theory as well as practice of the science of unveiling the real essence or the spirit.

It is necessary to clarify the limitations of any philosophical thought in general. It should be borne in mind that a philosophy, however lofty it may be, cannot formulate the absolutely correct interpretations of the transcendental truths revealed in the state of perfect unison with the ultimate reality. Sages, who perceive such transcendental truths through contemplative visions, are usually influenced by their own subjective moods in ecstasy. Moreover, they perceive these truths without any motive or reason, since their psycho-mental functions cease completely during such revelations. After coming out of the ecstatic state, it becomes difficult for them to interpret those experiences adequately and appropriately in words, since the intellect has its own inherent limitations.

This means that a philosophy, at best, can provide a somewhat rational picture of the spiritual realities and suggest general guidelines for directing an aspirant's spiritual efforts. It can serve the purpose of indicating just the rough plan or map of the spiritual path leading toward reality. A philosophy is merely the means to achieve the end and should not be substituted for the end itself. This holds good even in respect to the shad darshanas (the six classical systems of Indian philosophy).

These six systems are understood to be virtually three twin systems. The first twin is that of sankhya and yoga. The second twin is that of mimamsa (purva) and vedanta. The third twin is that of vaisheshika and nyaya. Each of these twins is considered to be merely two different aspects of one, like two sides of a coin. Each aspect of a twin serves as a complementary philosophy to that of the other aspect.

Sankhya and Yoga

The first twins, the sankhya and yoga philosophies, deal with the hierarchy of the tattvas (basic principles or categories), the evolution of prakriti (nature) through these tattvas, as well as the reverse process of dissolution of the tattvas into their original source, prakriti. While sankhya philosophy deals primarily with the evolutionary process that binds the individual soul into matter, yoga philosophy deals with the involution or the reverse process that releases the soul from the fetters of matter.

The meaning of the word sankhya is "enumeration." Since this system enumerates the tattvas (basic principles or categories), it is called sankhya darshana. In all, twenty-five tattvas are enumerated in sankhya philosophy. They are *purusha* (spirit or soul), prakriti (nature), *mahat* or *buddhi* (intellect), *ahankara* (ego), *manas* (mind), five *jnanendriyas* (cognitive senses), five *karmendriyas* (action senses), five *tanmatras* (subtle primary elements), and five *mahabhutas* (generic gross elements). According to sankhya, the whole phenomenal universe evolves out of these twenty-five basic principles or categories.

Out of these twenty-five tattvas enumerated by sankhya philosophy, only two are considered to be the most fundamental and eternal. They are purusha (spirit or soul) and prakriti (nature). Purusha is conscious spirit, while prakriti is unconscious primordial matter. Purusha is the positive primal principle, while prakriti is the negative primal principle. Purusha is a life-monad and is also known as atman or *jivatma* (individual soul or self). Purushas are multiple in number and are all separate yet identical life-monads.

When purushas or the positive primal principles interact with prakriti or the negative primal principle, the latter leaves its unmanifested state and evolves into twenty-three other metaphysical and physical categories or tattvas. As prakriti begins to evolve and unfold into these categories, it binds the purushas (individual souls) into subtle and gross matter. Sankhya philosophy provides the theoretical exposition of the twenty-five tattvas.

Yoga philosophy accepts this basic sankhya system in totality, but it adds one more tattva to those enumerated by sankhya and makes the total twenty-six tattvas. The additional tattva is that of Ishvara (divine being or God), the supreme ruler of the universe. This makes yoga philosophy theistic, in contrast with the atheistic approach of the sankhya system. That is why the yoga system is often called *seshvara sankhya* (theistic sankhya). The yoga system deals with the practical techniques of disintegrating and dissolving the tattvas in reverse order and isolating the purusha (individual soul) from its entanglement. When an individual soul is released from the fetters of the matter of prakriti (nature), it gains *moksha* (liberation), which is the ultimate goal of both sankhya and yoga.

Sankhya and yoga resemble each other very closely, except that the former is atheistic whereas the latter is theistic. But this is a very minor difference. Some critics exaggerate the difference in their methods of achieving deliverance. According to sankhya, the only way to attain liberation is through knowledge, while yoga prescribes definite psycho-physical techniques for achieving that goal.

It is true, no doubt, that the spirit can be unveiled and comprehended in its real essence by knowledge. But to substitute mere intellectual theoretical knowledge for true transcendental knowledge is a great blunder. Mere intellectual knowledge that is psychological in nature is often likely to be limited and fallible. But the kind of knowledge referred to by the sankhya system as the means to salvation is the true transcendental knowledge based on the actual experience of self-realization. Self is the substratum of true knowledge that is parapsychological in nature and unlimited and infallible in content.

This sort of transcendental knowledge cannot be gained without undergoing intense ascetic discipline through yoga techniques and thereby experiencing the real truth. It becomes necessary to first carry out the spiritual experiments prescribed by the yoga system in order to obtain the knowledge or revelation proposed by the sankhya system. Yoga techniques help transcend ordinary waking consciousness to reach the level of superconsciousness, and to experience true and complete knowledge referred to by sankhya. In short, it can be said that knowledge proposed by sankhya begins where the practice of yoga ends. Thus, sankhya and yoga are not different but complementary systems aimed at a common goal. Lord Krishna clearly states, "Only ignorant people speak of sankhya and yoga as diverse disciplines, but not the learned ones. Anyone firmly established in either of them duly attains the fruits of them both. Whatever goal is achieved by sankhya is reached by yoga too. He truly sees, who sees sankhya and yoga as one." (Bhagavad Gita V:4–5)

As regards purusha (individual soul), both sankhya and yoga hold that it is void of form, content, or attribute. It is pure life-monad, luminous, eternal, omniscient, all-pervading, and changeless. In its original form it is perfectly isolated and detached, but when engulfed in the lifeless matter of prakriti (nature), its omniscience is reduced to limited consciousness and it becomes involved in the life-process and in bondage. Purusha, though actionless, passive, uncreative, and not an efficient cause of anything, apparently seems to act, produce, and go through life-processes when masked by the matter of prakriti. As a matter of fact, purusha is only a catalytic presence in the material body, its role being that of mere activator of prakriti. But the actual activity, creativity, agitation, growth, decay, etc., belong to prakriti (nature), enveloping it.

Once purusha becomes associated with prakriti, its omniscience is obscured and its own true nature is forgotten. Then it begins to identify itself wrongly with ego, which is nothing but the subtle matter of prakriti. Subsequently that false ego-self remains ever-moving and agitated through the mind and its instruments. For attaining freedom from such a conditioned state, it becomes imperative to bring the turbulent mind to a state of rest. When the spontaneous activities of the mind are completely arrested, all obscurations caused by prakriti are automatically removed. As a result, purusha realizes its original true nature. That is the state of liberation.

Mimamsa (Purva) and Vedanta

Like the sankhya and yoga twins, mimamsa (purva) and vedanta also belong together. As a matter of fact, both are called mimamsa. They are considered to be two parts of a whole, or a complete philosophy representing the most orthodox exposition of the Vedic tradition. Together they explain the development, the aim, and the scope of the Vedas. They are the deeper reflections of a long search for basic unity underlying the formations of the outer worlds and the hidden forces of inner life.

The word *mimamsa* literally means inquiry or investigation. The first part of this twin philosophy is called purva mimamsa or simply mimamsa, while the second part is called *uttara mimamsa* or vedanta. Generally, in order to avoid confusion, they are better known as mimamsa (purva) and vedanta. Henceforth, these names will be used. Mimamsa (purva) deals mainly with *karma kanda* (ritual section). It narrates in detail the various sacrificial rituals and clarifies the liturgical aspect of the Vedas. It is often called *karma mimamsa.* Vedanta constitutes the *jnanakanda* (knowledge section). It is the contemplative part of the philosophy, dealing with the theoretical aspect of the Vedas. The word vedanta literally means the ultimate truth or *anta* (end) of the Vedas. Moreover, the vedanta system is based on the Upanishads that occur at the end of all the Vedas. That is also another reason for its nomenclature. It leads to the exposition of the ultimate reality, or Brahman. It is often called *Brahma mimamsa.* Since both of these parts deal with more or less exclusive aspects of Vedic philosophy, there is not much in common between them. Mimamsa (purva) deals with *shabda Brahman* (cosmic sound or word) which is endowed with names and forms and is projected in Vedic revelations (an aggregate of all hymns, mantras, prayers, etc.). Vedanta deals with *parama Brahman* (ultimate reality), which is transcendent and devoid of names and forms. One has to become well established in shabda Brahman before realizing parama Brahman.

In mimamsa (purva) the exposition of the liturgical aspect is done through the voluminous data presented in more than nine hundred *adhikarana* (topics or headings). Each adhikarana discusses a complete argument treating a particular subject. Adhikarana consists of five members: (i) *vishaya* (subject-matter), (ii) *samshaya* (doubt), (iii) *purva paksha* (prima facie argument), (iv) *uttarapaksha* (reply or refutation of erroneous views), and (v) *nirnaya* (conclusion). Thus, mimamsa (purva) elaborately defines the orthodox pattern of the Vedic liturgies.

Mimamsa (purva) does not recognize the existence of God, who might decide the fruits of karmas (deeds) of the individual souls. According to this system, the karmas, in themselves, are products of the fruits in one's life. Nevertheless, it is a polytheistic philosophy since it believes in the existence of a host of supernatural beings called devas (deities), popularly known as lesser gods. These devas reside in *svarga* (heaven). According to mimamsa (purva), an individual soul is considered to be liberated when it ascends to heaven. It stresses different kinds of ritual practices through which one can qualify for heaven after death. These practices include mainly the *yajnas* (sacrifices) of various types. Such yajnas are addressed to different deities who, when propitiated, bestow worldly favors as well as spiritual benefits upon the performer.

Mimamsa (purva) accepts the infallibility of the Vedas, which are considered to be not the product of conventional language but the emanation of reality in the form of shabda (word or sound). Hymns of the Vedas are the mantras (sacred formulas) with inherent meanings and powers to reveal the truth and work magic. During the performance of yajnas (sacrifices), specific mantras are recited along with sacrificial offerings. The effectiveness of yajna is based on the potency of these mantras. A yajna, performed with the proper incantation of mantras and appropriate rites, evokes the pleasure of the deities addressed. The latter are supposed to come to the site of the yajnas to receive their share of sacrificial oblations. When gratified with the offerings made to them, they bless the suppliant.

Mimamsa (purva) has not given much thought to cosmology. It mentions the six tattvas (categories): earth, water, fire, air, ether, and sound. According to this system, each succeeding category is the cause of the preceding one. Water is the cause of earth, fire is the cause of water, and so on. Thus, shabda (sound or word) is the sole cause of creation and only that category is eternal. All the remaining categories and their atoms are transitory in nature.

Mimamsa (purva) is an esoteric discipline. From the point of view of spiritual growth, it aims at attaining heavenly happiness by realizing shabda Brahman (cosmic sound). Yajna (sacrifice) is considered to be the means for achieving this goal. Here, the esoteric interpretation of yajnas is the controlling of senses and mind. This is achieved by controlling *prana* (vital air), with breath control. Giving away material possessions and using restraint through severe vows and austerities are regarded as essential for yajnas. Esoterically, *dravyas* (materials), *indriyas* (senses), vishayas (sense-objects), pranas (vital airs), etc., are the offerings put into the sacrificial fire, namely, the practice of the *atmasamyama yoga* (yoga of self-control). When the senses and mind are subdued, the inner subtle sound is realized as shabda Brahman. There ends the first phase of spiritual growth through mimamsa (purva). Thereafter, one becomes eligible for the second phase, mimamsa (uttara) or vedanta, which aims at the realization of parama Brahman (ultimate reality).

Vedanta represents pantheistic philosophy and regards the whole universe as synthetically derived from a single eternal principal essence called Brahman. It expounds the doctrine of advaita (nondualistic) philosophy, which considers that nothing really exists except Brahman. Even Ishvara (God), jivatmas (individual souls), prakriti (nature), and all phenomenal creations emanate from Brahman. All of them are merely the reflections of one and the same Brahman. Their separate existence is felt due to maya or *avidya* (illusion or nescience).

The word *Brahman* literally means growth, development, swelling, expansion, or evolution. Here it conveys the meaning of growth or evolution of the spirit. Brahman is the impersonal universal spirit. According to vedanta, though Brahman is divested of all attributes and action, it is the primal source from which all created things emanate and to which they ultimately return. Brahman is at once the efficient as well as the material cause of the visible universe. It is both creator and creation.

From a pragmatic point of view, this is known as *abhinna-nimittopadana-karana-vada* (theory of the sameness of efficient and material cause). According to this theory, Brahman creates the universe out of itself by itself. This means that the material for creation comes from Brahman alone and not from anywhere outside and Brahman is also the creator. An example of this is that of a spider that creates the cobweb with the help of saliva coming out of it. Here, the material cause of the cobweb, namely saliva, and the efficient cause, creator (spider), are not different from each other. This is called an instance of the theory of sameness of the efficient and the material cause.

Vedanta accepts the order of creation from the hierarchy of twenty-five tattvas (categories) as described in the sankhya system. But the former differs from the latter mainly on two points. First, vedanta expounds nonduality of the highest principle called Brahman, which is even beyond the world-supporting duad of purusha and prakriti mentioned by the sankhya system. Thus, vedanta is nondualistic while sankhya is dualistic in its approach to the highest and principal tattvas (categories). Another point of difference between these two systems is regarding their theories of creation. Sankhya accepts *parinamavada* (theory of transformation), while vedanta accepts *vivartavada* (theory of illusory manifestation).

According to the parinamavada of sankhya, the primal cause prakriti (nature), transforms itself into the form of creation. It is like the phenomenon of milk being trans-formed into curds. According to the vivartavada of vedanta, the universe is not produced at all. It is only Brahman, one-without-a-second, that appears in different forms as creation due to the illusion or ignorance of the *jiva* (embodied soul). It is like a rope appearing as a serpent due to illusion. This is called *adhyaropa* (attribution of something unreal to the real). It is the erroneous superimposition of one thing onto another. When the illusion of the serpent in the rope disappears, the rope is visualized in its true form. In the same manner, when the erroneous superimposition of the phenomenal world upon Brahman vanishes, the jiva (soul) realizes its true identity with it.

The real nature of Brahman is considered to be *satchidananda* consisting of three words: *sat* (eternal existence), *chit* (pure consciousness) and *ananda* (infinite bliss). This reality of Brahman is devoid of any attribute and is one-without-a-second. But Brahman has *shakti* (intrinsic power) called maya (illusory power), which is also known as avidya or *ajnana* (nescience or ignorance). This maya is also called prakriti. It is *anandi* (without a beginning) and eternally exists as the latent power of Brahman. Maya has no separate existence apart from Brahman, as the Sun's rays are not different from the Sun. Yet, when it becomes operative, it is capable of creating a *bhranti* (false impression) of being self-existent and different from Brahman. As it is difficult to describe Brahman, so also it is difficult to describe its illusory power, maya or avidya.

If Brahman is called the eternal reality, maya may be described as something that has the appearance of a transient reality. Brahman has no form, no name; but maya is *bhavarupa* (having capacity of becoming) and also *namarupa* (having names and forms) when projected as the spectacle of illusory phenomonal existence.

According to vedanta, maya or prakriti has two aspects: *samashti* (aggregate or whole), and *vyashti* (unit or part). Samashti is viewed as an aggregate constituted of units or parts, while in vyashti it is viewed as distinct units or specific parts of an aggregate. The samashti or aggregate aspect of maya (illusion) is attributed to Ishvara (divine being or God). The vyashti or partial aspect of maya is attributed to the jivas (individual souls). When Brahman, out of Brahman's own sweet will, assumes avidya (nescience) in the samashti aspect and fancies itself to be the universal God, Brahman feels endowed with a divine personality and the attributes of omniscience, omnipotence, universal sovereignty, etc. It is this self-deluded Ishvara (God) who becomes the efficient cause of creation, through the further projection of maya or prakriti. Brahman becomes instrumental in the evolution of cosmos. As Ishvara, Brahman pervades the entire cosmos and plays the role of a supreme creator, preserver, and dissolver in the forms of Brahma, Vishnu, and Maheshvara, the divine trinity. Yet as a matter of fact, the Supreme Brahman or Godhead remains untouched and attributeless, even beyond the apparent personal mask of godly nescience.

In spite of avidya (ignorance), the supreme consciousness of God is not circumscribed. It is not so with jivas (individual souls), whose waking consciousness is limited to small spheres. God possesses an omniscient mind since God is associated chiefly with *sattva guna* (quality of purity and knowledge), and is almost devoid of the other two gunas (qualities), *rajas* (activity and passion), and *tamas* (inertia and ignorance). On the other hand, there is a preponderance of rajas and tamas against sattva in jivas (individual souls) and so they are entangled in the snares of delusion. God, in spite of self-misrepresentation, remains omniscient and omnipotent and so does not get lost in delusion. God really knows that God's personal mask is merely for the sake of self-misrepresentation and therefore remains a spectator or a *sakshi* (witness) to God's own *lila* (divine play) of controlling the arrangements of all the worlds, directing the mental propensities of all sentient beings, and showering benignity for their good and pious deeds as also expressing wrath for their evil and impious deeds. Such is the distinction between Ishvara and jiva in the vedanta system.

According to vedanta, even the existence of the omniscient and omnipotent Ishvara (God) is not real. It is only the grandest of all spectacles of willful self-deception on the part of Brahman. So God is as much an illusion as the entire phenomenal world that emerges out of God's lila (divine play). Yet God remains fully aware of God's unreal and mere apparent entity, since God is the direct superego of Brahman. God cannot really be ignorant like the narrowly circum-

circumscribed human ego. God, or Ishvara, knows fully well that God is nothing but Brahman under the spell of self-misrepresentation through Ishvara's own illusory power, or avidya. Ishvara is the Lord of even maya and not its plaything like the jiva (individual soul). So Ishvara cannot be either lost in ignorance or caught in the snare of maya.

As a matter of fact, maya unfolds as shakti (power, energy, life-force) when actually associated with Ishvara. It remains only latent in the sublime, attributeless Brahman. Maya is the illusory attitude of *saguna Brahman*, or Ishvara (God), and not of *nirguna Brahman* which is attributeless. When Ishvara begins the lila (divine play), Ishvara enacts a cosmic role, and presides over the evolution of the cosmic plan by wielding wondrous power: shakti, prakriti, or maya. This very Lord who creates and rules the cosmos also becomes rooted in the hearts of all sentient beings, guiding and constraining their development. It is God, who from behind the curtain of God's maya, plays the role of a wire-puller making innumerable jivas (souls) dance like puppets on the immense and vast stage of the universe. Lord Krishna says in Bhagavad Gita.

"Ishvara (Lord), O Arjuna, abides in the heart-region of all beings, causing them to whirl round through maya (Ishvara's illusory power) as if they were mounted on machines." (XVIII:61)

Under the spell of maya (illusion), the jiva (individual soul) becomes trapped in the phantasmagoric forms and attractions or repulsions to false phenomena. To that soul, individual ego seems to be a reality. One becomes circumscribed by self-centered individuality. One fancies oneself to be distinct from all other beings, even from God. The limiting *adjuncts* (sheaths of the body) keep an individual soul apart from all the rest, both within and without, because they are not transparent coverings. Due to their opacity and dullness, the jiva is unable to perceive or realize the self-effulgent light of the Lord dwelling within his or her heart. God remains an unfathomable and unknown mystery to the individual soul.

Yet God acts as an inner guide and expects free cooperation, so that God can become the illuminator. God desires the jiva to become a transparent media for God's light, so that the darkness of ignorance can be dispelled. Only if that veil of ignorance is removed, can the jiva realize his or her own true nature, oneness with God, and finally identity with Brahman. When such a reunion with Brahman is achieved, the jiva achieves deliverance from the transmigrations, and the cycle of births and deaths comes to an end.

In order to break the bond of cause and consequence to attain perfect harmony and identity with Brahman, vedanta considers the removal of ajnana (ignorance) and acquisitions of *jnana* (true knowledge) a necessary prerequisite. Further, the vedanta system recommends the practice of yoga for attaining true knowledge by way of contemplative revelations. The path of yoga prescribed by vedanta is the *ashtanga yoga* (eight-fold system of yoga) formulated by sage Patanjali. That is why the vedanta system is often called *yoga vedanta* or *vedanta-yoga.*

This last pair of twin philosophies deals not only with cosmology but also with logical inferences. Its special feature is the atomistic doctrine used to explain cosmology.

While dealing with individual things in nature, the vaisheshika system recognizes seven *padarthas* (categories): (i) dravya (substance), (ii) guna (attribute or property), (iii) karma (action), (iv) *samanya* (generality), (v) *vishesha* (speciality), (vi) *samavaya* (cohesion), and (vii) *abhava* (nonexistence or negation).

The nature and characteristics of these seven padarthas are, in brief, as follows:

1. Dravya (substance): This category includes nine eternal substances: earth, water, fire, air, ether, time, space, mind, and soul.

2. Guna (attribute or property): This category includes twenty-four gunas: *rupa* (color), *rasa* (taste), *gandha* (odor), *sparsha* (touch), sankhya (number), *parimana* (dimension), *prithaktva* (severality), *samyoga* (conjunction), *vibhaga* (disjunction), *paratva* (propinquity), *aparatva* (remoteness), *gurutva* (weight), *dravatva* (fluidity), *sneha* (viscosity), shabda (sound), buddhi (intellect), *sukha* (pleasure), *duhkha* (pain), *ichcha* (desire), *dvesha* (aversion), *prayatna* (effort), dharma (merit), *adharma* (demerit), and *samskara* (subliminal impression).

3. Karma (action/movement): This category indicates activity consisting of motion, which are five types: upward, downward, horizontal, contraction, and extension.

4. Samanya (generality): This category indicates the association of the substances by common or generic properties.

5. Vishesha (specialty): This category indicates peculiarity, distinguishing property, or characteristic differentiation of each substance. Vaisheshikas have postulated a special theory of visheshas, from which the name of this system is derived. It is this category that is stressed by the vaisheshika system. In this category are the distinct features of the nine dravyas (substances). According to this system, earth, water, fire, air, and mind are held to be atomic; while ether, time, space, and soul are considered very special substances without dimension, extension, or visibility.

6. Samavaya (cohesion): This category indicates a special type of connection. Connections are considered to be of two types: *samyoga* (connection) and samavaya (permanent connection).

Samyoga is a temporary connection as that of *hasta-pustaka-samyoga* (hand-book connection), which comes to an end as soon as the book is put down from the hand.

Samavaya, on the other hand, is a permanent connection, and is destroyed only when one of the things between which it exists is destroyed. Such inseparable connections exist between the following five pairs that are called *ayutasiddhas* (inseparable entities).

1. *Avayava* and *avayavi,* part and whole: *pata* (cloth) and its *tantus* (threads/fibers).

2. Guna and *guni,* the quality and the object possessing it: *ghata* (pitcher) and its redness.

3. *Kriya* and *kriyavan:* the action and its performer; the horse and its action of running.

4. *Jati* and *vyakti:* the genus and the individual: the cow and its *gotva* (cowness).

5. Vishesha and *nityadravyas:* the eternal substances and their distinctive features. According to the vaisheshika system, the *paramanus* (atoms) of each eternal substance have some distinctive features that do not allow the atoms of one substance to be mixed up with those of another. The visheshas (distinct characteristics) remain in their respective eternal atoms by way of samavaya or inseparable connection.

6. Abhava (nonexistence or negation): This category indicates merely nonentity or nullity. All nameable things are classified as *bhava* (existent or positive), while nonexistent, nonentities are classified as Abhava. Strictly speaking, this category is not a separate predicament like the above-mentioned six categories. It is only a negative mode of arrangement.

The nyaya system presents its philosophy mainly according to the logical or syllogistic method. According to this system, *tattvajnana* (the true knowledge of the basic principles of reality) can be attained by way of vada (logical discussion). Its arguments consist of a combination of enthymemes and syllogisms. The syllogistic argument of the nyaya system has five avayavas (members): (i) *pratijna* (proposition), (ii) *hetu* (reason), (iii) *udaharna* (example or instance), (iv) *upanaya* (application to special case), and (v) *nigamana* (deduction or conclusion).

The nyaya system accepts four sources of true knowledge: (i) *pratyaksha* (perception), (ii) *anumana* (inference), (iii) *upamana* (analogy), and (iv) *shabda* (credible testimony). Anumana (inference) is said to be of three types: (a) *purvavat* (from cause to effect), (b) *seshvat* (from effect to cause), and (c) *samanyato drishta* (from perception to abstract principle).

The nyaya system puts great stress on anumana (logical inference) as the chief means of gaining knowledge. It considers udaharna (example or instance) to be the mainstay of anumana (inference). It is the logical approach from which the name of the system is derived; nyaya means logic.

The vaisheshika system also accepts a five-membered syllogism like the nyaya system, but it differs from nyaya in respect to knowledge sources. Vaisheshika accepts only two sources: pratyaksha (perception) and anumana (inference). Both systems, however, hold that knowledge comes through reasoning and external sources and not from within the individual.

The nyaya system recognizes padarthas or predicables involved in seeking knowledge in a logical way. These predicables are: (i) pramana (proof), (ii) prameya (object of knowledge), (iii) samshaya (doubt), (iv) prayojana (motive), (v) drishtanta (instance), (vi) siddhanta (conclusion), (vii) avayava (premise), (viii) tarka (reductio ad absurdum), (ix) nirnaya (determination), (x) vada (disquisition), (xi) jalpa (controversy), (xii) vitanda (cavil), (xiii) hetuabhasha (fallacy), (xiv) chala (perversion), (xv) jati (self-contradiction), and (xvi) nigrahasthana (refutation). All sixteen of these predicables are inclusive in the seven padarthas (categories) laid down by the vaisheshika system. The difference between them is only apparent, but not real.

Though the nyaya system is mainly devoted to logic, it does deal with soul, mind, body, cognition, the five senses, and their objects. Apart from that, it also discusses good and evil fruits of human karmas (deeds), volition, fault, pain, transmigration, and final liberation. The concepts of nyaya and vaisheshika in respect to all these subjects are more or less the same.

The special feature of the twin system of vaisheshika and nyaya is their atomistic doctrine. They accept the permanent existence of the atoms of the four mahabhutas: earth, water, fire, and air. They consider *akasha* (ether) to be eternal but without atoms. The minutest atoms called paramanus are not visible. When two such paramanus combine, one *dveyanuka* is formed. When three *dveyanukas* combine, one *tryanukas* is produced. The particles that are visible in a beam of sunlight entering through a small opening or a window are recognized as tryanukas.

At the beginning of creation, the movement of the atoms commences and in consequence they unite in various combinations, bringing forth the visible universe. Again, during cosmic dissolution, they disintegrate and become invisible. Hence there is no visible universe. The universe appears and disappears due to the cyclic periods of the combination and disintegration of atoms.

This atomistic theory of cosmology held by vaisheshika and nyaya differs basically from that of sankhya, yoga, and vedanta. The evolutionary theory of creation, according to the latter systems, is based on *satkaryavada*, the inherent existence of the effect in its cause; while the theory of integration of atoms, according to the former systems, is based on *asatkaryavada*, no latent existence of the effect in the cause.

Satkaryavada holds that there is the potential existence of the effect in the material cause even prior to the actual operation producing the effect. For example, the tree exists in seed in the latent form as an inherent potential effect. If it were not so, a seed would never evolve and grow into a tree. Satkaryavada is based on the idea that nothing can be produced out of the material cause if it does not hold those qualities or effects potentially even before the start of production. Satkaryavada also has two different aspects: (i) parinamavada (theory of transformation) is accepted by sankhya and yoga systems, and (ii) vivartavada (theory of illusory manifestation) is accepted by the vedanta system. Both of these theories, however, are intended to be inclusive of each other and not exclusively independent theories.

In contrast to satkaryavada, asatkaryavada holds that the actuality of the effect does not exist in the material cause prior to its production. According to this theory, there is a definite distinction between the states of the cause and the effect. It upholds the actuality of the effect and not the potentiality of it. From the point of view of this theory, an effect comes into existence only after the actual beginning of its production or materialization, and does not exist in its cause prior to that.

For example, the theory argues that tantus (fibers), which are the cause, are different from the pata (cloth), which is the effect. Cloth does not exist in the fibers or threads prior to its production, cloth. Effect is essentially a different entity from the fibers, or cause.

Again, the former differs from the latter in form, nomenclature, number, application, etc. Moreover, the help of the external means and agency, like a loom and a weaver, is necessary to produce the cloth out of the fibers or threads. If there was no difference between the cause and the effect (the fibers and the cloth), there would be no necessity for the external means and agency (the loom and the weaver) for production. Since the production is entirely a new creation, it needs some external agency and means for starting it. Thus, the effect comes into existence only from the moment its actual production begins, hence it is totally nonexistent prior to that. Therefore, asatkaryavada is also called *arambhavada* (theory of the beginning of actual effect).

This peculiar theory of arambhavada is adopted by the vaisheshika and nyaya systems for explaining the atomistic origination of the universe. According to their cosmology, the atoms (cause) are acted upon by Ishvara or God (external agency) and as a result there originates an absolutely new creation (effect). Further, this new creation or universe (effect) is essentially a different entity from the atoms (cause), differing in form, nomenclature, number, application, etc. Thus, there is a definite distinction between the states of the atoms and the universe.

Both vaisheshika and nyaya adopt a theistic view, though their God does not assume either a personal form or the role of a creator of matter. God is not a material cause but merely an efficient cause of the creation. This theology is very much in harmony with that of yoga. Vaisheshika and nyaya, like yoga, hold that God is a distinct soul. Other individual souls are also like God. All of them are eternal too, like God. God, however, is distinguished from them in respect to God's omniscience and omnipotence. God alone can govern the universe and can bestow the fruits of good or evil karmas (deeds) upon the individual soul. Since the individual soul lacks the attributes of God, it succumbs to the entanglement of its body, and the cycle of births and deaths, unlike the latter.

Another peculiarity of vaisheshika and nyaya is that they consider individual souls as substances, though eternal and all-pervading, not bound down to time and space. Their substance, however, possesses the atoms that are devoid of any dimension or extension, and hence remain invisible. Even during the absence of creation, these substances of individual souls exist, retaining their merits and demerits.

The nyaya system believes that moksha (liberation) is a state in which one does not experience either pleasure or pain. Vaisheshika holds that the destruction of all vaisheshika (distinctive characteristics) of the substances that bind the individual soul means liberation. However, both vaisheshika and nyaya believe that in the final stage of liberation, the individual soul is separated from its instruments of consciousness (the mind and body) and abides in a culminating condition of absolute and eternal unconsciousness. This is different from the state of superconsciousness or pure consciousness of a liberated soul according to the yoga and vedanta systems.

Six Systems Complement Each Other

We have considered, in brief, the six philosophical systems of India. There are certain differences in the theoretical statements of each system, and some of their viewpoints appear to contradict each other.

In general, they coincide in presenting the major aspects of the central doctrine of Indian philosophy. The differences that separate them on certain points are minor. When presenting experiences that are not in the reach of the senses, mind, or intellect, one has to depend on speculation and imaginative language, allowing room for some variations and anomalies.

The six systems of Indian philosophy also are the products of the honest observations of true spiritual experiences of the great sages. They are naturally arranged together as complementary projections of a single grand truth presented from different angles and planes of consciousness. Viewed in this light, the six systems are quite homogeneous and in general agreement. All of them accept the spirit as a transcendent and autonomous principle, but they proceed in different ways to prove its existence and explain its essence. Similarly, all systems accept that the involvement of the spirit with the forces of prakriti (nature) is the cause for its bondage, but they explain in different ways the manner of the participation of spirit with nature.

Yoga Links All Systems

We have seen that the six systems of Indian philosophy as a whole discuss reality—from an atom to the grand universe—and also deal with spirituality linking the individual soul with the cosmic soul, and finally identifying it with the transcendent Brahman.

Sankhya, yoga, and vedanta form an important trinity dealing with the truth of human existence and the mystery of the universe from the plane of spiritual and metaphysical realms. It is appropriate to study the metaphysics of these three systems in greater detail in the succeeding chapter. Mimamsa (purva) with its theological approach, describes chiefly the pious preoccupations and the formal rites that are considered to be the preliminary means for climbing the spiritual ladder. Vaisheshika and nyaya provide the analysis of the categories constituting the universe, mainly with the empirical data of manifest nature. They treat the subject from the point of view of logical reasoning on the plane of normal waking consciousness. Thus, vaisheshika and nyaya stand closer to the contemporary academic approach of modern philosophy.

Whatever the differences in approach or emphasis, the founding sages of all six systems were yogis. All of them accept yoga, in some form or the other, as the practical method for achieving the final goal laid down by them. Sankhya and vedanta clearly accept ashtanga yoga (eight-fold path). Mimamsa (purva) prescribes yajnas (sacrifices) and *nishkama karma* (action without attachment). Yajnas have esoteric significance and as such are part and parcel of atmasamyama yoga (path of self-control), while detached performance of actions is obviously karma yoga. Vaisheshika and nyaya, despite their realistic metaphysics and epistemology, recognize that a yogi with his or her supernatural perception is able to visualize even the subtlest atoms and study their properties. They also accept that right knowledge, detached living, and yogic meditation are the means to liberation. Yoga forms a link between all the six systems. It is the most effective practical technique for realizing spiritual truths.

chapter five

Metaphysics of Yoga

The major objective of all the philosophical systems of India, as seen earlier, is the liberation of the spirit or soul by disassociating it from matter. The cause of the soul's entanglement into material form lies in its association with prakriti (nature). Such association further leads the soul to participate in cosmic operations and the profane life. This degraded state draws the soul still further into the infinite cycle of births and deaths. One who seeks emancipation of the soul must thoroughly understand the metaphysics or the process of unfoldment of the subtle categories, and also understand the forms of prakriti and the laws governing evolution. Then one should make efforts to separate the soul from these binding forces of prakriti through the practice of yoga.

Keeping this objective in view, we shall try to understand the metaphysics underlying yoga philosophy and study cosmological evolution as it occurs out of the tattvas, (the metaphysical and physical categories) enumerated by the sankhya, yoga, and vedanta systems.

Dualistic and Nondualistic Approaches

There are two main approaches in respect to the fundamental tattvas or primordial principles out of which the whole universe is supposed to evolve. The sankhya system upholds the duad of purusha (individual soul) and prakriti (nature). The entire phenomenal universe is evolved from prakriti, because of the catalytic presence of purusha. The yoga system practically agrees with this dualistic approach of sankhya. The vedanta system, on the other hand, presents a nondualistic approach in which the duad of purusha and prakriti is integrated into a higher conception of a single reality called Brahman (ultimate reality or universal spirit). According to sankhya and yoga, both purusha and prakriti are real, eternal, and independent. According to vedanta, purusha or atman (individual soul) is identical with Brahman, while prakriti is unreal and nonexistent. In spite of this difference in approach, all three systems agree that purusha or atman becomes embodied in the subtle and gross elements of prakriti due to avidya (ignorance), and becomes involved in the cycle of births and deaths.

Purusha or Atman, Ishvara and Brahman

According to the sankhya system, purushas (souls) are multiple, changeless, independent, and aloof. They are solitary, individual entities not derived from any higher, omnipotent, universal force. They are completely passive and nonproductive. Innumerable, such purushas exist as if floating in a great whirlpool of cosmic matter of prakriti (nature), and getting involved in the process of evolution.

The yoga system agrees with this view of the separate existence of innumerable purushas (souls), but also adds one special purusha and calls it Ishvara (divine being or God). This divine being is eternal, unborn, undying, and unbound. Ishvara's power and preeminence are never equaled or excelled by any other purusha, even when the latter is liberated. That is why Ishvara is called purusha vishesha (a special kind of soul). Ishvara is the universal soul possessing omniscience par excellence.

Yet, Ishvara does assume a created mind-stuff out of compassion for the other purushas (individual souls). Ishvara does so to gratify living beings and to lift them out of the vortex of worldly existence by making them realize inner consciousness after removing obstacles. This created mind-stuff, however, which is voluntarily assumed by Ishvara with the above-mentioned motive, does not limit or bind Ishvara at all. The role of Ishvara is to provide help for other purushas to evolve, to unfold consciousness, and to attain liberation. Thus, though other purushas are in intimate relation with Ishvara in the realm of the inner life, they maintain their individual uniqueness and independent existence apart from Ishvara.

Vedanta philosophy does accept the existence of Ishvara (God), but merely as the projection of Brahman, the ultimate reality. Brahman is supposed to be nirguna, without attributes. It is not expected to act as a creative power by itself. It first has to assume saguna form, the form possessing attributes. In the initial stage of manifestation, Brahman projects itself as Ishvara possessing the attributes through its own illusory power, maya or avidya. So Ishvara is called saguna Brahman. The unborn, undying, unbound, and omniscient. Ishvara is God—the creator, the preserver, and the dissolver. The entire universe is nothing but God's appearance in prakriti. Ishvara is seen within prakriti, Ishvara is not touched by it. Ishvara is the Lord of prakriti. Thus Ishvara is the omnipotent, omniscient, all-powerful, sovereign divine being.

Introducing the special tattva (principle) called Ishvara by yoga philosophy is a bold attempt to bring reconciliation between the transcendental, nondual monism of vedanta and the pluralistic, dualistic, atheism of sankhya. The composite system of yoga philosophy brings the two doctrines of vedanta and sankya closer to each other and makes them understood as the presentation of the same reality from two different points of view. The nondual approach of vedanta presents the principle of *advandva* (nonduality of the highest truth at the transcendental level). The dualistic approach of sankhya presents truth of the same reality but at a lower empirical level, rationally analyzing the principle of dvandva (duality or pairs of opposites). Whereas, yoga philosophy presents the synthesis of vedanta and sankhya, reconciling at once monism and dualism, the supermundane and the empirical.

As regards the individual soul (called purusha in sankhya and atman in vedanta), vedanta philosophy holds that it is like a spark of the supreme transcendental essence known as Brahman (ultimate reality or universal spirit). As such, Brahman and atman are not different but identical. Atman is the manifestation of Brahman and so it is boundless, omniscient, omnipotent, and indestructible like Brahman. In contrast to sankhya and yoga which consider purusha to be inactive, vedanta considers Brahman, when shrouded with maya, as an active principle. Brahman, according to vedanta, dwells in individuals as atman, giving them life and enabling them to act and experience. Thus Brahman, in spite of its passivity, does participate indirectly as atman in the actions of creation. It does not, however, become involved in the processes or the consequences of those actions. It is beyond prakriti (nature) as the supreme transcendental essence.

Relationship Between Purusha and Prakriti

We have seen that sankhya, yoga, and vedanta differ in their viewpoints regarding the highest principles and the roles assigned to Brahman, Ishvara, and purusha or atman. Apart from this, they also differ slightly in respect to the relationship between purusha or atman (individual soul) and prakriti (nature). According to sankhya (and yoga more or less agrees with it), when purushas (souls) associate with prakriti (nature), the latter unfolds and evolves into subtle and gross metaphysical and physical categories, binding the former and involving them in continuous rounds of transmigration. The purpose of such voluntary binding or involvement on the part of purushas is said to be that of gaining complete awareness of their true nature by way of unfolding their inherent powers with the aid of prakriti. When bound, purusha becomes ignorant of its own true nature and confuses itself with ego. It can secure release from bondage by eliminating such confusion.

According to vedanta, prakriti or the phenomenal world is not a reality. It is merely an illusion caused by avidya (nescience) on part of atman (individual soul). Though atman is identical with Brahman (cosmic spirit), the maya (illusory power) of the latter makes the former subject to ignorance. Brahman by Its own power hides deep behind the veil of maya (illusion) and produces a spectacle of phenomenal illusion in the form of prakriti. Atman (individual soul) takes this phantasmagoric production of prakriti for real due to avidya (nescience). This avidya has the power of concealing as well as projecting. Through its operation it conceals the reality of atman and projects the illusory world as real. When right knowledge is attained, atman realizes that there is no prakriti or so-called phenomenal world. At the same time, the duality between atman and Brahman also vanishes making them one reality.

Both the sankhya and yoga systems believe that prakriti is real and eternal, like purusha, and that both of them are separate entities. The vedanta system differs on this point and considers only Brahman or atman to be real and eternal. Prakriti is only an illusory effect caused by Brahman or atman and has no existence apart from the latter. They cannot be separated as heat (or effect) cannot be separated from fire (or cause). Prakriti is the basic reality (as in sankhya and yoga) or as an illusory effect caused by basic reality (as in vedanta). We shall now try to comprehend the nature of prakriti's association with purusha or atman (individual soul).

As we have observed, sankhya, yoga, and vedanta accept the two fundamental principles, spirit and nature, and the association between them which is the basic cause of creation. All three systems agree in regard to the nature of the association between them. Purusha or atman (spirit) is *drishta* (seer or one who sees), while prakriti (nature) is *drishya* (seen or capable of being seen). The spirit with all its embodiments is the subject who sees or experiences the object that is the phenomenal world, or nature. When the consciousness of spirit becomes extroverted due to its embodiments, the relationship of drishta (seer) and drishya (seen) is established. Again, when the consciousness of spirit recedes inward, they begin to disassociate from each other. Finally, when the introversion of spirit's consciousness becomes complete, its association with nature comes to an end. Then there is no more existence of seer and seen or subject and object.

Whether prakriti is galvanized into phenomenal creation by the catalytic presence of purusha (as in sankhya and yoga) or is merely a phantasmagoric creation due to the ignorance of atman (as in vedanta), the association between them is that of seer and seen or subject and object. Though spirit is pure consciousness during complete introversion, it is cognitive of the phenomenal world when its consciousness is modified and dimmed due to the extroverted mind. It is because of psycho-mental consciousness that the spirit appears lost in the objective world or nature's manifestations. Thus, the elusive spirit seems to play a subordinate role to nature.

But, as a matter of fact, yoga philosophy points out that nature plays a subordinate role to the spirit that strives to grow or evolve. According to yoga philosophy, the association between spirit and nature exists for the sake of the growth of the former, while the latter serves the purpose of providing necessary experience and means leading to the emancipation of spirit. It is only with the help of nature that the spirit achieves the ultimate aim of self-realization.

Cosmological Evolution and Involution

According to sankhya philosophy, the association between purusha (individual soul) and prakriti (nature) results in the creation of the phenomenal universe. Purusha remains passive once the process of evolution sets in. Prakriti becomes active and expands into the empirical world through its latent forces and metaphysical and physical categories. There are twenty-three tattvas (metaphysical and physical categories) of prakriti according to the sankhya system, and the yoga system agrees with it. During the process of evolution, energy is transformed into matter bringing forth the phenomenal universe. Prakriti in its initial unevolved state is energy, while during the evolutionary process that energy is transformed into matter, manifesting the universe. Again, during the process of involution, matter is transformed into energy, dissolving the phenomenal creation and reducing it to the original state of unmanifested prakriti. Thus prakriri constantly undergoes the processes of evolution and involution.

Apart from the basic difference regarding the duality of purusha and prakriti, the vedanta system agrees with the sankhya and yoga systems in respect to the number and nature of metaphysical and physical categories evolving out of prakriti. Like the sankhya and yoga systems, the vedanta system also enumerates twenty-three metaphysical and physical categories that maya or prakriti unfold into the phenomenal universe. Particulars of these categories are also common to all three systems. Moreover, all three systems agree that the individual spirit or soul becomes bound by these categories of prakriti during the process of evolution through which the empirical world is manifested. In order to attain liberation, the spirit or soul must dissolve and transcend all these categories, one by one in reverse order, through the process of involution.

Forces Behind the Unfoldment of Prakriti

Prakriti (nature) as we already know, is the primordial, unmanifested, and most subtle metaphysical principle that has the potentiality to manifest into an enormous empirical universe. The whole universe remains in a potential state within prakriti so long as the three gunas (attributes) of the latter remain motionless and undisturbed. In the unmanifested state of prakriti, these three gunas are in *samyavastha* (perfect equilibrium). As soon as these three gunas are disturbed and set into motion, prakriti begins to unfold into other metaphysical categories resulting in phenomenal creation.

Though prakriti remains undifferentiated in its primordial state, it possesses the three gunas as latent attributes. These gunas remain in a dormant condition until the balance and harmony between them is maintained. When such balance is disturbed, any one of them becomes dominant over the other two, resulting in the beginning of the unfoldment of prakriti. Once the stability of the gunas is disturbed, they undergo restless dynamism, a seemingly unending interplay of perpetual change by way of entering into innumerable mutual combinations.

How is this balance between the gunas of prakriti disturbed? We have already seen earlier that there are two viewpoints in this regard. The sankhya system believes (and yoga agrees with it) that such imbalance is created through the catalytic presence of purusha (individual soul) with prakriti (unmanifested nature). Through such intervention of purusha, when the equilibrium of the gunas is disturbed, an inner dynamic movement is produced in unmanifested and motionless prakriti and the manifestation begins. Once the equilibrium of the gunas is broken, prakriti goes on unfolding and expanding through other metaphysical and physical categories. After providing the initial impetus, purusha (soul) remains a passive witness and all subsequent actions belong to prakriti.

Another view is that of the vedanta system, according to which prakriti is not real but illusory and so are its gunas. They appear to be real, however, when Brahman (universal spirit), out of its own sweet will, assumes avidya (nescience). Brahman causes prakriti and its gunas through assumed nescience. It is maya or avidya (nescience) that makes one believe, through distortion, that the balance between the gunas of prakriti is disturbed. Prakriti is not a reality but only a fake effect caused by maya.

Whichever of these two views we may accept, all these systems (sankhya, yoga, and vedanta) agree that the appearance of the phenomenal world is due to the unfoldment of prakriti through its twenty-three metaphysical and physical categories. They also agree that the process of such unfoldment sets in when the equilibrium of the three gunas of prakriti is disturbed, resulting in one or the other of them predominating over the remaining two. In short, unmanifested prakriti is merely a condition of the three gunas in perfect equilibrium with each other, while the manifested universe is nothing but an expression of these three fundamental attributes of prakriti interacting and combining with each other. The gunas underlie both noumenon as well as the phenomenon of prakriti.

Trinity of Gunas—Sattva, Rajas, and Tamas

Gunas of prakriti are three in number: sattva, rajas, and tamas. It is very difficult to explain what sattva, rajas, and tamas stand for. It is impossible to comprehend their real nature through ordinary human intellect since both mind and intellect also are the evolutes of these. Usually, the gunas are referred to as qualities, attributes, or properties. So sattva, rajas, and tamas can be regarded as the basic inherent qualities or attributes of prakriti (nature). Another meaning of the word *guna* is a string, a rope, or a strand of a cord. The three gunas of prakriti are comparable to three strands of a rope. Just as a rope is used for binding, so also is the three-strand rope of the gunas a binding of prakriti. It binds the multiplicity of the manifold universe and keeps all manifestations under complete control. Moreover, these gunas of prakriti not only bind the matter and objects of the manifested universe but also bind the purushas (individual souls) into subtle and gross bodies of matter.

Though the connotations of the term *guna* are manifold and the true nature of sattva, rajas, and tamas can be known only through higher spiritual experiences, it is worthwhile to attempt to understand their characteristics. For the sake of clarity, the essential characteristics and peculiarities of each of the three gunas of prakriti that vary in different contexts can be classified under various aspects.

Aspects of Guna as Motive	Sattva	Rajas	Tamas
(i) Powers of evolution	harmonic vibrations; uniform tension	mobility or activity	static resistance or inertia
(ii) Phenomenal radiations	luminocity or radiation; white or bright yellow in color	haziness or dimness; red in color	darkness; black in color
(iii) Spiritual expressions	divine or angelic; rising to higher, heavenly planes	humane; staying on earthly plane	demoniac; dragging down to hell or lower planes
(iv) Reflections of awareness	illumination; discriminative knowledge	scepticism; mundane knowledge	illusion or ignorance; groping in the dark
(v) Mental conditions	peace; serenity; stability	restlessness; state of flux	dullness; fickleness
(vi) Motivations of life	dispassion; devotional outlook; spiritual pursuits	higher passions; pleasure-seeking; worldly pursuits	lower passions; mirage-chasing; idle pursuits

Aspects of Guna as Motive	**Sattva**	**Rajas**	**Tamas**
(vii) Forces of bondage	fondness for comforts and learning	liking for various goal-motivated undertakings	given to indolence, slumber, and heedlessness
(viii) Ensuing symptoms	steadiness; intellectual growth; quickened understanding; purity; spiritual fervor; health; happiness; goodness; humility; uprightness; love; compassion; charity; truthfulness; forgiveness; fortitude; tenacity; contentment; enthusiasm; cheerfulness; fearlessness; gentleness; self-restraint; moderation, etc.	activism; flared-up senses; passion; greed; craving; hoarding; attachment; self-conceit; arrogance; ostentation; unjustness; contempt; slander; prone to joy and sorrow; boastfulness; competition; tendency of likes and dislikes ambition, excess, etc.	sluggishness; infatuation; confusion; stupidity; delusion; aversion; malice; anger; fear; harshness; recklessness; bewilderment; irrationality; inadvertance: obstinancy; deceit; procrastination; despondency; vulgarity; grief; anxiety; pain; hatred; violence; deficiency, etc.

Lord Krishna says in Bhagavad Gita, "Sattva, rajas, and tamas are the (three) constituent aspects that originate from prakriti (primordial nature); they bind down within the body, O mighty-armed Arjuna, the imperishable dweller (soul) of the body." (XIV:5)

Sattva being pure and luminous, binds to happiness and knowledge. Rajas being impure, causes passion and cravings and binds to activity. Tamas, being of the lowest type, causes ignorance, inertia, and bewilderment, and binds to indolence and illusion. Sattva facilitates enlightenment. A yogi should increase sattva and purge out rajas and tamas from his or her individual nature in order to know reality. Sattva gives rise to dharma (merits or virtues) in individual nature, while rajas and tamas produce adharma (demerits).

Once the equilibrium of the trinity of gunas is disturbed, a constant interplay of these gunas begins. As a result, the three gunas combine and cross-combine with each other in innumerable ways and in different proportions. Such combinations of gunas convert the undifferentiated stuff of prakriti (primal nature) into differentiated matter. To put it another way, it can be said that pure energy is transformed into subtle matter. The restless dynamism caused by the unending interactions of the trinity of gunas provide the basic motive power for the evolutionary creation.

Reflections Cause Imbalance Among Gunas

Brahman is chit (pure consciousness) or absolute awareness. It is known as *chidatma* (spiritual conscience). When this chidatma is reflected in the samashti avidya (universal nescience), it assumes the role of Ishvara (God). In the same way, when it is reflected in the vyashti avidya (individual nescience), the role assumed is that of jivatma (individual soul). Both God as well as the individual souls are nothing but *abhasas* (mere reflections) of chit (pure consciousness of the Brahman) into the avidya (nescience) that is the basic characteristic of prakriti (nature). There is a distinction between the two types of reflections. God or the universal reflection is the Lord of prakriti, while the individual reflection or soul is liable to the bondages of prakriti.

When chit becomes reflected as cosmic conscience in the form of God, it does not lose omniscience and omnipotence. God remains unconditioned and beyond the bounds of prakriti. In fact, God governs the latter. On the other hand, when chit is reflected as individual conscience, it degenerates from absolute pure consciousness to a limited individual consciousness. This conditioned consciousness is called *chitta* (individual conscience). The cosmic conscience, God, initiates the macrocosmic manifestation of prakriti (nature), while the individual conscience initiates the microcosmic manifestation. The conscience at the macrocosmic as well as the microcosmic level, due to its reflections in avidya (nescience), cause imbalance in the three gunas of prakriti, setting evolutionary forces into motion.

Order of Evolution of Prakriti

When chit or pure consciousness of Brahman is reflected in avidya (nescience), it appears as *chidabhasa* or individual soul. Unlike its cosmic counterpart, God, the individual soul is liable to stick to the defilements of the gunas of prakriti. No sooner does it stick to the gunas that it loses its purity and gets defiled into chitta (individual conscience). The animating principle of life begins the order of evolution of prakriti. This order of evolution in both the macrocosmic and microcosmic manifestations is more or less similar.

In both macrocosmic and microcosmic manifestations, prakriti evolves through its twenty-three tattvas (categories): mahat or buddhi (intellect), ahankara (ego), manas (mind), five jnanendriyas (cognitive faculties), five karmendriyas (action faculties), five tanmatras (subtle elements) and five mahabhutas (gross elements). As mentioned earlier, the reflection of chit (pure consciousness) as chitta (individual conscience) results in a loss of purity and omniscience on the part of the spirit or soul. Subsequently, due to avidya (nescience), it sticks to the gunas of prakriti and gets further defiled and entangled in the above-mentioned tattvas. In this way, the order of microcosmic evolution begins binding the individual soul into the snares of twenty-three evolutes of prakriti (nature). Initially, it is enveloped in the *antahkarana* (internal instrument) and subsequently into *bahyakarana* (external instrument) as well as the subtle and gross elements. We shall, now, discuss this process in detail.

Antahkarana (Internal Instrument)

The first step toward evolution is the emergence of antahkarana or the internal instrument consisting of four categories: chitta (individual conscience), mahat or buddhi (intellect), ahankara (ego), and manas (mind). Chitta, as discussed earlier, is the defiled reflection of pure consciousness of spirit and as such is transcendent and immaterial. On the other hand, the remaining three categories of the antahkarana are subtle matter.

Mahat literally means "great." It is the great cause or the fundamental stuff of the vast phenomenal universe. This great principle is also known as buddhi (intellect). It is the power of comprehension. It helps not only to comprehend the material world, but also to communicate with the spirit or self, as it is closely linked with chitta (conscience) and thereby with the animating principle. Chitta virtually serves as a seat for buddhi (intellect).

Ahankara (ego) is the next direct evolute from mahat or buddhi. Ahankara is sometimes mistaken for chitta (conscience). Ahankara functions on the extroverted plane of subject-object relationship, but chitta is not conditioned by such distinctions of subject and object. Chitta (conscience) is unconditioned self-awareness, while ahankara is conditioned by ego-sense or self-concern. As a matter of fact, the true self is beyond and behind the screen of ego, which is nothing but an aspect of avidya (ignorance). The real self remains completely circumscribed and beclouded by ahankara (ego), and is discovered only when self-concern is totally dissolved. With the dissolution of ego, the subject-object distinctions also disappear and transcendental awareness dawns. That is true self-awareness.

Though both buddhi (intellect) and ahankara (ego) are the evolutes springing from the combination of all three gunas, buddhi precedes and is superior to ahankara. This is because the former is characterized by the predominance of sattva while the latter has the predominance of any one quality at a given time. The gunas are not manifested one by one or individually; they are present in all the evolutes of prakriti at once, though they are distributed in unequal proportions. They exist in samyavastha (equal proportion or equilibrium) only in the undifferentiated and completely homogeneous primordial substance of prakriti. This original state of perfect equilibrium of gunas characterizes prakriti as avyakta (invisible, unmanifest, or undeveloped).

Ahankara (ego) has the potential to transform according to the predominant proportions of the three gunas. So it becomes distinct as sattvic, rajasic, and tamasic categories. Out of *sattvic ahankara* evolve manas (mind or the faculty of thinking) and jnanendriyas (the five cognitive senses), *rajasic ahankara* develops into karmendriyas (the five action faculties) and *tamasic ahankara* produces tanmatras (subtle primary elements). From ahankara the process of evolution branches off in three different directions, according to its three classes.

The first three evolutes of prakriti, buddhi (intellect), ahankara (ego), and manas (mind) form the three-fold instrument, called antahkarana (the internal instrument). Sometimes chitta (conscience) is also considered as the fourth constituent of this inner organ. This antahkarana is considered to be of *madhyama parimana* (medium size), neither immense nor small. It is the so-called inner psychic shell that normally closely overlies purusha or atman (the individual soul). It assumes a powerful and commanding position in relation to the other evolutes of prakriti. It forms the innermost center with all the conditioning attributes of the individual personality. It is the real center governing all psycho-mental processes. With the help of this inner instrument, an individual proceeds toward the various experiences of the outer environment through the exterior senses of perception. It can be said that antahkarana (internal instrument) controls an individual much more than he or she can control it. This is the reason why it actually shrouds the individual self and makes the latter undertake the hallucinatory role of being involved in the life-process. The individual soul is dragged into an illusory relation with the psycho-mental processes of life through antahkarana.

Bahyakarana (External Instrument)

We have already seen that ahankara branches off into three more evolutes apart from manas (mind), jnanendriyas (five cognitive senses), karmendriyas (five action senses), and tanmatras (five subtle primary elements).

Now we shall discuss the cognitive and action senses. Jnanendriyas or the cognitive senses are the five perceiving faculties: hearing, sight, smell, taste, and touch. The corresponding body parts through which these faculties work are ears, eyes, nose, tongue, and skin. Karmendriyas, or the action senses, are the five action faculties: speech, grasping, locomotion, evacuation, and reproduction. The corresponding organs through which these faculties work are tongue, hands, feet, rectum, and genitals. The faculties of perception and action form together a part of the subtle body, while the organs of perception and action form a part of the gross body. In other words, the faculties of perception and powers of action are the products of subtle matter, while the corresponding physical organs, through which they are effected, are made of gross matter.

The ten sense-faculties (five cognitive and five action) together, are known as bahyakarana (the external instrument). They are so-called because they function outward. Though they are not perceptible, being of subtle matter, their presence can be inferred from their working. Sattva is the predominant guna in the faculties of perception, while rajas is predominant in the faculties of action. The faculties of perception make for the attitude of *bhokta* (enjoyer or recipient) in an individual, while the faculties of action make him or her *karta*, (doer or one who acts).

Coordination Between Internal and External Instruments

The bhokta is one who is endowed with the faculties of perception through which he or she receives and assimilates various vishayas (sense-objects), and as a result experiences pleasant or unpleasant feelings and sensations. This means that the bhokta, in order to enjoy sense-objects and experience the spheres of sense-perceptions, needs the help of the "inner instrument" (conscience, intellect, ego, and mind). These four components of the inner instrument and the perceptive senses function together in a coordinated manner to provide worldly experiences to the bhokta (recipient). The consciousness of the bhokta is turned outward through the doors of the senses. The other principle of karta (doer) also remains in effect simultaneously with that of bhokta. Karta constantly and spontaneously carries out activities through the action senses in cooperation and harmony with the bhokta. An individual is enabled to continue life-processes through the joint functioning of the principles of karta and bhokta.

The ten sense-faculties (bahyakarana or external instrument) function as the doors, while antahkarana or internal instrument (conscience, intellect, ego, and mind) function in a coordinated manner to open and close these doors seeking, apprehending, and reacting to the external environment. First of all, the mind collects the outer experiences through the ten sense-faculties and presents them to the ego, which appropriates them and subsequently delivers them to the intellect for further analysis and judgment. Finally, these experiences are reflected in the conscience or the inner self. The impressions of the outer universe so received and reflected in the mirror of conscience, produce the world of visions, dreams, and mirages, weaving delusion on the part of the purusha (individual soul). As a result, the individual becomes confused and bewildered. His or her higher consciousness becomes veiled and comprehension becomes limited.

All life-processes are governed and directed by antahkarana (internal instrument) and are executed through bahyakarana (external instrument). Among the four constituents of antahkarana, it is the mind that remains in immediate contact with and operates directly through the ten sense-faculties of bahyakarana. Therefore, some scholars also include the mind among the sense-faculties and recognize eleven sense-faculties in all. They differentiate the mind by calling it *antarendriya* (internal sense faculty), while the other ten are considered the *bahyendriyas* (external sense-faculties).

Purusha (soul) is not the real activator of the life-process, yet it feels engaged into that hallucinatory role of karta (doer) and bhokta (recipient). Ahankara (ego) is the real center and prime motivator of all life-processes. But through *abhimana* (conceit) it causes the purusha to believe that it is the individual soul (purusha) who acts, enjoys, suffers, etc. Actually, purusha is devoid of any modification or action. All psychic and physical experiences of the phenomenal realm belong to ahankara (ego). Through the misconceived notion of "I consciousness" produced by ahankara, purusha is misled to wrongly appropriate to itself whatever the former initiates. Purusha feels false concern as the originator of all actions, and the recipient of all joys and sorrows, whereas the real commander behind the veil is ahankara.

Ahankara (ego) carries out its activities through the five jnanendriyas (cognitive sense-faculties) and five karmendriyas (action faculties). In doing so, it uses manas (mind), and the five pranas (vital airs). All the activities proceed through the harmonious functioning of all those products of ahankara (ego). Like karmendriyas, the five pranas are also the products of rajasic ahankara (active ego). Though these pranas perform very important functions in the human organism, they are not clearly specified among the hierarchical categories evolving out of prakriti (nature). Some texts mention them, while others do not. All three philosophical systems: sankhya, yoga, and vedanta accept the reality of prana (vital force) and its significant role in the actual practice for self-realization. This vital force is generic prana, out of which five different vital airs are derived.

The five vital airs are: (i) prana (ascending vital air), (ii) *apana* (descending vital air), (iii) *samana* (equalizing vital air), (iv) *udana* (elevating vital air), and (v) *vyana* (pervading vital air). The first vital air, prana, derives its name from the generic prana (vital force) and its seat is in the chest region. Apana is located in the lower abdomen, and samana is centered in the stomach and the navel region. Udana is effective from the throat to the skull, and vyana prevails in the entire body. These five pranas are often wrongly identified with the air that we breathe. The air of the breath is considered to be grosser than these five vital airs. Pranas are, in fact, not the winds but the subtle powers that build up and sustain the systems of the subtle body of the human organism. They should not be confused with the air that we inhale and exhale. Pranas are subtle forces that derive their power directly from the central source of life-energy that manifests in the human body by virtue of the presence of purusha (soul).

Subtle and Gross Elements

So far, the evolution of prakriti (nature) has proceeded in the direction of unfolding the inner and outer equipments (antahkarana and bahyakarana) useful for perceiving phycho-mental phenomena and the subconscious biomotor activities. Subsequently, the unfoldment of prakriti occurs in the direction of producing coarser and denser categories, which make the objective experiences possible. The equipment for both subjective as well as objective experiences evolved out of one and the same homogeneous mass of energy, prakriti. As such, the subjective and objective phenomena have a single substratum and a common matrix in prakriti.

We have already mentioned earlier that out of tamasic ahankara (dull ego) are produced five tanmatras (subtle primary elements). Now let us understand the nature, order of appearance, and further transformation of tanmatras into five mahabhutas (generic gross elements).

The five tanmatras are (i) shabda (sound), (ii) sparsha (touch), (iii) rupa (color/form), (iv) rasa (taste), and (v) gandha (smell). Tanmatras are the most rudimentary stable elements that can be apprehended only in manifold sensations. Their true nature, however, can be realized through the experiences of the subtle body. Since these rarefied elements have the potentiality of being transformed into gross elements, they serve as the potential material for the formation of the phenomenal universe. They can be considered the subtle components of the ultra-atomic particles, forming the nuclei of the physical world.

There is a specific order in which these five tanmatras evolve. They appear neither simultaneously nor in random order. First of all, shabda (sound) originates. Then sparsha (touch), rupa (form/color), rasa (taste), and gandha (smell) come into existence in succeeding order. Each succeeding tanmatra retains the quality or qualities of the preceding ones. This means that the later the appearance, the more qualities exist in a tanmatra. Accordingly, shabda has the solitary quality of sound. Sparsha possesses two qualities: touch and sound. Rupa has triple qualities: form, touch, and sound. Likewise, rasa has four qualities, and gandha has all the five qualities.

Out of these five tanmatras evolve the five mahabhutas (generic gross elements): (i) akasha (ether), (ii) *vayu* (air), (iii) *teja* or agni (fire), (iv) *apa* or *jala* (water), and (v) *prithvi* (earth). Generally, each tanmatra is linked with a corresponding mahabhuta. Sound is linked with ether, tangibility with air, shape and color with fire, taste and flavor with water, and odor with earth. Each mahabhuta, however, is not merely a product of any single tanmatra. Each of them, in effect, is a compound of all the five tanmatras, one of them dominating in each. For example, sound dominates in ether, touch in air, form in fire, taste in water, and smell in earth.

The mahabhutas also evolved in the same order as their corresponding tanmatras. That means akasha (ether) is the first to appear, followed by air, fire, water, and earth in succession. Again, like the tanmatras, each succeeding mahabhuta possesses the quality or qualities of the preceeding ones. Though mahabhutas are considered gross elements, they are not yet visible at this stage. Still, they are in their generic forms. In their pure states they are in ultra-atomic forms and are not visible. They should not be confused with chemical elements known to modern science. In fact, all the chemical elements of modern science are derived out of the combinations and condensations of these five generic gross elements, or mahabhutas. In other words, the mahabhutas can be considered the essential states of matter.

Visible creation comes into existence only after the process of *panchikaraṇa* (quintuplication) between the five mahabhutas takes place. This quintuplication is a principle of compounding each generic mahabhuta with the rest of the four in specific proportion. Uncompounded, mahabhutas cannot produce the gross object or the physical world. In order to create the visible universe, they have to go through the quintuplication process as described below.

Each of the five mahabhutas is divided into two equal parts. Then one of the halves of each mahabhuta is further split into four equal parts. One quarter of each of the remaining four mahabhutas is added to the undivided half of each mahabhuta. Thus, in each newly formed mahabhuta there will be a constituent part of all the five original generic mahabhutas in definite proportions. Accordingly, the newly constituted ether will have 50 percent of the original generic ether and 12.5 percent of each of the remaining four: air, fire, water, and earth. Likewise, all the other newly constituted mahabhutas will have 50 percent of their own generic substance and 12.5 percent of the remaining four mahabhutas. Only such compounded mahabhutas possess atoms and participate in the formation of all the gross objects, bodies, and the whole universe. These mahabhutas are the last evolutes of prakriti. Thus, all animate and inanimate creations and all life-processes are dependent on the hierarchical evolution of the twenty-five metaphysical and physical categories (tattvas) discussed in this chapter.

Classification of Tattvas (Categories)

We have discussed the process and order of the unfoldment of prakriti (or *pradhana* as it is often called in the sankhya and yoga systems) through the expressions of its triple gunas (attributes). We have mentioned earlier that there are twenty-five tattvas (categories) according to sankhya.

In terms of cause and effect, these twenty-five categories are classified into four groups: (i) *avikriti* (not an effect), (ii) *prakriti-vikriti* (cause-effect), (iii) *vikriti* (effect only), and (iv) *na-prakriti, na-vikriti* (no cause, no effect). Those groups are further explained below:

1. Avikriti (not an effect): the *mula prakriti* (primordial nature) is called avikriti or uncaused as it is not produced by anything. In other words it is only the cause and not an effect.

2. Prakriti-vikriti (cause-effect): seven categories are such that they are produced from other causes (categories) and they in turn are the causes of further products (categories). Thus they are both cause as well as effect. These seven categories are mahat or buddhi (intellect), ahankara (ego), and the five tanmatras (subtle primary elements). Mahat is the product of prakriti and produces ahankara, which in turn produces five tanmatras. These tanmatras also produce mahabhutas (generic gross elements).

3. Vikriti or *vikara* (effect only): the following sixteen categories are only the effects and not the cause. They are themselves the products but do not produce anything. These are the five jnanendriyas (cognitive senses), the five karmendriyas (action senses), the five mahabhutas (generic gross elements), and the manas (mind).

4. Na-prakriti, na-vikriti (no cause, no effect): purusha (spirit or soul) does not produce anything, nor is it produced by anything. Hence it is neither the cause nor the effect.

The yoga system offers a more or less similar four-fold classification of the twenty-four categories evolving out of prakriti or pradhana.

Keep in mind the four levels or stages of development or differentiation among nature's triple gunas. In yoga, the twenty-four categories are broadly classified into four divisions: (1) *alinga* (unmarked or signless), (2) *lingamatra* (only marked), (3) *avishesha* (nonspecific), and (4) vishesha (specific). These four divisions are briefly explained below:

1. Alinga (unmarked): undifferentiated prakriti is considered to be unmarked. Being noumenon, it is signless. So far its latent gunas (attributes) exist in samyavastha (state of equilibrium), and it remains characterless and nonproductive. Moreover, that being the primordial state of prakriti, it is not resoluble into anything else. Therefore, there is no operation of the evolutionary force at this initial level.

2. Lingamatra (only marked): at the next level, phenomenal creation actually begins. Out of alinga (unmarked) prakriti evolves mahat (also called buddhi, intellect). This mahat is the first and only evolute from which the entire further evolution proceeds and is resoluble into prakriti. Being the resultant effect of prakriti, it is marked with differentiated characteristics. Hence it is called lingamatra (only marked).

3. Avishesha (nonspecific): this third group includes six categories, ahankara (ego) and its further products, the five tanmatras (subtle primary elements). These six categories that are products as well as their causes are considered to be avishesha (nonspecific). They are merely archetypal and not particularized. In the course of further evolution they become reflected into specific or particular categories that are far more specialized in their characteristics and functions.

4. Vishesha (specific): in the fourth and final level of unfoldment, ahankara (ego) produces eleven more categories: manas (mind), five jnanendriyas (cognitive sense-faculties), and five karmendriyas (action faculties). Similarly, five tanmatras (subtle primary elements) produce five mahabhutas (generic gross elements). All these sixteen categories produced at this level constitute an aggregate of vishesha (specific). There is no further transformation of these into any more categories. From this level onward the process of cosmic manifestation involves only mutual combinations of all the evolved tattvas (categories). The last sixteen categories that evolve at this fourth level of unfoldment are clearly particularized and highly specialized. Therefore they are called vishesha (specific).

Like the four-fold classifications of the tattvas (categories) of prakriti (nature) in the sankhya and yoga systems, there is a three-fold classification in the vedanta system, also. According to vedanta, the categories unfolding out of prakriti or avidya are classified into three broad groups: (i) *avyakrta* (not manifested), (ii) *amurta* (invisible or formless manifestation), and (iii) *murta* (visible manifestation with names and forms). Avyakrta is the unmanifested state of prakriti with its triple gunas in equilibrium. The second division, amurta, includes all the subtle, invisible, and formless categories. They are buddhi (intellect), ahankara (ego), manas (mind), the five cognitive senses, the five action faculties, the five vital airs, and the five tanmatras (subtle primary elements). The last group, murta, includes the five mahabhutas (generic gross elements), through the cross-combinations from which the entire visible universe is created.

Difference Regarding Primordial Principles

To sum up the discussion of the metaphysics of the sankhya, yoga, and vedanta systems, it may be said that there are some differences between their speculative thoughts.

The first difference is in regard to the fundamental and eternal principles that cause the whole drama of the unfoldment of the phenomenal universe. Sankhya and yoga regard purusha (individual spirit) and prakriti (nature) as two independent and eternal principles, while vedanta carries its speculation a step further, integrating the duad of purusha and prakriti into a higher conception of a single nondual principle of Brahman (transcendent spirit).

Another difference is regarding the nature of purusha. Sankhya and yoga believe in the multiplicity of purushas, while vedanta dissolves such multiplicity by identifying the individual soul (atman) with Brahman.

The third difference is in respect to the reality of prakriti. Sankhya and yoga consider prakriti to be real and eternal; but vedanta dismisses it by explaining it as an illusory manifestation of Brahman through its maya power. According to vedanta, prakriti has no real independent existence. It is merely a distortion of Brahman, appearing as the misread subjective experiences of individual souls, which again represents the same Brahman under the spell of avidya (nescience).

Such differences in conceptualization of philosophical thoughts are but natural and inevitable, since the human intellect, itself being a product of prakriti, cannot fully comprehend the higher principles. These minor differences, however, do not seem to present any real contradiction in the speculation of the three systems on the whole. Sankhya, yoga, and vedanta are in complete agreement that in order to attain liberation, the purusha (individual soul) must become totally isolated from the fetters of prakriti (nature), whether this latter is real or illusory.

Difference in Metaphysical Approaches

The six philosophical systems of India, together, exhaust the rationally possible standpoints of metaphysics. Their metaphysics, with ontological categories and cosmology, is connected to a theory of knowledge and ethical orientation. It revolves around the concepts of universal and individual essences and the doctrine of harmony or oneness of both. Since all the six systems stand on the common ground of the Vedic orthodox tradition of Indian philosophy, in spite of the differences in their hypotheses their metaphysical core has more or less a similar structure.

In this chapter we have considered in detail the systematic evolution of a series of twenty-four metaphysical categories enumerated by sankhya and accepted by yoga and vedanta. The metaphysical standpoints of these three systems have a great deal in common. Of course, sankhya and yoga put forth dualistic metaphysics, while vedanta presents a monistic approach. The remaining three systems, vaisheshika, nyaya, and mimamsa (purva), expound pluralistic metaphysics.

In the previous chapter, we have already observed that vaisheshika puts forth the theory of pluralistic metaphysics involving seven categories (padarthas). These categories have nine dravyas (substances) and twenty-four qualitative attributes (gunas) that are either generalized (samanya) or particularized (vishesha). The relation between these categories and attributes is that of inherence (samavaya). Vaisheshika does not agree with the concept of evolution of categories out of a single primordial principle like prakriti (nature). Its approach to metaphysics is realistic and atomistic. It holds that the coming into being of the universe is the result of the movements of the atoms manipulated by God. The activity (karma) of the atoms and their aggregation is the cause of the origin of the universe. Vaisheshika acknowledges the reality of only the external world consisting of innumerable atoms.

Nyaya took over vaisheshika theory as its metaphysical foundation, though it developed sixteen padarthas (categories). Actually, all of these categories of nyaya are included in those of vaisheshika. Similarly, mimamsa (purva) also stepped into the ready framework of the pluralistic-realistic metaphysics shaped by vaisheshika. It deviated slightly in the number and nature of categories. As a matter of fact, mimamsa (purva) bears only a slight metaphysical stamp on its doctrine, which mainly explains the Vedic rituals.

From the point of view of metaphysics, sankhya, yoga, and vedanta have a great deal in common, while vaisheshika, nyaya, and mimamsa (purva) share many characteristics. In spite of their differences in monistic, dualistic, and pluralistic approaches in presenting their metaphysical doctrines, the six systems should not be regarded as independent philosophies. They are merely different schools representing the same thought by elaborating its different aspects.

Their common emphasis is on the ultimate aim of attaining moksha (liberalization) through self-realization. They seek the highest or complete perfection of self here and now, while still alive, and not after death. Further, as a means toward achieving this aim, all these systems unanimously recommend the practice of the various techniques of yoga.

chapter six

Similarity of Macrocosm and Microcosm

We have already seen that there are in all twenty-five metaphysical and physical categories that are instrumental in cosmological evolution. The whole manifest material world evolves out of one unmanifest primordial power and finally dissolves into it after ages through the process of involution. Once again, after a very long pause, the unmanifest power begins to manifest into the phenomenal universe. The cycle of cosmogony, creation and dissolution, or say, evolution and involution, goes on eternally.

Everything in this phenomenal universe is derived from the combinations of the twenty-five metaphysical and physical categories. Due to the continuous combining and recombining of these categories, the whole universe goes on changing every moment. New things come into existence and old things decay and disappear. It is the case with the animate world. New lives are born and old ones die. During the process of evolution, purusha or atman (individual spirit) is fettered with the remaining twenty-four categories of prakriti (nature) and undergoes the rounds of birth and death. In order to liberate the fettered soul from bondage, it becomes necessary not only to know these categories, but also to transcend them through an involutionary process. Yoga is the practical system for realizing this end.

In fact, the human soul strives continuously to shake itself free from the entanglement of prakriti, but unfortunately becomes so much involved in life-processes and their consequences that it forgets its real objective. As a result, it succumbs to death before realizing the goal of liberation. Again it is born, along with all its merits and demerits acquired during the previous births. It can go on being born again and again, millions of times, if it never succeeds to know and transcend the categories that bind it.

Both sankhya and vedanta philosophies believe that moksha (liberation) can be attained through *vidya* (knowledge of the self) and that such knowledge cannot be obtained from outside but from within, through the process of yoga. Knowledge of the self is already present within us, but because of the entanglement into the categories of prakriti due to avidya (nescience), it is forgotten. Revival of this knowledge of the self is possible through the systematic practice of yoga. When all the categories of prakriti (nature) that bind the individual human soul are known and transcended through various techniques of yoga, the true nature of the self is realized and liberation from all bondages is attained.

Macrocosm and Microcosm

The entire process of creation and the embodiment and conditioning of the spirit by the twenty-four categories of prakriti (nature) occurs in three levels: (i) karana (causal), (ii) *sukshma* (subtle), and (iii) *sthula* (gross). The spirit, both in its universal and individual aspects, becomes embodied and conditioned at these three levels. In other words, the spirit is covered with three types of bodies, each conditioning its consciousness to varying degrees. These three bodies, according to their varying grossness, are called *karana sharira* (causal body), sukshma or *linga sharira* (subtle body), and *sthula sharira* (gross body). The first is most subtle, the next is subtle, and the last is gross. The first two are not visible, while the last is visible as an empirical reality.

These three bodies condition the spirit with three relative states of consciousness. In the gross body, consciousness is limited to *jagrati* (waking state). In the subtle body it is limited to *svapna* (dream state). In the causal body it is associated with *sushupti* (deep-sleep state). This holds good for the spirit in both aspects—universal and individual. When it is embodied in the universal aspect, it assumes the form of *Brahmanda* (macrocosm) with extraordinary universal consciousness. On the other hand, in the individual aspect, it assumes the form of *pindanda* (microcosm) with ordinary individual consciousness.

From the macrocosmic point of view, it is regarded as the aggregate or totality of being—the cosmic self, while from the microcosmic standpoint it is the individual self.

Indian philosophical thought proclaims the identity of the individual self and the cosmic self. As such, it believes that whatever is found in the human organism is also found in the universal organism. It visualizes the direct and close link between the microcosmic form of human existence and the macrocosmic form of universal existence.

Sheathing Structure of Human Organism

Before we embark on a detailed review of the cross-relationship between the microcosmic essence and the macrocosmic essence, it is necessary to get some idea about the sheathing structure of the human organism, pindanda, or microcosm. According to yoga philosophy, the human organism is constituted of purusha or atman (self) enveloped in three overlapping vestures: karana sharira (causal body), sukshma sharira (subtle body), and sthula sharira (gross body). The causal body is the innermost vesture around the human soul and the gross body is the outermost vesture. The subtle body is the intermediate vesture and forms a link between the causal and the gross bodies. The gross body is perishable after the normal human lifespan. The subtle body sustains for a very long time. But the causal body endures the most and is comparatively more or less permanent, because the same causal body is carried forth through many lives.

According to vedanta philosophy, there are five superimposed layers or vestures enveloping the human soul. The first which is the innermost is known as *anandamaya kosha* (sheath of joy or bliss). It corresponds with the causal body mentioned above. The next three layers are called *vijnanamaya kosha* (sheath of intellect or knowledge), *manomaya kosha* (sheath of mind), and *pranamaya kosha* (sheath of vital airs). They jointly correspond with the subtle body mentioned above. The fifth is *annamaya kosha* (sheath of food), which corresponds with the gross body.

This sheathing structure of the human organism hides the purusha or atman (self) deep within, falsely projecting itself as the microcosm and bringing forth the illusion of the world as the macrocosm. This two-fold appearance of microcosm and macrocosm is in effect only as a phantasmagoric production because of avidya (nescience) that overwhelms the intuitive and perceiving faculties of human beings. The bodies or sheaths thus obstruct the true comprehensive knowledge about the concealed self. Such knowledge, which is already present within, is recollected when the sheathing structures of the human body are swept away. When this obstruction is removed, the self is realized and the apparent creations of the microcosm and the macrocosm are immediately undone. Such realization can be achieved through the practice of yoga. During profound meditation, a yogi visualizes in his own organism (microcosm) the magnified image of the entire universe (macrocosm) distinctly by stages. Thereby he or she realizes that the essence of microcosm with all its modifications and stratifications, gross and subtle, matter and form, is one and identical with the essence of macrocosm.

States of Microcosm

Now we shall understand the different states of microcosmic consciousness and the nature of the experiences in these distinctive states as they evolve. The microcosmic essence, purusha or atman, has four padas (states of being). They are known as (i) atman, (ii) *prajna,* (iii) *taijas,* and (iv) *vishva.* The first state of atman is the omniscient and the eternal indwelling self that is the sole controller of the microcosm. The second state is that of prajna (knower) with undivided consciousness, as in deep sleep. The third state is that of taijas (luminous or shining one) having its field of operation in the dream state. The fourth state is that of vishva (extroverted consciousness) which is an individual moving and living in the waking state in the phenomenal world. The last three states of microcosmic consciousness are identified with the three bodies: causal, subtle, and gross bodies, respectively.

This analysis of the microcosmic states of being also brings out the three-fold nature of experiencing. Microcosmic or human experiences can be broadly divided into three states: the waking state, dream state, and deep-sleep state. Each of these three states has distinctive characteristics. In the waking state, the gross body functions as the embodiment of the jiva (soul) and the experiences of the external phenomenal world are obtained through different sense-perceptions. In the dream state, the subtle body with indriyas (all sense-faculties) and antahkarana (conscience, ego, mind, and intellect) functions as the embodiment of the soul. In this state, all perceptions are internal and based on the impressions of the previous experiences that are deposited in the mind. Only the past impressions lodged within are revivified. Though these experiences are merely internal and subtle, they are shaped and projected as if they are real, like the experiences of the waking state.

In the deep-sleep state neither the sense-faculties nor the mind function, the determinative intellect lapses into its causal condition, and consciousness is withdrawn into itself. Hence it does not set up any presentation of experience.

In this state, the self is restricted to the embodiment of the causal body only. In the deep-sleep state, though consciousness is drawn closer to the inner self, there is no real self-awareness because atman is still covered by avidya (veil of ignorance), which is the root cause of all three states: waking, dreaming, and sleeping. Unlike the waking and dreaming states, however, the ego or the non-self does not function in the deep-sleep state.

There is no intervention of any cognition in deep sleep and stream of consciousness is arrested within itself. But this is still not the transcendental state or the fourth state known as *turiya,* in which the consciousness merges into the atman (self).

States of Macrocosm

We have observed that the microcosmic essence, atman, has four different states of consciousness. Likewise, the macrocosmic essence, Brahman, also has four distinctive states: (i) turiya or avyakta, (ii) Ishvara, (iii) *hiranyagarbha* or *sutratma,* and (iv) *virat* or *viraj.*

The first state of Brahman is indescribable because it is *avyakta* (imperceptible or unmanifest) and beyond the three states of normal human consciousness (wakefulness, dream, and deep sleep). That is why it is called turiya (the fourth or absolute state). It is the supreme culmination of the transcendental state in which the mystery of Brahman is centralized. It is the state of undifferentiated potential power that is advaita (nondual), nitya (everlasting), *swayambhu* (self-existent), eka (one-without-a-second), and avinashi (imperishable). It is an utterly tranquil and most blissful state of Brahman, the macrocosmic essence.

The next state is that of Ishvara (God). This is the state known to be the great cause of the *jagatkarana* (universe). It is both the beginning as well as the end of all beings. It is the great omniscient source as well as the controlling center of all of phenomenal creation. It is associated with its own maya (illusory power) from which everything has manifested in the past, is manifesting in the present, and will be manifested in the future. Maya or prakriti constitutes the causal body of Ishvara.

The third state is hiranyagarbha or the presiding deity of the macrocosm invested within the subtle body. It is also called sutratma (thread-soul of the universe) because it binds all the constituents of the universe together. It is the consolidating power that penetrates through all creation like a subtle thread holding the universe like a multitude of shining gems woven upon a string. It holds all creation in and out as it spreads through the void.

The last state is virat or viraj (universal or cosmic form). It is also called *vaishvanara.* It is known as the all-pervading transfiguration of the divine being. It is the omnipresent universal form encompassing all the aggregates of the visible and tangible phenomenal world. It is the fully manifested macrocosm. It is what human eyes perceive as the gross universe, wherein all manifestations of time and space appear and perish. Yet this macrocosmic form is not the complete manifestation of infinite avyakta (imperceptible) or turiya (absolute) Brahman (reality). It is produced out of the association of only a fragment of absolute Brahman with its maya (illusory power).

Macrocosm Vis-a-vis Microcosm

When macrocosmic evolution begins, avyakta or turiya Brahman (absolute reality) first manifests as Ishvara (God). This is the universal soul of the macrocosm having the causal body of maya (willful nescience). It is the efficient as well as the material cause of the universe. Then it assumes the form of hiranyagarbha having the subtle body binding the universe with its subtle threads. Finally, it emerges as virat with the gross celestial form, encompassing the entire universe. This is the gross body of the macrocosm.

Likewise, during microcosmic development, the atman or purusha (individual soul) first manifests as prajna (knower) enveloped in the causal body of avidya (ignorance). Then it further takes over the subtle body and manifests as taijas (luminous one). Finally, it assumes the vishva form, enveloped into the gross human physique and endowed with normal waking consciousness of human existence.

The four states of macrocosmic evolution roughly correspond with the four states of microcosmic development. The initial stages of both are purely spiritual, while the remaining ones involve the combinations of spirit with matter (prakriti). The four states of macrocosm and the corresponding microcosmic states are compared briefly in the next section.

Turiya or Brahman is the universal spirit. It is the highest and purest state of divine existence. It is the ultimate reality and the noumenon behind all metaphysical and physical phenomena. It is beyond all worldly existences, the supra-cosmic reality. It is one-without-a-second. It is absolute, eternal, unmanifest, unborn, omniscient, omnipresent, omnipotent, immutable, inconceivable, undefinable, all-pervasive, and all-inclusive. When associated with its maya power, it assumes the following three macrocosmic states:

1. Ishvara

It is the manifestation of the cosmic Lord or God. It is the great spirit that is the source of all conscious souls as well as ever-productive nature. It projects the universe from itself and again withdraws it. It is the source as well as the end of all manifestations. It includes the totality of consciousness. As such, it is universal consciousness. It is the great cause of creation and it is associated with the aggregate of all the causal bodies in the universe. It effects everything through maya and then remains a sovereign witness to everything. It is the omniscient controller of maya as well as all beings.

2. Hiranyagarbha or sutratma

Ishvara is cosmic Lord, while hiranyagarbha is cosmic self. The former is the higher nature of the great spirit, while the latter is its lower nature. The former includes all conscious souls, while the latter includes the totality of unconscious nature. The former is the great cause of creation, while the latter is the presiding deity of the cosmos. As such, the whole universe with all its becoming is projected through the universal energy or cosmic force of hiranyagarbha, which permeates the entire creation. The whole universe is held together as shining pearls are strung on a golden thread. This luminous thread-power permeates everything in and out, weaving a shining fabric of subtle stuff. Behind this luminous fabric of the subtle stuff, the face of God remains hidden. Hiranyagarbha loses omniscience due to false identification with the universal ego-sense. As the cosmic ego, it assumes the subtle and luminous cosmic body and becomes associated with all the subtle bodies in the universe collectively.

3. Virat

It is the all-pervading celestial form of the divine being. This universal transfiguration encompasses the aggregate of all gross bodies of the phenomenal world. Virat is the end product of the macrocosm within a fully evolved empirical universe.

Purusha or atman is the individual spirit or self. It is the pure state of individual existence. It has no relative existence since it is beyond the three states of human consciousness: wakeful, dream, and deep-sleep states. It is imperishable and devoid of characteristics like Brahman. When under the spell of maya (illusory power), however, it undergoes deceptions and succumbs to *upadhis* (conditioned states) of the triple bodies (causal, subtle, and gross). These three microcosm states with limitations are described below:

1. Prajna

It is the manifestation of jiva (individual soul) in the causal body. As such, it is associated with Ishvara (God), who is the aggregate of all causal bodies. It can be considered to be the partial aspect of Ishvara, who is the source of all conscious souls. As Ishvara controls and supervises the macrocosm or the larger universe, so also prajna is the controller and supervisor of its microcosm or the small universe of the human organism. Its consciousness is *ghana* (homogeneous or undifferentiated) like that of deep, dreamless sleep, but it is limited due to avidya (ignorance).

2. Taijas

It is the manifestation of jiva (individual soul) in the subtle body. It remains ever active and in a state of perpetual flux because its subtle body is magically fluid and shining. It develops a false identification of the self with ego. This ego-sense keeps it tied with the subtle body. Taijas operates through the egoistic impulses with the aid of the sense-faculties and the vital airs. Its consciousness is turned inward, enjoying exquisite dream memories. Because of the subtle body, it corresponds and remains associated with the hiranyagarbha state that is an aggregate of all subtle bodies of the world.

3. Vishva

It is the final manifestation of jiva (individual soul) in the gross human organism that is subject to growth, decay, and death. Its consciousness is turned outward through the doors of the senses. It is completely bound and conditioned by matter. It is associated with virat, or the phenomenal world.

Individual Consciousness in Microcosm

Individual consciousness, first, identifies itself with the causal body, and thereafter with the subtle body. But while identifying with the subtle body, it does not give up its identification with the causal body. In the same way, it manifests into the gross body without giving up identification with both the previous bodies. The consciousness of the vishva state of microcosm identifies itself not only with the gross body but also the subtle as well as causal bodies. The consciousness of the waking state remains identified with all the three bodies because it functions through the external organs and also brings into play the internal sense-faculties.

When individual consciousness withdraws from the gross body and becomes identified with the subtle body, the waking state disappears and the dream state ensues. During this dream state, the external organs become inactive and so also the sense-faculties because they cannot function without mutual aid. Consciousness remains restricted to antahkarana, the four-fold inner instrument (conscience, intellect, ego, and mind). In the dream state, individual consciousness carries on its functions through modifications of this four-fold instrument. Experiences of the dream state are generally the products of desires arising from leftover impressions of the waking state. Individual consciousness feels content in playing the double role of both the subject and the object, appearing to satisfy desires in an illusive manner. This dream world is *tejomaya* (full of light) and hence the identification of the individual consciousness with it is called taijas (luminous one). This state of consciousness identifies itself not only with the subtle body, but also the causal body.

When individual consciousness is further withdrawn even from the subtle body, it becomes identified with the causal body. As a result, the deep-sleep state is experienced. In this state, all the functions of even the antahkarana (conscience, intellect, ego, and mind) come to a standstill and consciousness remains bound up with the causal condition, avidya (nescience or ignorance). In this state the individual self experiences itself as merely a reflection of atman (self); but such a reflection is not the real comprehension or self-realization. There is still the possibility of the experiences of the dreaming and waking states springing up once again from such a reflection. Therefore, the individual consciousness associated with the deep-sleep state and the causal body is called prajna (knower), as differentiated from atman (self).

Finally, when individual consciousness is divested of the identification with all the three adjuncts of microcosmic existence (gross, subtle, and causal bodies), nescience is removed and the state of superconsciousness is attained. Then the individual becomes fully aware of his or her pristine nature and realizes the true self or atman. This is turiya or the fourth state beyond the three states of waking, dreaming, and sleeping. In order to attain self-realization, it is necessary to first resolve waking consciousness into dream consciousness, which in turn should be resolved into deep-sleep consciousness. Finally, even deep-sleep consciousness should be resolved into superconsciousness or pure consciousness of atman (self). When atman is realized, Brahman (supreme spirit) is automatically realized because they are one or identical.

Significance of the Syllable Aum

In the Vedas, the monosyllable aum is considered to be the very essence of Brahman. In Vedic philosophy this sacred symbol is highly glorified. "I am aum in all the Vedas," says Lord Krishna in the Bhagavad Gita. (VII:8) Aum is the mysterious formula that is revelatory of Brahman (ultimate reality). It is a composite expression of name as well as a form of the highest truth. It is called *pranava* which stands for the transcendental state, while its three different letters stand for the three phenomenal states. *a* stands for the gross body and the waking state, *u* for the subtle body and the dream state, and *m* for the causal body and the deep-sleep state in the microcosm or the individual human being. Similarly, in the macrocosm, *a* signifies virat or the gross manifestation of the celestial form, *u* signifies hiranyagarbha or the subtle metaphysical manifestation of the universe in the form of the cosmic force, while *m* represents Ishvara or the cosmic Lord in the form of the great primal cause of creation.

The fusion of these three constituents (*a, u,* and *m*) into one integral syllable of aum (or pranava) represents the most fundamental principle of being, both at the microcosmic as well as the macrocosmic level. The process of gradual resolution of all the three states of phenomenal existence, mentioned above, leads to the fusion of the triple constituents of aum into the transcendent integrality of pranava. Such fusion results in the direct spiritual realization and disembodied liberation that is the fourth state, turiya. This is why in Vedic literature aum or pranava is elaborately prescribed as a sacred symbol for contemplation or as a sacred formula for repetition.

In Katha Upanishad, Nachiketas requests Yama (Lord of death): "Tell me that which thou see it as neither this nor that, as neither the cause nor the effect, and as neither the past nor the future."

To this Yama replies: "I tell thee briefly—it is the word *aum.* It is this word that all the Vedas record, all the penances proclaim, and all the spiritual aspirants desire. That syllable means the highest, the Brahman. One who knows it gains whatever he desires. This (aum) is the best and the highest support (for spiritual practice). By knowing this support, one becomes magnanimous in the world of Brahma (Lord the creator)." (I:II:14–17)

In Yoga Sutras, sage Patanjali also has described aum as the designator of Ishvara (God). Thus it has the inherent power of revealing the divine being or supreme consciousness. All yogis and all Indian scriptures attribute great potential and mystic power to this monosyllable aum. It carries hidden within it tremendous power, but only an experienced yogi knows how to release it.

Progressive Resolution of All States into One

All the states of microcosm as well as macrocosm, although they appear to be different, are merely manifold divisions of one and the same reality, Brahman. In order to realize Brahman, it first becomes necessary to identify them with each other and then to resolve them one into the other. A yogi, by contemplating deeply on aum, begins with the identification of the vishva state of microcosmic self with the virat state of macrocosmic self. Then the yogi proceeds to identify taijas with hiranyagarbha and prajna with Ishvara. Thus during contemplation on aum, a yogi experiences the three individual states of consciousness that are identical with the three universal or collective states of consciousness. As a result of such nonexistence of difference between the microcosmic and macrocosmic states, there remains only three states of consciousness instead of six for that yogi.

Having established the identity between the microcosmic and macrocosmic states, a yogi proceeds further to reduce even the remaining three states into only one. The yogi resolves them progressively in order of gross, subtle, and causal states. First of all, the gross state of the mutually identified vishva and virat, symbolized by *a,* is resolved or merged into the subtle state of the mutually identified taijas and hiranyagarbha, symbolized by *u.* Then this latter state is resolved into the causal state of mutually identified prajna and Ishvara, symbolized by *m.* Finally, for the realization of the state of pure consciousness, even the causal state has to be resolved into atman which is identical with Brahman.

This is how a yogi reduces his or her microcosmic personality as well as the macrocosmic universe into atman Brahman, which is of the nature of pure consciousness and infinite bliss. Then the yogi has nothing more to achieve. This final stage is turiya, the fourth state. In this turiya state, a yogi perceives nothing but Brahman everywhere. For him or her the phenomenal world is unreal, and only Brahman is real. He or she is a true *jivanmukta* (one who is liberated while still living). Even though such a yogi may involve him or herself in worldly activities, he or she remains forever free from bondages. The whole yogic process of resolving the three bodies, while repeating aum and thereby realizing Brahman, is briefly but aptly stated by Lord Krishna thus: "Restraining all the gateways of the body, confining the mind within the heart, fixing prana (the life-force) in the crown of the head, becoming established in yogic concentration, uttering the monosyllable aum—the (symbol of) Brahman, and contemplating upon Me, whosoever departs from the body (resolves the three embodied states) attains the highest goal (Brahman)." (Bhagavad Gita, VIII: 12-13)

chapter seven

Theory of Rebirth

Yoga philosophy believes in the principle of the immortality of the soul and the theory of its transmigration. It deals with life not only here and now but also with life hereafter. The implications of the principle of the immortality of the soul are that though the human being is finite, his or her spirit is unborn and undying. The spirit is entirely different from the physical and psychological complexity of human existence. Further, according to the theory of transmigration, such an immortal spirit becomes reborn after each death in an unending series of lives, one after the other. Such continued passage of the spirit in the cycle of births and deaths is called *avagamana* (coming and going). Though the spirit is otherwise considered to be immortal, as jivatma, (an embodied soul) it appears to be dying and reincarnating when involved in the wheel of *samsara* (mundane existence).

The final objective, according to yoga philosophy, is to find a way to escape from this wheel of samsara and secure moksha (liberation) for the soul. Though, according to the principle of immortality, the soul survives even after the death of the body, such survival after death is considered to be merely the temporal freedom of the soul and not real liberation. In that instance, the soul, with all the subliminal impressions of the merits and the demerits acquired during the previous life and stored intact in the subconscious as samskaras (innate complexes or predispositions), awaits rebirth into a new body. The soul's survival after death automatically suggests the existence of a life after death. Such post-existence of the soul indicates transmigration and freedom on a lower plane. But there is another higher concept of immortality and freedom from rebirth. According to this concept, the soul, becoming free from all its physical and psychological adjuncts, rises above all temporal planes and ascends to the highest plane of timelessness, or eternity. Thereafter it is not reborn. This is eternal freedom and real liberation of the soul.

The theory of transmigration or rebirth is based on the law of karma (action). Whether a rebirth will be for a better or a worse life as compared to the previous life will depend upon the nature and quantity of the rewards and punishments that are due on account of the past karmas (deeds).

Personal responsibility accounts for everything. It even explains the original differences of birth, heredity, environment, circumstances, etc., among human beings. It fulfills the need of moral and ethical justice, which is expected to square up all the karmas of all the lives through appropriate rewards and punishments before the final dissolution of the universe. The doctrine of karma is discussed in detail in the succeeding chapter. It is mentioned here only briefly in connection with the theory of rebirth.

Clinging to Life

From the depths of each heart of every living being there arises the universal desire to continue the present existence. One does not intend or like to face death.

Most beings shrink back from the horrible pangs of death. When a being is forced into death, its soul is lonely, forlorn, and fearful.

Consequently, the soul's immediate impulse is to become surrounded with company once again. Such a longing drives each soul to reach out for a new body at once. The basic impulse or craving for life is sustained not merely during earthly existence but is carried on across the gulf of death and even up to a rebirth or to another conditioned existence. Such desire for continued existence is the chief cause of samsara (rounds of births and deaths) and its inseparable sorrows. The fundamental impulse of clinging to life keeps the cycle of conditioned existence going on and on from life to life for every jiva (soul).

The desire to live and the fear of death go hand in hand in the theory of transmigration or rebirth. These two impulses are ever-present among all creatures, from the worm to the human being. Every creature, even a child, quivers at the idea of death. Though one has not experienced death in the present life, a person infers the fear of death as a result of his or her experience of death in a previous life. The painful death experience in a previous life persists in his or her memory through latent samskaras (subliminal impressions) during the current life that generate the fear of death and the desire to cling to life. These two basic impulses establish a connection between the previous and the present life.

Unless the fear of death is overcome, the desire to cling to life is not eradicated. Both impulses remain eternally present unless they are simultaneously mitigated through the practice of yoga. One can obtain release from these impulses and simultaneously from the entanglement of the web of samsara (conditioned existence) through yoga, which makes one free from the clutches of disease, old age, and death. Through the practice of yoga, one attains everlasting freedom not only from psychological impulses and drives such as the fear of death and the desire to live, pleasures and pains, love and hatred, etc., but also from the embodied existence itself. As a result, one attains the most *kaivalya* (perfect form of isolated existence), which is higher than not only human existence on earth, but also angelic existence in heaven. It is an unfettered, omniscient, and perfect state of existence of atman (individual spirit). Such a perfected and isolated pure spirit does not succumb to bondages and sufferings anymore and is permanently released from the rounds of transmigrations. That is moksha (liberation).

Transmigration to Heaven, Hell, or Earth

Heavenly beatitude should not be mistaken for real everlasting freedom, or moksha. Existence in the heavenly sphere is equally illusory in character as is life on the terrestrial plane. It is no less a delusion than even the descent to purgatorial hell. All three types of existence are merely the continuance within the sphere of the transmigratory worlds of the cycle of repeated births and deaths. One who is genuinely desirous of obtaining everlasting freedom from the realm of births and deaths should not be interested even in the enjoyments of a heavenly life. As a matter of fact, the conditioned existence, whether on Earth or in Heaven or Hell, is illusory and hence undesirable. Heaven, Earth, and Hell are merely parts of the phenomenal universe and therefore the conditioned existence in any of these spheres necessitates rebirth or transmigration.

Whether a person will be reborn on Earth or in Heaven, or Hell, depends upon his or her karmas (deeds) in the present existence. Good deeds qualify a soul for a rebirth in a higher sphere, or Heaven. Evil deeds make a soul descend to a lower sphere, or Hell. Balancing good and evil deeds entitle a soul for another birth on Earth. It is true that the good deeds bring pleasures as their fruits, while evil deeds result in sorrows. Neither the good deeds nor the evil deeds, however, are capable of yielding release from the perennial circulation of transmigrations. Of course, no one would like the horrible and painful existence of Hell. All would prefer the joyful life of the higher celestial sphere in Heaven, even as compared to the Earthly life, which is a mixture of joys and sorrows. Only a few genuine aspirants desire to attain a still higher and infinitely better state of existence from where they will never be reincarnated in any form whatsoever. This highest and most blissful state is known as *kaivalya* (isolated existence), wherein temporarily lost "self-awareness" is fully restored to the soul.

Interlude Between Two Lives

Generally, a soul does not transmigrate into a new incarnation immediately after death. There is usually an interlude between the previous existence and the next incarnation. During such intermediate existence, a soul dwells in the two inner bodies, the subtle and the causal bodies. After death, it gives up only the gross body, retaining the other two. The interlude following death and preceeding rebirth is like a prolonged state of dreaming. It is as illusory as the dream state experienced while living in the gross body. Perhaps it is a much more hallucinatory state than the latter. A departed soul exists in an intermediate state in the subtle body (also having the causal body within), seeing this and the other worlds while floating in the void, going up and down and experiencing a mixed feeling of both pleasure as well as pain. As a fish moves floating in the water between the two banks of a river, so also a departed soul with the subtle body moves between this world and other worlds.

The duration of such after-death intermediate existence will depend upon the deeds and desires of a soul in the previous life. It will remain in that floating state, deeply immersed in delusional and apparitional experiences for a specified time. When the hour for its rebirth strikes, it proceeds toward some world and the womb, as determined by the divine judge Yama (Lord of death) after adequate evaluation of its karmas (deeds). The soul's future destiny is decided during this interlude between two lives. Before entering a new womb for the next life, its consciousness sinks slowly into nescience, the causal body. Its memory of the previous life also fades, stage by stage. This process is a sort of "dying another death" in the subtle body, as it had died previously in the gross body. The only difference between the two deaths is that this second death in the subtle body is a reverse process of the first death in the gross body. The first was for quitting the gross body, while the second is for assuming a new gross body.

Process of Death

At the time of death the soul abandons its physical sheath or gross body. When the physique becomes weak through old age or illness, it is unable to hold fast to the two inner bodies, the subtle and the causal bodies. The inner bodies become severed from the gross body. The soul is carried within the inner bodies and the gross body separated from them remains in a lifeless state. We call this "death." Now let us understand the process of death in detail.

When a person is on the verge of expiring, first the functioning of the pranas (vital airs) in his or her body becomes disturbed. Their force is weakened and they begin to subside gradually. As a result, the organs of action slowly become defunct. Subsequently, the cognitive senses are severed from the corresponding organs of perception. Then the cognitive senses begin to sink inward and become cut off from the related sense-organs. Concomitantly, the perception of objective things and cognition of forms of the external world stops. Then the principle of consciousness is withdrawn into the heart and the dying person sinks into a state of subconsciousness.

After that, the four gross elements in his or her body begin to sink, one by one, into the order of earthy, watery, fiery, and airy elements. First of all, the earthy element loses its coherence as organic matter resulting in a state of coma or loss of body consciousness. Then the watery element begins to dry out and the throat region becomes parched. When the fiery element begins to subside, the body becomes cool, losing its natural warmth. Finally, when the airy element ceases to function, with the last exhalation of the breath, the soul leaves the gross body and is carried away into the ethereal or subtle body. This is the sign of the final moment of the death process.

After-death Intermediate State

The condition of a deceased person in the after-death intermediate state will depend upon his or her temperament and tendencies formed in accordance with his or her karmas (deeds). His or her reactions to the circumstances of the after-death existence will be commensurate with his or her self—culture, character, and willpower developed by the soul through the deeds performed by body, speech, and mind during the earthly life. Moreover, the soul's experiences during after-death existence will prove to be either educative or punitive, depending upon the dominance of virtues or defects cultivated during the life that has just ended. In short, a packet of these predispositions, inherited by him or her through the karmas performed during the earthly life will be awaiting suitable opportunities to discharge appropriately good or bad experiences during the after-death existence.

During this intermediate state, a deceased person remains immersed in subconscious visualizations of his or her own thought-forms projected into the void. The soul considers such hallucinations to be real, external, and alive. As in a dreaming state, the soul creates in the after-death state, through mental imagery, any type of unreal entity—godly or demoniac, human or non-human, animate or inanimate—and awaits favor or suspects danger from it. The whole phantasmagoric phenomenon occurs like a mysterious drama of mental imagery performed on an awe-inspiring stage of wild void.

The phantasmagoric creations emanating from the complex thought-forms of a deceased person affect him or her for good or ill. Generally, when a person is about to die, his or her mind becomes restless and confused. It is entangled in all types of desires, attachments, and aversions. So a dying person is worried about leaving all his or her worldly possessions, relatives, and friends behind. At the same time, he or she experiences great agony of death. The person's intelligence becomes quite obscured and he or she falls into a state of panic. Under such circumstances, a person will be sad and afraid. As a natural consequence, he or she undergoes terrifying experiences after death during the intermediate state of existence.

Sometimes the soul visualizes that a mad elephant is chasing him or her. Or the soul feels as if he or she is falling headlong into a very deep well. Sometimes the soul experiences that a person who was his or her enemy during earthly life comes to take revenge of some previous grievance. The enemy victimizes the soul, piercing his or her body with a glistening sword. Or the soul feels that the hungry wolves and vultures are eating away flesh from his or her body until only the skeleton remains. At other times the soul visualizes some animal-headed, wrathful devil drinking his or her blood and then chopping his or her body into pieces and feeding the dancing ghosts around the scene with his or her flesh. As a matter of fact, all such terrifying experiences are created phantasmagorically by the soul due to delusion and evil traits gathered during the earthly life. Such horrible fantasies, appearing in an uninterrupted series, are the creations of impure mind.

Of course, the fear-causing apparitions occurring in the after-death state provide the deceased person with an opportunity to square up his or her pending obligations and repay the karmic debt of the past life. So, instead of getting frightened, if he or she analyzes these apparitions quietly and thoroughly, he or she will have all his or her karmas cleared. Thereby the soul will be capable of gaining freedom even from the subtle body and proceeding further toward emancipation. But such discrimination and courage remain a far cry for ordinary human beings. Only those who are trained in yoga while incarnate on Earth, can face the after-death experiences with proper discrimination and sufficient courage.

It is not that a deceased person visualizes only the horrible sights all the time in the after-death intermediate state. Terrifying apparitions are the results of his or her evil karmas. But everyone does have some good karmas. Even if a deceased person's evil karmas are in excess, the soul does undergo pleasant experiences also in lieu of whatever small amount of good karmas are to his or her credit. So, along with horrors, the soul occasionally enjoys pleasant apparitions. Manifold pleasant dreams are shaped in his or her vision, making the soul happy, laughing, and rejoicing.

Sometimes he or she soars in the sky between this world and the other heavenly worlds previously unseen, enjoying their glamour from a distance. At other times, the soul feels in a fanciful apparition that he or she has amassed a great amount of wealth and is living a happy and leisurely life. Or the soul feels flattered by the prestige he or she earns by doing many charitable acts or performing heroic deeds, though they are mere fantasies. Sometimes the soul sees various farcical scenes providing good entertainment. All such apparitions are the results of his or her noble desires and good deeds of the past life.

Seeking Rebirth

A deceased person moves between the Earth and the other worlds in the subtle body, sometimes rejoicing and sometimes feeling frightened, depending upon past karmas and desires. The soul may continue in this intermediate state of existence until his or her piled up karmas are exhausted. But that remains only next to impossible for almost all souls. In the shorter or longer run, every deceased person, except those who are yogically trained, become miserably frightened. So the soul hastens toward the world, in which he or she is destined to be reborn according to the divine judgment passed by Yama, the Lord of death. The only way to flee the horrors of the after-death existence is to enter some womb and seek rebirth. This invariably is the fate of all persons, except the yogis and the holy persons with many pious deeds to their credit. But the fortunate souls of the latter type are always very few, if not rare.

To whatever world a soul is granted admission for being reborn, he or she immediately rushes there and enters the womb earmarked for him or her. The soul has no power to exercise any choice for a particular womb. With the soul, he or she brings the two inner bodies and the unpaid balance of past karmas (deeds) and unsatisfied desires. Thus the soul makes his or her own destiny for the coming life. If the soul has lived a predominantly sattvic life in the previous existence, cherishing noble desires and performing charitable acts, the soul will be directed to one of the higher worlds (Heaven) for the new birth. If he or she has indulged mainly in rajasic desires and activities in the previous life, the soul will return to this Earth-plane once again. But the soul will be thrown to any of the lower demoniacal worlds (Hell), if he or she was predominantly tamasic, with evil tendencies and deeds in the former life.

Upon entering the new womb for a rebirth, the soul forgets all intellectual knowledge acquired by it in the previous life. The soul loses the memory of all events and everything pertaining to the former life, including even the identity of his or her own self. Now the soul becomes a different person with a new identity for the coming life. But the soul still carries the old legacy of the karmas (deeds) and the desires of the former life, in the form of samskaras (subliminal impressions). These samskaras form the prenatal tendencies that play a very important part in his or her new life also. He or she is likely to turn out to be a good or bad person, intelligent or dull, rich or poor, happy or miserable depending upon the samskaras carried forward from the previous life to the new womb. Thus the soul reaps the fruits of past karmas and desires, good or bad, even in the new life. That keeps the wheel of the soul's samsara (conditioned existence) rotating continuously.

chapter eight

Causes of Bondage and Suffering

The word *samsara* literally means "temporal or mundane existence." Since existence is linked with the transmigration of the soul from one life to another, samsara also connotes "realm of births and deaths"; "worlds of rebirth"; "wheel of ceaseless becoming"; "chain of bondage"; and "realm of phenomena and duality." Samsara is a continuous process of births and deaths. It is endless and at the same time transitory and of no avail. It is the product of avidya (nescience) and hence full of the pairs of opposites and false distinctions between all worldly things. It is dream-like, unreal, and full of unbearable sufferings and inconsequential pleasures. Neither its sorrows nor joys yield redemption. In short, samsara is the vortex in which, under the sway of ignorance, a soul undergoes an unending series of dramatic dreams of worldly lives, spellbound by its own passions, fears, and desires.

So long as a soul remains subject to avidya (nescience), it retains the mundane consciousness within the world in which it is born, whether it is in the higher worlds, human world, or infernal worlds. For the soul, the wheel of samsara goes on turning and out of every death there springs forth another birth through avidya. Its mundane mind is deluged by false concepts and their consequent pairs of opposites; hence it indulges in desires and activities that create fast bondage. Its limited consciousness keeps it enslaved in profane desires and drives, impulses and emotions, sentiments and activities, and drags it away from a moral, pious, and spiritual mode of living. As a result, a soul develops a special attraction to worldly wealth, power, and sense-enjoyments, which it strives to attain even by committing sins.

Samsara has its basis in the theory of rebirth on one hand, and the doctrine of karma on the other. Its modus operandi is explained through the eternal nature of a soul and the principle of its transmigration, while it is justified in light of the continuousness of the effects of karmas (deeds). A soul's ego-personality during its phenomenal existence is merely a karmic conglomeration of different characteristics acquired through the experiences of innumerable lives. Samsara is merely a soul's worldly existence, conditioned by karmic effects.

A soul in its embodied existence becomes a hypothetical carrier of karmas in the form of samskaras (subliminal impressions). It carries the impressions or traces of all the desires and deeds of past lives in its subconscious. The subtle effects of the desires cherished and the karmas performed are carried forward as samskaras along with a soul's transmigration to the next samsaric existence. Samsara is nothing but an entanglement of a soul in the web of desires and deeds. The desires create the intentions to fulfill them and the intentions drive an embodied soul to become occupied with karmas. In this manner, desire provides a foothold for the mind and the intention for its fulfillment supports the mind's direction to the body to become occupied with the relevant karma. So far as there are desires, there is a foothold for the mind; and so far as there are intentions supporting the mind's activities, there are resultant karmas. The origin of samsaric existence of a soul is due to avidya (nescience); its continuity is due to mental conformations, and consequent karmas, while its perpetuity is because of the mundane mind that grows on the food of desires and cravings to satisfy them through actions.

Indian philosophy teaches that the mind is the cause of both samsara (conditioned existence) and also moksha (liberation). It produces the bonds of existence and also becomes instrumental in the release from bondage. When it is directed toward worldly desires and ambitions due to ignorance, the result is the continuity of samsaric existence or bondage. But when the same mind is directed toward pious and spiritual aims and efforts, with proper understanding, it leads to the freedom from bondage or samsara.

Dual Role of Samsara

During any particular human existence, a person remains so much deluded by his or her limited consciousness and mundane mind that he or she is unable to remember everything about his or her past years in the same life, let alone the memory about his or her former lives. The soul knows practically nothing about former lives and so he or she is unable to learn any lesson out of the experiences of the former lives. The person does not realize that all former lives were on the whole nothing but sufferings and pains with only intermittent and momentary episodes of happiness, which in a way act to bind the person rather than help to gain release.

A person, in any particular existence, remains much fascinated and spellbound by worldly pleasures due to ignorance. He or she becomes forgetful about the real nature of his or her own pure, unbound, and immortal being and tries to seek pleasures offered by the illusory objects of the phenomenal world through the extroverted senses. The person does not use introspection and turn his or her mind inward to realize his or her true 'self.' He or she remains linked with the tough and durable filaments of *vasanas* (desires) and karmas (deeds), succumbing perpetually to the wheel of samsaric rounds of birth and death.

The soul keeps on transmigrating from one existence to another: celestial, earthly, or infernal according to the destiny built up by him or her in the previous existence. The soul is normally unable to break away from this involvement in the wheel of samsara. However, God is kind to provide the soul with an opportunity to turn a vice into a virtue. Thus a human being can turn the sorrowful samsara into the means for overcoming his or her own bondage. Samsara, through its anguish, sufferings, and despairs, awakens a person to introspection and self-analysis and stimulates his or her spiritual efforts. It provides an opportunity to drown out unhappiness, to rise above all deceptive feelings, and to reach the pure spiritual state of supra-mundane existence. It establishes a golden link between the lower realm of sorrow and the higher realm of bliss. One rises with the help of the same thing, samsara, by which he or she falls and obtains release with the help of the same thing by which he or she becomes bound. In this manner, samsara has a dual role to play for the sake of helping the spiritual growth of individual souls, so that they may gain final emancipation.

Awakening and Release from Samsara

When in some lifetime an individual becomes bored with his or her endless rebirths, one after the other, acting different career roles aimlessly, he or she begins introspection and self-analysis. He or she presents the self with questions like—Who am I? Why am I bound? What makes me endure destiny? Am I ever to obtain rest and peace or am I to keep going on with the endless course of transmigrations? When such pertinent questions strike his or her mind, the spiritual search begins and with this awakening he or she decides to resign the interminable roles of samsaric existence. Then the person seriously strives to throw away the mask of ego-personality in order to realize his or her true hidden nature. The person voluntarily exiles himself or herself from the external forces of the temporal life in order to explore the veiled force of life within.

Mere awakening is not sufficient, however, for finding an escape from samsara (temporal existence) and attaining moksha (liberation). For that one needs to be properly qualified. In order to attain moksha one is required to increase one's virtues by meritorious conduct in many earlier births. The Indian sages have taught that for bringing the day of salvation nearer, one should continuously endeavor to live a moral and pious life. One should not entertain excessive attachment in daily life. One should break away from the worldly desires of seeking wealth, power, and sense-enjoyments. At the same time, one should try to conquer the undesirable emotions, impulses, sentiments, and passions. All these are hurdles to spiritual attainment. One should free the self from these demerits and then adopt the practices of yoga.

Means for Transcending Samsara

It is very difficult to accomplish release from continual samsaric existence. The only way leading to the cessation of samsara and its consequential sufferings is the practice of yoga. A yogi transcends samsara by way of practicing severe austerities and progressive meditations. The yogi tries to integrate into consciousness the entity of the real self underlying his or her ego-personality and physical frame. Consequently, through persevering efforts, the yogi becomes capable of attaining an unfettered state, freedom from samsara, and becomes endowed with perfection and omniscience. Then he or she rises above all bondages and limitations, bringing an end to the conditioned existence (samsara) forever.

First of all, an aspirant of yoga expiates all his or her sins, such as *kama* (lust), *krodha* (anger), *lobha* (greed), *moha* (attachment), etc., by practicing special austerities. Such austerities qualify the yogi for a rebirth into the higher, heavenly spheres after death. But a genuine aspirant must understand such results as mere byproducts of the yogic path and should not be interested in such intermediate stations. Though the rebirth into the heavenly sphere may mean quite a happy and pleasurable existence enduring for thousands of years, it still represents only another round of samsaric existence. A genuine yogi does not merely preoccupy himself or herself to ameliorate the present life but also to avert the possibility of either the descent into the infernal worlds or even the ascent into the higher worlds in the next life. The yogi proceeds further to transcend all the worldly illusoriness that necessitate rebirth.

A genuine yogi is not interested in the enjoyment of the fruits of his or her austerities.

Sacrificing all the alluring rewards of hard austerities, the yogi proceeds further with progressive meditations for achieving the complete purification of mind, intellect, and consciousness. The yogi completely subdues his or her senses and constantly tames the mind to single-pointedness, achieving a state of profound ecstasy. A person who has not tamed his or her mind and also controlled the senses in this manner is impure in consciousness and does not reach the transcendental state of superconsciousness. Such a person is again carried away into the whirlpool of death and rebirth. But a yogi, whose heroic efforts in progressive meditations bring to him or her the state of superconsciousness, transcends the illusion of phenomenal existence (samsara), becomes divined with perfection and omniscience, and is completely released from the rounds of birth and death. Thus, a yogi escapes from samsara and attains moksha (liberation) even before the final dissolution of the entire phenomenal universe.

Samskaras: The Seeds of Becoming

Samsara or phenomenal existence is merely the creation of the mind. Though actually the phenomenal universe is nonexistent, jiva, an embodied soul, regards it as real due to its limited mental powers. Such mundane mind is impure because of the subliminal impressions, samskaras, of the acts done and desires cherished in the former state of existence. These samskaras, or the traces carried by the mind in the form of latent memories or subliminal impressions of past lives, are the cause of "becoming" or rebirth.

Unless and until a person is liberated, he or she is not able to abandon the two inner bodies, the subtle body, and the causal body. They are more or less his or her permanent accompaniments. They remain continuously with him or her throughout the process of his or her evolution. Such permanent clinging of the two inner bodies is the basic condition of rebirth. This is because the inner bodies are the carriers of the germs of rebirth in the form of samskaras. These samskaras are the subliminal impressions or the latent traces left on the subconscious mind by the acts performed and the desires cherished by a person, not only in the present life, but in innumerable former lives. The coverings of the two inner bodies constantly restrict the plane of consciousness of the soul and keep it drawn toward worldly existence.

The two inner bodies are the reservoir into which the samskaras (subliminal impressions) of all that we desire and do in the present life are constantly being poured. These impressions are carried with these inner bodies through future lives and at opportune moments and in favorable conditions they are transformed into good or bad experiences. Samskaras are the causes that set the dormant desires in motion and drive one to act. They are the seeds of vasanas (desires) and karmas (deeds). As a tree yields seeds that in turn produce many trees, even so, the present life yields seeds in the form of samskaras (subliminal impressions) that in turn become the cause of many future lives.

Since the two inner bodies are not formed afresh with every rebirth they build up a sort of permanent and cumulative record of all that a person thinks, feels, desires, and does during each life. In the next or future lives, when an appropriate contact is established with this record of the dormant samskaras, by natural impulse the person is driven to strive to satisfy the vasanas (desires) that remained unfulfilled in past lives. Vasanas provide the motivating force for karmas. They drive the mind in all possible ways, dragging it irresistibly toward the favorable conditions in which their purpose will be satisfied. The human mind thus remains incessantly active under the continuous pressure of vasanas (desires). That is why the mind is said to be the cause of samsara (rounds of birth and death).

Causes of Bondage

As we have seen, the samskaras (subliminal impressions) carried forward by the inner bodies from one life to another set the previous unsatisfied vasanas (desires) into motion in subsequent lives. These vasanas provide the motivation for fresh karmas that are performed not only by physical actions but also by way of thoughts, feelings, and speech. These new karmas, in turn, produce new samskaras and vasanas. Thus, an unending vicious circle is established, forming a complex network for the fast bondage of the soul in the samsaric existence. To attain liberation one must bring an end to this vicious process.

Samskaras, as the potential seeds of karmas (thoughts, feelings, words, and deeds) form the roots of this vicious cycle. One must square up all karmas and burn away all their seeds. But this is an uphill task. Not only should one rectify all the past karmas by way of suffering, but at the same time one should abstain from committing new karmas. The first proposition seems impossible to attain during one lifetime, and the second proposition sounds almost impossible to practice even for a day. That means there must be some other method for dealing with this problem of karma. Indeed, there is one, and that is the method prescribed by the ancient yogis of India.

Yogis have tried, and with success, to approach the problem of karma in an indirect way. They found that the basis of all kinds of latent karmas is the five *kleshas* (afflictions or sources of afflictions): (i) avidya (nescience), (ii) *asmita* (mundane consciousness), *raga* (attachment), (iv) dvesha (aversion), and (v) *abhinivesha* (desire to live). These kleshas are responsible not only for the embodiment or the bondage of the soul, but also for its status and condition in the present life depending upon the merits and the demerits acquired by it during the past lives. They impair pure consciousness and weaken the mind. So long as roots exist, a tree grows and bears fruit. Similarly, the latent karmas bear fruit as long as their roots in the form of kleshas exist. The yogis annihilate the latent karmas by way of removing their foundation, the kleshas. Just as a burnt seed cannot germinate, so also the burnt seeds of the latent karmas cannot sprout. They render the latent karmas unfit for further propagation by cutting their roots, the five kleshas (sources of afflictions).

What are the Kleshas?

The first, avidya (nescience), is the lack of knowledge about reality on the part of an individual soul. Through ignorance the individual soul forgets its true nature and recognizes what is impermanent, impure, and painful to be eternal, pure, and pleasant. This veiling, caused by avidya, is the main kleshas (source of affliction) from which the remaining four kleshas are issued forth. It provides the soil on which the rest of the kleshas grow.

The second, asmita (mundane consciousness), is the awareness of the individual entity or ego-sense on the part of the individual soul. It imparts a sense of "I-am-ness" to the soul. Loss of pure consciousness caused by avidya further leads the soul to identify its existence as the embodied self, though the cover consists of the thinnest and the subtlest layer, the causal body. This happens as a result of the blending together of the knower and the power of knowing, or the seer and the power of seeing. Pure consciousness that is really singular appears to be dual in mundane consciousness. It is, however, only a deception caused by avidya (nescience).

The third of the kleshas, raga (attachment), is the attraction toward an object of pleasure or endearment of any person. It includes affections of all types that are accompanied by happiness. It issues forth every time there is a recollection of pleasure or happiness connected with any object or person.

The fourth, dvesha (aversion), is the repulsion, antipathy, or dislike for an object or a person. Contrary to raga, it brings pain, misery, and unhappiness. It arises out of the memory of pain or unhappiness connected with any object or person. Both raga and dvesha constitute a pair of opposites, the positive and negative feelings.

The fifth and last of the kleshas is abhinivesha (desire to live). It indicates both the will to live and the fear of death. It is the natural instinct to cling to life. Such craving for unending existence is universal and eternal. The fear of death remains present in a living being permanently until it is eradicated through the practice of yoga.

Kleshas Appear in a Link

These kleshas (sources of afflictions) are interconnected, more or less forming a chain of linked causes and effects. This chain begins with avidya (nescience), which gives birth to asmita (mundane consciousness) as a subsequent effect. Asmita produces the feeling of personality that finds expression in raga (attachment) and dvesha (aversion). Strong personal attachments and aversions have a direct impact upon one's attraction to the mundane life. This results in abhinivesha (desire to live) which is the final expression in the series of kleshas. Once this chain is put into motion by the appearance of avidya, the rest of the kleshas arise automatically as subsequent effects, and continue to exist in an endless flow, until the initial cause, avidya, is removed.

Kleshas Cause All Sufferings

When the human soul, owing to the power of maya or avidya, gets involved in subtle matter, its consciousness becomes identified with that veil or covering of matter. As a result, the pure consciousness of the soul degenerates and becomes identified as asmita (mundane consciousness), which is merely a limited awareness of an entity. Avidya and asmita proceed together, hand in hand, as twin sisters. Though theoretically avidya precedes asmita, both of them appear more or less simultaneously like the two sides of a coin. In other words, it can be said that the latter is the immediate result of the former.

When the pure consciousness of the soul begins to descend from the subtler to the grosser matter, it continues losing awareness about its true nature and simultaneously goes on increasing its association with mundane existence. The pure consciousness of the soul falls from its highest state and becomes a limited and a weaker expression in the form of asmita (mundane consciousness). When it descends from the causal body down to the subtle and the gross bodies, each intervening veil of the covering sheath conditions it with relative limitations. This means that the expression of consciousness becomes increasingly vague as the entanglement of the soul proceeds from the subtlest vesture to the grossest one. Asmita becomes strongest when the human soul is finally enclosed in the physical body. Asmita provides the common link between the causal, subtle, and gross bodies.

During outward consciousness, asmita functions in association with the gross body. When consciousness identifies with the inner entity, asmita functions in association with the subtle body at the mental or intellectual level. But when consciousness is identified with willpower or intuition, the level even beyond that of the intellect, asmita in its most refined form functions in association with the causal body. Asmita functions in its varying aspects in association with the different bodies, resulting in a very complex process. This produces multiple problems that are very difficult to deal with and that bring innumerable human miseries and sufferings.

All the problems of human existence ultimately filter down to the pairs of opposites or two biases represented by the kleshas, namely raga and dvesha. These two appear as the immediate effects of the functioning of asmita at various levels. They create bondage for the human soul and condition the life to a great extent. They keep human beings constantly tied to the limited levels of mundane consciousness through expressions of attractions or repulsions toward the external environment. They deeply permeate human life and distort the field of consciousness and intellect, destroying peace of mind.

Raga and dvesha are to be regarded as mental perversions. They are generated continuously and involuntarily throughout one's phenomenal existence. They strengthen the ego and obstruct consciousness. They conceal the serene state of one's true self and uninterruptedly build up an illusory frame of individual persona. They breed vasanas (desires) and produce distortions in the mind. Among many other desires, there arises a strong desire for life, abhinivesha. In the series of kleshas, avidya (nescience) is the cause or the beginning and abhinivesha (clinging to life) is the result or the final expression. All the kleshas, thus, operate together bringing innumerable miseries and sufferings to human beings.

Various States of the Kleshas

These five kleshas (afflictions) may exist in four different states. They may be dormant, attenuated, interrupted, or sustained. They remain in any of these four states depending upon the favorable or unfavorable situations that are operative. All these are mere modifications or changes in the manifestation of kleshas. When a klesha fixes on an object and finds a favorable situation becoming fully operative with its outward expression, it is said to be in the sustained state. This condition of the kleshas is generally present in all ordinary persons whose psychological forces are not subjected to any kind of control or self-discipline.

Two opposite types of psychological forces cannot manifest at the same time. Love and hatred cannot find expression simultaneously. When love prevails, hatred is overpowered and does not arise. In this case, hatred is said to be in the interrupted state. Similarly, when hatred is manifested, love remains in an interrupted state. A klesha can be in an interrupted condition even when the psychological forces are not opposite in nature. For example, a man may be loving two women. When he expresses love toward one, his love for the other is not manifested or operative simultaneously. He may express it later on at another time. In such a situation, though the psychological forces are not contradictory, one finds expression at a given moment while the other remains interrupted. Among ordinary people the kleshas appear and disappear in turn, according to favorable and unfavorable situations, attaining either a sustained or an interrupted state.

But through the practice of yoga, these kleshas can be reduced to very feeble psychological forces. When rendered weak through yogic discipline, the kleshas are overpowered and generally remain in an attenuated condition. They may, however, be awakened or become sustained, though in a milder form, when a yogi comes face-to-face with stimulating situations. This means that the kleshas in the attenuated state can be reiterated under favorable situations. They remain in the dormant condition only until there is lack of proper stimulation for them to become operative. When not involved in any purposeful activity, a yogi's kleshas exist merely potentially as dormant psychological forces in his or her mind, but they revert once more to the sustained state and become operative when brought face-to-face with various sense-objects.

Yoga Aims at Total Destruction of Kleshas

The kleshas can be rendered completely sterile only when a yogi attains *viveka khyati* (discriminative discernment) through *para* vairagya (highest detachment). Due to the lack of perfect nonattachment, a yogi can fail to attain real cognition and still persist under the spell of avidya (nescience). Such failure leads to the repeated confrontation of the kleshas that exist in his or her subconscious mind in vestigial forms. The kleshas exist in the attenuated state as germs or seeds that can germinate again under suitable conditions. Only when, through intense practice, a yogi reaches the highest degree of detachment and gains discriminative knowledge about ultimate reality are these germs or seeds of the kleshas burnt up. As the burnt seed cannot sprout, the dormant kleshas cannot come into operation again, because their potential power of manifestation is destroyed. In such a yogi, the kleshas are said to exist in the fifth state which is beyond the dormant, attenuated, interrupted, or sustained states described above. In this fifth state, the kleshas merely exist without any potential power to reappear. Such a yogi is a fortunate person indeed.

Under all circumstances, the kleshas should be rejected. Throughout a human being's existence, these kleshas become dominant or recessive at one time or the other, depending upon the individual's nature and the environmental situation. They flare up when provided favorable conditions, and they become inactive in unfavorable conditions.

Unless and until these kleshas are completely destroyed, there is always the possibility of their becoming active again. It is necessary, therefore, to eliminate them totally, destroying even their potentialities. They should be rendered absolutely incapable of germinating any further.

The kleshas are so interrelated with each other that it is impossible to nullify or remove any one or a few of them without touching the rest of them. This means that one must destroy all of them or none at all.

Yoga discipline teaches how all the kleshas can be completely and permanently destroyed. A yogi attacks them gradually and overpowers them step by step with immense patience and perseverance. In the initial course of a yogi's self-disciplining efforts, they begin to fade, slowly becoming less and less effective. In the intermediate stage of his or her disciplining, they are nullified and made temporarily inoperative. They flare up anew, however, more or less unconsciously, on being supplied with a motivating force by the sense-objects. But during the final spell of self-disciplining, a yogi attacks them at their roots which are grounded in the major kleshas, namely avidya (nescience), and reduces them to practically nothing.

It is due to avidya that the other four kleshas become apperceived, but when avidya itself dwindles, all of them dwindle away simultaneously.

Thus the whole technique of yoga is designed to remove all the kleshas (sources of afflictions) in totality and thereby eliminate all samskaras (subliminal impressions), and vasanas (desires), and to burn away all the seeds of karmas (deeds) automatically. When this happens, the vicious process of bondage and sufferings comes to an end, releasing a yogi from future incarnation or rebirth. Thus, a yogi cuts off the cycle of births and deaths through self-discipline and attains the summum bonum of life—the unity of atman (self) with Brahman (ultimate reality).

chapter nine

Doctrine of Karma

It becomes obvious from the discussion in the previous chapter that a soul is bound to the wheel of births and deaths on account of karmas (deeds), samskaras (subliminal impressions), and vasanas (desires). All of these are closely interconnected, forming a sort of network of latent conditions for the bondage of the soul. This network becomes more and more complex as a soul passes on from one life to the next. After many lives, the network assumes a highly complicated and bewildering form that seems to defy any solution for the release of a soul from its bondage.

During each earthly existence, a soul performs innumerable karmas by way of thought, speech, and activity. These karmas leave behind the corresponding samskaras and vasanas. Both the latter are carried forward along with the subtle body from one life to another. When these latent samskaras become activated at opportune moments in any future lives, they awaken the dormant unfulfilled vasanas (desires), which in turn lead the soul to perform new karmas. The karmas of the present life lead to the karmas of the next life, or future lives. They establish a continuous and unending cyclic chain.

The samskaras are the storehouse of all karmas. When the accumulated stock of karmas ripen in this storehouse during any lifetime, the soul reaps good or bad fruits according to the nature of the ripened karmas. The karmas are the underlying cause of all kinds of experiences not only in the present life, but also in future lives. They are the seeds of individual ignorance and future existence. Until these seeds of karmas are burnt up, they go on sprouting into new karmas that consequently leave new samskaras and vasanas, building toward a destiny for still another existence of delusory performances and rewards. But when the karmas are completely burnt up and done with through the practice of yoga, all the records of samskaras and vasanas, accumulated during a long period through a series of lives, get spontaneously demolished. As a result, the inner illumination unfolds and the soul realizes its true identity with Brahman (ultimate reality).

Karmas Cause Rebirths

A soul continuously struggles to evolve from the inanimate to the animate life and from the lower form of animal life to the higher form of human life until, at last, it attains self-realization and is liberated from the cycle of births and deaths. During this long journey through thousands or even millions of rebirths, it remains subject to the law of karma. Through each incarnation, it slowly evolves into a higher being, moderating actions, building up essential virtues, and reforming values that generally aid the process of spiritual upliftment. Yoga philosophy teaches that a series of reincarnations of the soul is designed only for providing proper experience that will help the soul's spiritual development; such spiritual growth is otherwise not possible. Every soul has to learn the lessons through tutelary experiences sooner or later. These lessons and experiences formulate the basic framework of the soul's earthly existence through many incarnations.

Ever since the beginning of the present creation of the phenomenal world, each soul has undergone innumerable births and deaths. Each soul might have existed as insects, birds, beasts, and finally as human beings. Human birth is considered to be the best among all living creatures, since it offers the scope for the liberation and union with Brahman or the ultimate reality. According to Indian philosophy, it is karma that determines the species and the circumstances in which a soul is born.

The karmas performed in a previous life or lives determines the status of the present incarnation. If a soul has performed highly good deeds, it may even be reincarnated in heaven. In the same way, very evil deeds might cause a soul's rebirth in hell. A soul receives rewards for highly good karmas during its stay in heaven. Likewise, it undergoes punishment for very evil karmas in hell. But after completion of its period of existence in either heaven or hell, it has to be reborn on this earth, for there is no scope for liberation except during human existence,

Inexorable Principle of Karma

The basic principle underlying the philosophy of karma is that karmas are productive and they yield good or bad fruits in terms of happiness or sufferings. They either build up hurdles or accelerate speed on the path of enlightenment for the soul. The process of the fruition of karmas is not interrupted by deaths or rebirths. Every karma performed in the current life leaves its mark or trace in the form of samskaras (subliminal impression) that follow the soul like a shadow in the next life. One cannot get rid of it without getting rewards or undergoing punishment, whichever is the appropriate result for it. Only a yogi who has advanced to a high state is capable of dissolving the karmas and obtaining freedom from their effects.

Ordinary human beings are not likely to be able to wipe out or square up all their karmas in a single lifetime. They generally leave this world with many karmas unaccounted for. They are bound to come back to this earth to taste the fruits of residual karmas.

The karmic balance of one life is carried forward to the next life. Thus the past karmas of a person condition his or her present state and the present karmas shape his or her future state. The principle of karma is based on natural justice, since every person is thereby made responsible for his or her existing condition at all times. It permits no excuse or grievance for fate, which is the product of one's own karmas.

Life or existence, therefore, is an unbroken actualization of the consequences or effects of one's karmas performed during earlier existences. The karmas condition the untransmissible specificity of the individual character and determine the individual's structure of instincts. These karmic products are transmitted directly or indirectly through the physical and intellectual heritage in the succeeding lives of the individual.

Karma Philosophy Is Not Fatalistic

We have seen that according to the philosophy of karma, everyone receives the appropriate reward or punishment for one's own intentionally performed good or evil deeds by way of happiness or sufferings, respectively. The law of karma is essentially the law of cause and effect, or action and reaction. One has to reap exactly what one sows. In karma philosophy there is an objective reality of the action and its result. Everything that happens in one's life is either the effect of a previous cause, or the cause of a future effect.

This, however, does not mean that a human being is hopelessly bound to a predestined fate and that he or she is helpless in either moderating or avoiding it in any way. It is indeed regrettable that some people misunderstand and misinterpret this law of karma. They argue that if the past karmas determine the future of an individual, it means that everything is supposed to have been planned out in advance and one can do very little to alter one's life and make progress. They mistakenly believe that everything that goes to make one's present existence is but an unavoidable outcome of one's previous karmas and one cannot do anything to improve or alter it. Though there is partial truth in the argument, it is not a completely rational approach. It is a partly fatalistic or negative approach.

It is no doubt true that according to the principle of karma, the results of the karmas already committed previously cannot be annulled or escaped. To that extent, the present life is indeed predetermined. But merely tasting the fruits of past karmas is not all of the present existence. One builds up a large stock of new karmas as well during each life. One does have the right of free will in performing such fresh karmas and making one's own destiny. One can certainly mold these karmas that are yet not performed, and map out one's own future and alter adverse trends in current life. One is the maker of one's own destiny by performing either good or evil karmas. In this sense, one is the architect of one's own future and not a slave of destiny.

As a matter of fact, destiny is nothing but the result of the efforts made in past lives. Similarly, the efforts made in the present life are nothing but the cause of destiny in a future life. Instead of sitting back passively, accepting fate or destiny, one should actively try to improve one's lot by performing fresh karmas with proper understanding about the operation of the law of karma.

Various Aspects of Karma

Generally, karma is understood to be an act that one performs physically, but according to Indian philosophy, the term *karma* has a wider connotation. It includes not only physical acts but also spoken words and conceived thoughts. Mere hurting words spoken toward another person constitutes karma as much as an act of hurting the person physically. In the same way, even thinking of partaking of some food is karma as much as actually eating it.

One way of classifying the karmas is in accordance with the time of their performance and the period of their fruition. Such classification of karmas is three-fold: (i) *kriyamana* or *vartamana karmas* (present deeds), (ii) *prarabdha karmas* (past deeds fructifying now), and (iii) *sanchita karmas* (previous deeds yet to ripen).

The first, kriyamana or vartamana karmas, are those that one is currently performing in the course of the present life. Here there is full scope for using one's free will and thereby moderating or reforming the fresh karmas. One can make appropriate decisions and exert the choice for right actions and avoid wrong ones. Through proper discrimination, one can utilize every opportunity for spiritual advancement and unfoldment.

The second type, prarabdha karmas, are those that are performed in previous lives, but are now ripening and yielding results in the present existence. These type of karmas provide tutelary experiences so that one can learn lessons from them and improve future performance, devoting oneself to spiritual practices.

Everyone must undergo the resulting experiences of prarabhda karmas without fail; there is no escape from them.

The third type, sanchita karmas, are past karmas performed during previous lives. They remain in the storehouse of the subconscious as samskaras (subliminal impressions) until they become ripe and begin to fructify in some future life. These karmas fructify in a lifetime in which there are appropriate conditions and a suitable environment for their expression. There are not enough opportunities in one lifetime for all the karmas performed during the previous lives and also during the present life to ripen and give fruit. Those karmas that have not yet been worked out are accumulated as sanchita karmas for fruition when the time is ripe in another lifetime.

Sometimes a fourth type is added to the above-mentioned three-fold classification of karmas. The fourth type is called *agami karmas,* those karmas that are not yet contacted but that will be performed at the appropriate moment during the course of the present life. Here, also, one has the opportunity to use one's free will and educate one's own mind for making the right choice of karmas to be performed.

Another mode of classifying the karmas is in accordance with the initiative and the motive behind them. Accordingly, the karmas are of two types: (i) *sakama karmas* (deeds performed with desire) and (ii) nishkama karmas (deeds performed without desire).

It is already understood that a soul has to reap the good or bad fruits of all that he or she thinks, speaks, or does during temporal existence. Atman (self), however, does not perform karmas; only a jiva, an embodied soul, performs karmas. All karmas are performed by a jiva through the body, mind, and senses. So long as atman (self) remains in the bondage of the body, mind, and senses, it forgets its true nature and behaves as an embodied entity, or jiva. Through ignorance, a jiva believes that he or she is the doer of all karmas, though, in reality, as atman, jiva is not the doer. Such a misconception on the part of the jiva arises because of ahankara (ego). When the karmas are performed with ego, there are bound to be some kind of initiatives and motives behind them. Hence, the jiva performs them with some underlying desires and attachments. Such karmas are called sakama karmas and they are bound to yield good or evil fruits, causing the cycle of births and deaths,

On the other hand, a yogi who realizes his or her true self, performs all karmas, controlling all solicitations of the senses without any selfish motive. Such a self-realized soul performs all karmas in a disinterested manner without any hope or expectation. He or she does not cherish any desired end and is not affected by infatuation while performing the karmas. Such karmas performed without desires or attachments are called nishkama karmas. They do not cause any bondage to a soul.

In order to escape the results of karmas, or bondages, one should perform karmas without desires, attachments, selfishness, and expectations of their fruits. A self-realized person alone is endowed with the ability to exercise full control over the sense-faculties and perform such nishkama karmas. He or she is a yogi in the real sense and is not fettered by karmas. While performing karmas, the yogi fully understands that he or she does not do anything by personal initiative or ego but it is divine will that directs him or her to act that way.

Still another way in which the karmas are classified is based on the principle of do's and don'ts. According to this mode of classification, the karmas are divided into three types: (i) *nishiddha karmas* or *vikarmas* (forbidden deeds), (ii) *vihita karmas* or *kartavya karmas* (deeds that ought to be done), and (iii) *kamya karmas* (deeds performed with desire or motive). Let us examine each of these three categories of karmas in brief.

Nishiddha karmas are those deeds that are prohibited by the scriptures. Such karmas include theft, lying, adultery, violence, cheating, chicanery, hurting others, partaking forbidden food, idle occupations, etc. These karmas are also called vikarmas. One should refrain from engaging in these karmas.

Vihita or kartavya karmas are those deeds that are prescribed or enjoined by the scriptures as obligatory. They ought to be performed as one's duty. A long list of such deeds can be found in Indian scriptures. Some of them are devotion to God, practicing austerities, giving alms, worshipping, performing sacrifices, serving parents, discharging family obligations, supplying the bare minimum needs, and satisfying hunger, thirst, etc., for maintaining the body, and so on. According to the orders or the commands of the scriptures, these kartavya karmas are more or less incumbent on everybody and they should be performed as obligatory duties.

Kamya karmas are those that are prompted by some self-interested motive or desire. They are generally performed to gain some particular object and with a view to future fruition. For example, the karmas performed for securing children or riches or for getting rid of an ailment or a calamity are all kamya karmas. They are not "musts" and are certainly not necessary for those who are seeking spiritual upliftment, because they keep one's mind restless and constantly worried about receiving the fruits of these deeds. They often result in frustrations and sometimes even lead to engaging oneself in forbidden deeds. Therefore, these karmas should be avoided as far as possible.

Riddle of Akarma (Inaction)

We have seen that according to the principle of karma, every act, performed intentionally, binds the soul to the result, affecting its future existence. Keeping this fact in view, some people think that it is better to give up all karmas since they are the source of bondage for the soul. This reasoning sounds good but is not practicable. It is impossible for any human being, except a fully realized yogi, to refrain from karmas. For ordinary unrealized persons, the karmas are unavoidable.

In Bhagavad Gita, Lord Krishna says, "One cannot live even for a moment by giving up all karmas."

So, it will be a vain illusion to think that one endowed with a body can afford to avoid the performance of karmas totally. At best, one can avoid increased involvement in karmas or disregard their consequences. But an embodied soul is inevitably caught in the network of karmas that at once binds him or her not only to present existence but also in after-death existence. Only a realized yogi is capable of performing karmas without becoming involved in their consequences. But for ordinary human beings, karma and its result is inevitable.

To live means to be active in mind and body. A karma means any thought, speech, or action. One may succeed to some extent in giving up physical actions or in observing silence; but it is next to impossible to exercise control over thoughts. Only a yogi of a high order can achieve it, but not the ordinary person. That is why in Bhagavad Gita, Lord Krishna enjoins not to refrain from the karmas but to perform them without attachment to them and without desire for their fruits. Real *akarma* is not the abstention from karmas but the renunciation of ego, personal interest, desire, and attachment while performing the karmas. When the sense-centers are controlled while one is engaged in performing a karma, it amounts to akarma (inaction). Such a self-controlled person is not involved in the results or consequences of the karmas. He or she does not flee from action, but acts with complete inward detachment. Such action becomes a yajna (sacrifice) and does not cause any bondage. Akarma does not really imply inaction, but the action performed in such a manner that it does not incur any karmic debt or create bondage.

Akarma is an action performed as a detached witness. That is why, in Bhagavad Gita, Lord Krishna says, "He who sees action in inaction and inaction in action, is a wise man and a yogi; he is fully accomplished in karma."

A yogi who has attained mental control and inner composure performs all actions in a detached spirit. He or she is not bound by the results thereof. Such nonbinding actions are in a real sense as good as inaction. Moreover, a yogi knows that his or her real self is not the "doer" even when performing karmas. The yogi also sees inactivity of the real self in the activity of the embodied self. Likewise, a yogi also understands that true inaction is the result of *atmajnana* (self-realization).

Ordinary persons who have not realized the true nature of the self believe out of ignorance that inaction is the turning away from action. This is a false conception on their part. Since they lack mental control, even when they sit quietly without indulging in any apparent outward action, inwardly they continue to brood over sense-objects. So there is really action in their apparent inaction. They are deluded persons who have failed to grasp the true meaning of akarma (inaction). It is rightly said in Ashtavakra Gita that "for a stupid person even inactivity is activity and for a wise person even activity is as good as inactivity since it is devoid of the resulting effect, bondage."

As a yogi sees inaction in action, he also sees action in inaction. When a yogi is observed in meditation, although he or she sits steady in one place, still the yogi is capable of moving in any part of the universe and doing any activity. But other ordinary human beings would see the yogi seated inactively in the same place. The yogi, however, is conscious about his own activity during inactive meditation. A yogi sees action in inaction and inaction in action, and he or she is, as such, the knower and doer of all actions.

The riddle of karma is, thus, very obscure and complicated. Even wise persons become puzzled and confounded in understanding its true meaning. One cannot grasp its real feature even with the highest reasoning. In order to comprehend it truly and fully what is required is spiritual experience and intuitive knowledge. For that, one first has to transcend the realm of karma itself and become a self-realized, action-free person. Such a person is a yogi, perfect in knowledge, and untouched by the laws of karma. For the yogi, all distinctions between karma and akarma cease to operate. The yogi seems to live like other human beings performing various karmas, and yet he or she is not bound by the fetters of karmas like ordinary persons. Even while immersed in active life, the yogi has the full realization of the true actionless nature of his or her real self.

chapter ten

Operation of Karmic Law

The doctrine of karma is scientific and its implications are as incontrovertible as those of the law of cause and effect. It is closely connected with the time factor since it involves an interminable chain of causes and effects in evolutionary progression through countless millions of years. According to yoga philosophy, life or samsara (mundane existence) is not merely physical but also a psychic phenomenon. This psycho-physical view of human existence is closely related or rather inseparably connected with the doctrine of karma. The Indian sages believed that behind the apparent physical existence of a human being there is also another real psychic existence still undetected by modern science. They postulated that if a human intends to know himself or herself fully, he or she must recognize both types of existence and within the fullness of time. They found that a person is at present the outcome of what he or she thought and did in the past and so shall his or her future status also be determined by how he or she thinks and acts now. They examined thoroughly the hidden side of a human being's nature through the practice of yoga and ultimately discovered that a person and all his or her faculties are governed by the immutable laws of karma.

Karmic Forces Cause Bondage

Through the veil of maya (illusion) the human soul considers its phenomenal shadow, ego, to be real. Ego is nothing but the karmic conglomeration of various characteristics acquired by the human being through innumerable existences in the phenomenal world. Real "self" is beyond the realm of phenomena or prakriti (nature). It cannot be realized while one is immersed in the ego-sense. It is only when one is able to soar beyond ego-sense that the soul is absolved from the network of karmic forces and is led to self-realization. The atman (self) can be realized by breaking every fetter binding the individual to samsara (mundane existence).

For such realization, one should acquire merits by performing good deeds and avoiding evil deeds, and resort to yoga. It is by treading the path of yoga that the chain of bondage to samsara (mundane existence) is broken, ending all karmic debt of the past and preventing even the arising of karma in the future. Then the soul is set free from the samsaric existence to experience the bliss of self-realization. All striving of temporal existence, even birth and death, come to an end. Bhagavad Gita rightly teaches that a realized or perfect yogi, who performs all actions without desire and attachment and only for the welfare of the other beings, is not bound by them. For the yogi, no future karma leading to rebirth arises. If he or she reincarnates at all, it is only voluntarily and as an *avatara* (willful incarnation).

Factors Contributing to Temporal Existence

Human beings are bound to the treadmill of several mutually interconnected and interdependent causes and effects. This happens as a result of their previous karmas. Once entangled into the net of samsara, they are reborn interminably, each time falling victim to sorrows, sufferings, illness, old age, and finally death.

According to Indian philosophy there are twelve essential factors that contribute to the character and problems of our mundane existence. They are: (i) avidya (ignorance), (ii) samskara (subliminal impressions), (iii), asmita (mundane consciousness or ego-sense), (iv) *nama-rupa* (name and form), (v) *bhavarupa* (life or phenomenal existence itself), (vi) indriyas (ten sense-faculties and mind), (vii) vasana (desire), (viii) *upadana* (indulgence), (ix) *anubhava* (experience), (x) *janma* (birth), (xi) *jara* (old age), and (xii) *mrityu* (death).

We have already discussed earlier the first three, avidya, samskara and asmita. Here we shall obtain some idea about nama-rupa and bhavarupa. *Nama* means "name," *bhava* means "becoming," and *rupa* means "form, shape, color." Nama-rupa means all that has form, shape, color, and name. That denotes the entire external world of the subjective and objective realm, which includes all perceived and known forms or all the objects of perception. Similarly, bhavarupa means "the form of becoming." That denotes the transient phenomena of mundane existence itself, including all life that has a beginning and an end. It binds the soul to the everlasting rounds of births and deaths, being ephemeral and perishable in character.

Indriyas and vasanas were also discussed earlier and need no further explanation. Upadana (indulgence) and anubhava (experience) are mutually correlated and they jointly denote a thinking, acting, and experiencing individual endowed with indriyas (mind and sense-faculties). Together, these three, combined with vasana (desire) are instrumental in the clinging of the soul to the normal world consciousness and its participation in a fuller phenomenal life.

The meanings of the last three factors, janma (birth), jara (old age), and mrityu (death) are self-explanatory and easily understandable.

Of these twelve factors contributing to mundane existence, the first two are linked with past karmas, the next four are linked with present effects, another three are linked with present karmas, and the last three are linked with future effects. When these causes and effects begin to operate in an individual, they produce subtle karmic matter in his or her constitution. With every thought, act, and experience, a fresh influx of karmic substance is produced. This karmic substance is finer and more tenacious than any known substance. Being of a subtle nature, it flows through the subtle vehicles and channels in the human framework. The karmic law operates through all the three (gross, subtle, and causal) bodies of the human being.

How Does Karma Affect the Gross Body?

According to *ayurveda,* Indian medical science, there are seven *dhatus* or essential ingredients of the body: chyle, blood, flesh, fat, bone, marrow, and semen. Sometimes ten ingredients are enumerated, adding hair, skin, and sinews to the above seven. Apart from these, there are three humors of the body: phlegm, bile, and wind that are also essential for life.

Out of the essential ingredients, rasa (chyle) is the primary juice or constituent fluid formed from food that one eats. This is subsequently changed into blood when mixed with bile. Likewise, it is converted into the remaining essential ingredients in combination with the three humors.

The gross body is affected by the karmas one performs because all the secretions of the body are affected by one's thoughts, speech, and actions. Depending upon the nature of karma performed, the bodily secretions are predominated by any one or two of the humors.

Such shifts in predominance of one or the other of the three humors affect the colors of the secretions too. For instance, the color of the secretion is white when phlegm is predominant and the other two are subordinate. It is yellow when bile is predominant and the other two are subordinate. It is bluish when wind is predominant and the other two are subordinate. It is green when phlegm and wind are predominant and bile is subordinate. It is red when all the three humors are in equal proportion. In this manner, even the colorings of the secretions in the body are affected by the karmas.

Influx of Subtle Karmic Substance

As the karmas bring about changes in the secretions of the gross body, they also influence the subtle and the causal bodies through subtle karmic substance. Every thought, word, or act involuntarily produces some kind of subtle karmic substance that flows through the subtle body and is finally accumulated in the subconscious in a concentrated form. As the chyle, blood, and other secretions flow through the passages of the physical body, the karmic substance flows through the 72,000 *nadis* (subtle channels) of the subtle body. It is further communicated to the subconscious through extremely subtle channels called *hita nadis,* which are hardly one-thousandth part in thickness as compared to the human hair.

The karmic substance gets accumulated in the subconscious and entails future joys or sorrows when transformed into the specific circumstances of life. In due time the stored-up old karmic substance is consumed, like the fuel of the life-process, but at the same time, fresh karmic substance is reinforced. The old stock of karmic substance is used when it ripens into the fruits of success or calamity for the soul, and the fresh stock is poured into the subconscious as the new material for future fruits. The process of consumption and production of the karmic substance is kept in operation continually, clearing and restocking the storehouse of the subconscious.

Categories, Smell, and Colorings of Karmic Substance

The process of the continuous influx of karmic substance blends different characteristics, smells, and colors in the subtle body. The emanation of radiation, color, and odor is popularly known as the aura of the body. Generally, such auras are visible only to those who possess psychic powers. The brightness or dullness, colorings, and odors of the human aura depend upon the nature and character of the karmic substance affecting the subtle body. The performance of acts and the subsequent changes in mental attitudes of a person are reflected as the corresponding changes in his or her aura.

According to Indian philosophy, a person's attitudes are expressed through one's (i) jati (status by birth), (ii) *sanjnu* (deeper state of mind), (iii) gunas (natural qualities), and (iv) kriyas (activities). Jati is the outcome of past karmas that decide the varied conditions of present worldly life. Sanjna is the recent state of being, depicting the person's degree of awakening, or say, evolutionary status. Gunas are the sattvic, rajasic, or tamasic tendencies indicating mental harmony, restlessness, or sluggishness respectively. Kriyas are actions in the current life. Again, sanjna is primarily depicted by the subconscious, and gunas find expression mainly through the subtle body, while kriyas are performed by the gross body.

The influx of karmic substance in the subtle body is characterized by the three gunas (qualities) and may be sattvic, rajasic, or tamasic. Sattvic influx of karmic substance brings peace, happiness, and knowledge and results in good, holy, or pious activities. Rajasic influx of karmic substance generates restlessness, cravings, and selfishness, and leads to sensual and pleasure-seeking activities. Tamasic influx of the karmic substance brings dullness, miseries, and ignorance and results in evil or sinful activities.

The gunas are not just qualities but the very substance or the finest matter of prakriti (nature). According to Bhagavad Gita, "The gunas are born of matter and bind the immortal dweller of the body (soul) fast in the body." (XIV:5) The gunas combine with karmic substance while influxing the subtle body. Such combinations determine three different categories of karmic substance: sattvic, rajasic, and tamasic as described above.

As the fire lends the glowing red color to the hot iron ball, the influx of karmic substance in the subtle body communicates different colors to the aura. The type of the color so communicated to the aura depends upon the category of the karmic substance poured in. Six different types of colorings are communicated to the aura. They fall into three pairs, each corresponding precisely to the three categories of karmic substance mentioned above. Moreover, each category of karmic substance is accompanied with a specific smell or odor, either pleasant or unpleasant.

The color and the smell, either refining or polluting the aura, depend upon the nature of the karmic substance influxed. Sattvic influx produces light colors and good odors. Rajasic influx lends gaudy colors and pungent odors. Tamasic influx produces dark colors and bad odors.

Sattvic influx has a fine fragrance and its colorings are *shukla* (white) and *pingala* (tawny). Rajasic influx is pungent and its colorings are *lohita* (red) and *harita* (green). Tamasic influx has a bad odor and its colors are *nila* (bluish) and *krishna* (black).

Karmic Substance Obstructs Liberation

The influx of karmic substance as mentioned above, and the colors and smells communicated by them to the human aura indicate the purity and the spiritual status of the individ-

purity and the spiritual status of the individual soul, sattvic being the highest, rajasic the intermediate, and tamasic the lowest. The influx of any kind of karmic substance should be avoided if liberation is to be attained. Even the sattvic influx, though produced by good or pious acts, obscures the aura and keeps the soul linked to the world. No doubt these ties are gentler than those produced by the rajasic or tamasic influx. But since it creates bondage for the soul, even the sattvic influx should be stopped.

It is very difficult to stop the influx of karmic substance completely. Only a yogi of high attainment can do that. A yogi who has transcended the three bodies (gross, subtle, and causal bodies) and the three gunas (sattva, rajas, and tamas qualities) is able to stop the influx of karmic substance completely. Such a yogi has burnt up all past karmas and has also gained freedom from the bondage of any new karma performed. He or she abides in the colorless, odorless, pure, and luminous atman (self) that remains untouched and unpolluted by karmic substance and its colors and odors. For the yogi all karmic necessities of further birth and death also come to an end. Thus, it is only through yoga that the forces of karma and the influx of karmic substance can be controlled and nullified. When the "seed" of karma or the karmic potentials stored in the subconscious in the form of samskaras (subliminal impressions) are burnt out through yoga, the influx of karmic matter is completely stopped, abolishing the cycle of births and deaths.

Piling up the Karmic Debt

All the karmas performed in the present life do not ripen and bear fruit in this life only. Some of them yield results somewhat later, either in the next or in some future life. The karmas that are not squared up in the current life are piled up as a karmic debt conditioning an individual's jati (status), *ayuh* (span of life), and *bhoga* (experiences in terms of joys and sorrows). The karmic debt determines one's circumstances and environment in the next and future lives. This is the reason why all human beings are not born with equal opportunities in life.

The karmas prompted by some kind of desire or attachment are bound to bear fruits and incur karmic debt. Such debt can be paid either by way of worldly enjoyments or by sufferings. Bhogas (experiences) include all pleasant and unpleasant experiences one goes through as a result of the ripening of his or her previous karmic debt. Good deeds lead to enjoyments, while evil deeds bring sufferings. Both enjoyments and sufferings, however, are the result of karmas performed with desires and attachments. They create bondage for the soul and should be avoided.

Both pleasant and unpleasant experiences are relative and relevant as dvandva (pairs of opposites) to all ordinary human beings. But to a person advanced spiritually and possessing pure discrimination, all the experiences, even pleasures, are painful. He or she knows that these pleasures are not only temporary but are conducive to enhancing the sense-cravings and to bind him or her to the illusions of worldly existence. Yoga philosophy believes that all is suffering for the wise person. The very existence in the mundane world engenders suffering. Even worldly pleasures, of whatever character, are sufferings because they ultimately lead to sorrows and pains.

Suffering is Universal

According to Indian philosophy there are three types of *tritapas* (sufferings): (i) *adhidaivika* or heavenly, (ii) *adhibhautika* or earthly, and (iii) *adhyatmika* or inner. Heavenly sufferings are provoked by the devas (deities or lesser gods). Earthly sufferings are caused by prakriti (nature); inner sufferings are caused by the organic body and the senses. All sentient beings, whether a lesser god or a human being, or an animal, or an insect, are prone to suffering. Suffering is universal. It is a cosmic modality to which everything, having a life term, is subjugated.

This view of universal suffering should not be regarded as pessimistic. Instead of floundering in despair, it stimulates one to rise beyond the sufferings by nullifying karmic debt through the redemptive techniques of yoga. So the wise person or a yogi regards suffering as a precondition of liberation, and not as a painful condition of existence. The sufferings unceasingly remind him or her of the futility of worldly wealth and ambition and lead the yogi to detachment and ascetic practice in order to attain freedom from sufferings, or liberation.

Indian philosophy teaches that suffering is not to be rejected or dreaded, since it is the means of liberation. Indian philosophy reveals that karmic debt of whatever magnitude can be paid up by way of sufferings. This provides hope and confidence even to a sinner to ameliorate his or her spiritual status by exhausting or putting an end to his or her karmic debt through sufferings. Such a prospect of redemption changes a person's outlook, preparing him or her to undergo the sufferings cheerfully rather than grumpily. A person becomes aware that he or she suffers because of previous sins. At the same time, he or she is sure that the current suffering is going to bring future well-being and deliverance in the course of time, when his or her karmic debt is squared up completely.

The philosophy of universal suffering prompts a person to lead a pure and perfectly moral life, free from evil tendencies. It makes a person cheerful and happy here in this life and also well-prepared and better disposed for the life beyond. A person awakened to this higher nature strives to obtain freedom from the bondage produced by karmic debt through the practice of yoga. In the course of time, he or she attains pure discriminative knowledge and thereby freedom from the bonds of karma. He or she becomes a self-realized or liberated yogi.

Need to Accept Karma Doctrine

From the foregoing discussion it becomes quite evident that the law of karma operates in a logical way, though mainly on a subtle plane. It is of the utmost importance for a genuine seeker of the truth to accent and believe in the doctrine of karma. That enables him or her to renounce worldly attachments through proper distinction between good and evil karmas. He or she knows for certain that whatever one thinks, speaks, or does leaves behind it corresponding samskaras (subliminal impression) in the subconscious. A person's good karma produces favorable samskaras and bad karma leaves adverse samskaras. Consequently, he or she adopts only good karmas and rejects the evil ones. Further, becoming more conscientious, he or she is able to put forth utmost zeal and energy in his or her spiritual pursuit.

As he or she feels terribly guilty of the sins already committed, he or she exerts in earnest devotion and with great perseverance, giving up all attachments to the worldly life. On the other hand, those who disbelieve karmic laws go on committing impious acts, piling up heaps of unlimited sins throughout their lives. They are certain to fall into the miseries of the lower worlds hereafter. Since they are much involved in mundane pleasures and worldly attachments, they lack the intention or the zeal for spiritual pursuit. It is quite necessary for a spiritual seeker to establish belief and keep a firm faith in the doctrine of karma and to tread the path of righteousness. Those who disbelieve in the doctrine of karma, in fact, disbelieve in God, because it is through the operation of the laws of karma that the justice of God prevails.

ॐ

chapter eleven

Human Life and Its Purpose

No doubt, in all material creation, the human being is the brightest creature since he or she is made in the image of God. It is a great fortune to be born a human being, since moksha (liberation) can be attained only in this form of existence. Only the human body is considered a fit vehicle for obtaining salvation.

The level of human existence is considered to be between the devas (lesser gods) and the animals. The devas have only subtle bodies and so they cannot endeavor liberation. Though they have only happiness to experience and no misery, theirs is not an existence free from the bondage of karma. They have attained birth in that higher heavenly realm due to good karmas in their previous human lives. What they are enjoying is the fruit of such fine deeds. When the stock of their good karmas is exhausted through heavenly enjoyments, they return to this earthly plane and are born as human beings.

Animals, though they possess gross bodies, lack the contemplative mind and discriminating intelligence that are of utmost importance in the process of realizing God. It is possible for them to obtain a human birth after a very long evolutionary process. It may take thousands or perhaps even millions of years to attain that level of development. Until then they cannot hope for salvation.

But the human being is gifted with an adequate instrument in the form of the triple bodies (gross, subtle, and causal bodies). Such a body, if properly devoted to spiritual endeavors, is capable of bringing divinity to the owner. There is the possibility for a human being to visualize his or her image in God and to realize likeness with God. A human being can be said to be a would-be-god, provided he or she strives properly and sincerely for the highest goal of life, God-realization. There is no moksha (liberation) without this attainment.

Types of Human Endeavor

According to Indian philosophy, the objects of human efforts are classified into four types: (i) *artha,* (ii) kama, (iii) dharma, and (iv) moksha.

Artha means economic pursuit aimed at earning a livelihood; acquirement of wealth and material possessions. It is concerned with the economic, social, and civic life of the individual.

Kama means the pursuit of married life aimed at the satiation of desires and establishing family life through which love and pleasure find expression.

Dharma means the pursuit of ethical, moral, and religious duties aimed at maintaining proper harmony in the personal as well as social life.

Moksha means the pursuit of spiritual development aiming at the release from all kinds of worldly bondages and the final redemption or liberation of the soul.

The first three objects of human endeavor cover the legitimate rights and duties of an individual. It is through the protection of these rights and the fulfillment of these duties that the welfare of the individual, his or her family, and his or her society is derived. These are the efforts or pursuits of worldly life and general well-being. The last or the fourth object of endeavor is for the final human good. It is regarded as the highest and the ultimate aim of human life.

From the foregoing discussion it becomes evident that a rare human birth, with a healthy body, discriminating intellect, and the right endeavor to use them properly for attaining everlasting happiness and peace, are the necessary prerequisites for moksha (liberation). Real happiness and unending peace can be obtained only through freedom from all kinds of bondages. Real happiness, bliss, eternal peace, freedom from bondage, liberation, etc., are synonymous terms or phrases indicating the highest state of existence.

Where Does Real Happiness Lie?

There is no real happiness in the embodied life which is limited and subject to the pairs of opposites, such as pleasure and pain, happiness and misery, knowledge and ignorance, heat and cold, light and darkness, success and failure, and so on. Real happiness is bliss and that lies in freedom from all pairs of opposites.

All pairs of opposites are nothing but false concepts of the mundane mind. One comprehends duality as a result of false discrimination. In order to transcend duality, one should go beyond the pairs of opposites such as good and evil, light and darkness, true and false, heat and cold, attachments and aversions, birth and death, etc. When that is achieved, one is able to comprehend nonduality, making no distinctions between things but realizing that everything includes everything else. Duality is a synonym to the illusion of mundane mind while nonduality is the supra-mundane comprehension attained by way of spiritual enlightenment. Real happiness can be experienced only in that perfect nondual state of mind.

Every human being longs and strives for happiness. One makes attempts to find happiness according to his or her capacity and level of development. One adopts the way to search for happiness according to his or her understanding and discrimination. Of course, most people seek happiness through bhoga, sense-enjoyments. They try to satisfy the physical and emotional aspects of their personality. These persons are called bhogis or those seeking worldly pleasures. They can obtain only momentary happiness, which is usually followed by gloom and misery.

Only few persons seek happiness by way of disciplining the body, mind, and intellect. Those who can make these three function at their best and harmoniously, can attain real, lifelong happiness. They are called yogis, whose object of endeavor is moksha, the fourth and highest object of human efforts. Yogis do not consider the other three human pursuits to be worthwhile, since they cannot bring everlasting happiness and peace.

Throughout the ages, saints, yogis, and sages have been proclaiming that real and everlasting happiness can be obtained only by overcoming all human limitations, and sufferings can be overcome only through God-realization, the experience of the universal spirit that is the source of all life, powers, and bliss. They also proclaim that human beings can rise above all limitations and escape all sufferings through the practice of yoga.

Ego-personality and Limitations

Paramatma (universal spirit) is always pure, perfect, shining, spotless, eternal, indestructible, and beyond all limitations, pairs of opposites, and sufferings. A spark of this universal spirit dwells in every being as jivatma (individual spirit). As a partial expression of the universal spirit, the individual spirit is also endowed with all the qualities mentioned above. In its true nature, the individual spirit also is without sins, limitations, and sufferings, and beyond all pairs of opposites.

When the individual spirit, however, becomes embodied in material form, its consciousness is lowered and the ensuing limitations, with regard to space, time, and matter, lead it to acquire sins, and undergo sufferings. When clothed in flesh, the human being forgets the true nature of his or her inner self or spirit. The body, mind, emotions, intellect, comprehension, in fact, his or her whole nature and personality become limited. Through illusion a person considers his or her surface self or the ego to be the real self. But that "surface self" or the ego-personality, expressing itself in words and actions at the normal level of human consciousness, is bound by limitations. As a result, he or she is constantly tossed between various opposites of nature, and feels pleasure or pain, joy or grief, love or hatred, happiness or despair, etc. In the course of time, he or she deteriorates physically, mentally, intellectually, and emotionally, and finally dies, once again to be encased into a new temporal envelope. He or she will be reborn according to the karmic debt in order to atone for old sins. This cycle of reincarnation continues till he or she becomes perfect and realizes the true, indestructible, and eternal nature of his or her spirit. Only such self-realization can bring deliverance from all kinds of sufferings. The leitmotif of Indian philosophy is the human desire to rise beyond all limitations and to escape all sufferings. According to Indian sages and yogis, no knowledge is worthwhile if it does not help a human being transcend his or her limitations and obtain deliverance from sufferings. This can be achieved through the redemptive techniques of yoga.

Final Goal of Life: Yoga and Not Bhoga

We have already seen that the goal of human life and endeavo: should be the perfect manifestation of the inner self, unfolded through perfect consciousness by way of transcending all limitations. We have also seen that the individual soul can be perfected and the individual personality can rise above all limitations only by integrating the opposites of nature, breaking the barriers created by the ego or the false surface self, and realizing the difference between the ego-personality and the true self. Such development of the inner being is possible only in an upward direction through the practice of yoga, and not in a downward direction by indulging in bhoga (sense-enjoyment). Yoga is the spiritual way of life, while bhoga is the worldly way of life.

Human beings, through delusion, fall prey to the deceitful pleasures of the sense-objects. They hardly have any idea of real eternal happiness or bliss. Hence, they feel satisfied with the ordinary pleasures of sense-objects. It is just like mistaking the mirage to be water. Sense-objects are like the bait that initially appears attractive to a hungry fish but ultimately proves painful when swallowed. All the sense-enjoyments are thus illusive and create nothing but misery. They form the very basis of samsara (earthly existence) for mortal beings. Only those with spiritual inclinations wisely avoid this poison in the form of bhoga (sense-enjoyments). As they grow spiritually, through yoga, they obtain a glimpse of real, unlimited happiness or bliss. One who tastes real bliss always remains internally fully satisfied and peaceful. Subsequently, he or she never gives himself or herself to bhoga. Real happiness and eternal peace can be secured by escaping from the clutches of bhoga and being intently set in yoga.

Bhoga: Outcome of Desires

Due to tamas (ignorance), one entertains vasana (desires) and *trishna* (cravings), and pampers the senses by indulging in their objects. The desires and cravings lead to bhoga (sense-enjoyments). They are the source of discontent. When the desires and cravings are not fulfilled, the mind becomes disturbed and restless. Such a discontented mind breeds anger. All these jointly work to destroy mental peace and make happiness impossible. They destroy the very roots of knowledge, leading one to disregard truth and sink in the mud of doubts and illusion. Hence, the wise person should not entertain desires and cravings and should refrain from indulging in the senses.

Of course, when a particular desire is satisfied, one temporarily feels contented and happy. But this illusory feeling of desirelessness and happiness soon lapses into the original condition of discontent and unhappiness. Under normal circumstances, the fulfilled desire is not totally eliminated, but it runs and hides temporarily in the subconscious mind. This does not permit *santosha* (perfect contentment) and real happiness to prevail.

Yoga: Fruit of Contentment

In order to be happy one should overrule needs, desires, and grievances. One should be satisfied with whatever comes to him or her in natural course or of itself. Whether one gets comforts or discomforts, he or she should remain contented. One should not have any complaints in regard to any happening in life. Only such a contented soul is fit to attain the high state of equanimity through yoga.

Sage Patanjali says, "Supreme happiness can be gained from santosha (contentment)." (Yoga Sutras, II:42) This means that in order to be established in yoga and obtain supreme happiness, one should try to overcome thirst, hankering, and desires that are the sources of discontent. Real happiness will appear when these sources of discontent disappear. It abides in a contented and balanced state of mind, because it is to be felt as a joy from within and within and not through the gratification of desires. Perfect happiness or bliss is inherent in every soul, since it is one of the three basic aspects of atman (spirit). It can be experienced only when all kinds of desires are eliminated and the mind becomes perfectly contented and calmed through the practice of yoga.

Spiritual Life Is Worthwhile

The human soul, while in bondage, loses its direct experience of the inner *ananda* (supreme happiness or bliss) and gropes after petty, temporary pleasures in the external world. But while pursuing such ordinary pleasures, it is dragged further into unhappiness that is quite opposite to the inherent nature of atman (spirit). It is wise not to waste one's efforts and lifetime in such futile worldly pursuits in the vain hope of gaining happiness from them.

Precious human life should not be frittered away in worldly pursuits that are spiritually profitless and hence worthless. It should not be wasted in heaping up perishable goods and accumulating worldly riches that merely result in unhappiness rather than real, everlasting happiness. They bind the soul fast to samsara (mundane existence), which is slavery and not freedom. Instead of striving for the acquisition of worldly wealth, one should dedicate life to the seeking of the ananda (supreme happiness or bliss) existing within, by winning spiritual enlightenment.

Keeping this purpose in view, one should endeavor for a holy, spiritual life rather than a pleasure-seeking, worldly life that affords neither real nor permanent gains. One should not be lured by worldly wealth, comforts, name, fame, etc. Instead of exerting worldly powers one should devote life to cultivating one's own innate and hidden spiritual powers. A single lifetime spent in spiritual quest is far better than even thousands of lifetimes frittered away in worldly pursuits. It is worthwhile giving up all prospects and concerns of worldly aims and objects and dedicating life to spiritual development.

Course of Ideal Human Life

According to Indian philosophy, the ideal life-course of an individual should be divided into four stages: (i) *brahmacharyashrama,* (ii) *grhasthasrama,* (iii) *vanaprasthasrama,* and (iv) *sannyas ashrama.*

Brahmacharyashrama is studentship. During this stage one must devote himself or herself to studies or learning and observe strict *brahmacharya* (celibacy). The second, or grasthasrama, is householdership. During this phase, one has to fulfill his or her due role in worldly life as a responsible householder, enacting all types of social and professional duties. The third, or vanaprasthasrama, is retirement. During this stage, one should gradually withdraw from worldly activities and turn toward the search for spiritual enlightenment. The fourth and last, or sannyas ashrama, is renunciation. During this phase, one has to completely renounce worldly life, severing all ties with family, home, property, etc., and wholeheartedly enter the path of the spiritual quest.

This means that an individual should be involved in social roles and worldly activities only during the first half of one's life (all stages of life being equal in duration). During the latter half, he or she should devote life to the more arduous task of the inward spiritual quest.

Taking into consideration the four different stages of the lifespan it can be said that the first stage is preparatory to the second stage of a responsible adult life, while the third stage is preparatory to the fourth stage of reunciating life.

It is difficult to maintain both worldly pursuits and spiritual pursuits simultaneously. Therefore, the lifespan has to be divided equally for each kind of pursuit.

Those who cannot turn away from society and worldly ambitions, throwing off all possessions and concerns and breaking from all expectations and anxieties, should remain content by fixing only a modest goal for themselves on the spiritual path. Moksha or the wholehearted spiritual pursuit aimed at liberation is not for them.

It is meant for only those who are able to enter upon the last two stages of life, turning away from the worldly way of living. Even out of those who enter the third stage of retirement and withdrawal from the responsibilities of the family, very few reach the final phase of complete renunciation. Real sannyas (renunciation) is not just running away from normal responsibilities, nor is it a carefree lifestyle. Apart from casting away all earthly ties and material possessions, a sannyasi (renunciate) is expected to be genuinely free from all worldly desires and ambition, which is very difficult for most people. Only those who can rise above personal motives and selfishness are fit to enter the phase of sannyas ashrama, which is considered the highest way of life.

Real Road of Life

Indian philosophy suggests the total rejection of worldly wealth, power, enjoyments, social affairs, economic pursuits, and all worldly activities in order to embark wholeheartedly upon a great spiritual adventure. One has to become literally dead to time and every concern of life in order to cultivate perfect virtues in thought, speech, and action. Yet such renunciation is not the goal but only a stepping-stone for reaching perfect quiescence, experiencing divine bliss, and attaining freedom from bondage. From the point of view of Indian wisdom, the real and ultimate purpose of human life is to secure quiescence, bliss, and liberation. Indian sages have also suggested the way to reach this goal, and that is the classic path of yoga.

chapter twelve

Supreme Bliss and Worldly Joys

Brahman (ultimate reality) is unity in trinity and prakriti (nature) is trinity in unity. The trinity of Brahman includes sat (eternal existence), chit (pure, absolute consciousness), and ananda (supreme bliss). On the other hand, the trinity of prakriti includes sattva (harmony), rajas (activity), and tamas (inertia). Unlike the trinity of sat-chit-ananda that are all of equal value, the trinity of sattva-rajas-tamas possesses unequal value, being superior, intermediate, and inferior qualities respectively.

Sat-chit-ananda are not the attributes of Brahman but are mere three-fold aspects. They are not separate, but one and the same. Though they appear to be a trinity to ordinary human understanding, they constitute a unity known as Brahman. On the other hand, sattva-rajas-tamas are not one and the same but different qualities supporting each other.

Brahman, when reflected in various forms of life, is known as atman (individual spirit), which abides in the heart of all sentient beings. Atman, being part and parcel of Brahman, has the same three-fold aspects: sat-chit-ananda. When atman is reflected in different bodies, it appears to be of innumerable forms. Though it enters the bodies, it also exists beyond them. Atman is reflected more clearly with its triple aspects in pure forms and hazily in impure forms. This means that the reflection of sat-chit-ananda is prominent and clear in the pure sattvic matter of prakriti. It is less evident in rajasic matter, and quite dim in tamasic matter.

Nature and Power of Maya

When Brahman or atman is mixed up with matter, whether sattvic, rajasic, or tamasic, it becomes conditioned by maya (illusion). Avidya (ignorance or nescience), klesha (affliction), sorrows, and sufferings form the nature of maya. It is the veiling power of Brahman, hiding the real and making the unreal to appear as real. However, it is in itself neither sat (real) nor *asat* (unreal). It is existent but does not abide forever. It is unreal and yet it is not mere void or nonexistent. It can be said that maya is both real and unreal at the same time or neither real nor unreal. This sounds quite paradoxical. But maya is simply indescribable and inconceivable.

When intermingled with matter, the atman (self) forgets its essentially divine nature owing to the *avarana shakti* (veiling power) of maya. Subsequently, atman begins to identify itself falsely with forms or bodies on account of the *vikshepa shakti* (projecting power) of maya. As a result, nonexistence or nothingness begins to appear as existing and real, conditioning pure consciousness to shrink and become limited mundane consciousness. Such reflection of atman through maya makes it jivatma (embodied soul). In the same manner, when Brahman (universal spirit) is reflected in maya, it becomes Ishvara (God or supreme being). The only difference is that a jiva (soul) forgets its real nature and becomes conditioned by maya, while Ishvara remains unaffected and unconditioned. Jiva has a feeling of impermanent existence, with a limited and extroverted mundane consciousness and is attracted to ordinary sense-pleasures. Ishvara, on the other hand, being the perfect embodiment of Brahman, possesses unconditioned consciousness and enjoys sublime bliss.

Through the vikshepa shakti (projecting power) of maya, there emerges the hallucination of the world of entities, with 'I-ness' in them, and innumerable objects with different names and forms. Such hallucination is the play of Brahman who creates maya and drowns its own sparks, atman, into superficial existence, conditioned consciousness, and common pleasures. Due to such conditioning, inherently eternal and indestructible, atman begins to consider itself subject to origin and destruction.

False Identification with Ego-personality

Through the power of maya, atman begins to identify itself falsely with the body, mind, and intellect in which it is enveloped. Subsequently, it struggles for existence in whatever form or body it has obtained. Such struggle necessitates the use of mental and intellectual equipment. The oscillations of mind and exercise of intellect create desires and attractions to worldly objects and sense-pleasures. Thus the embodied soul plunges into the sea of worldly affairs. Then onward it goes on fighting innumerable battles of life, undergoing endless cycles of births and deaths. It constantly remains in search of peace and bliss, no doubt, but out of ignorance a soul goes on chasing restlessly after the enjoyments of sense-pleasures. Joys derived out of worldly objects are all fleeting and impermanent in nature. A permanent source of joy is atman itself, but it has forgotten its own true nature because of embodiment in the material form. In order to obtain everlasting joy or bliss, the individual soul must attempt to transcend its body, mind, and intellect, and know itself as eternal and indestructible atman, which is also the source of inexhaustible bliss.

An individual soul is credited with three bodies (gross, subtle, and causal bodies) and five sheaths (gross, vital, mental, intellectual, and bliss sheaths). Atman is beyond these bodies and sheaths. When these bodies and sheaths are transcended through the practice of yoga, a jiva becomes free from all limitations, realizes its true nature in the form of atman, and gains the great experience of sat-chit-ananda. There ends jiva's manifested life and identification with ego-personality, yielding place to self-realization, which enables it to merge back into the final source of all manifestations, Brahman (ultimate reality).

Impermanent Worldly Joys

As already observed, ananda (supreme bliss) is one of the three-fold aspects of Brahman (ultimate reality). All joys that are enjoyed by ordinary human beings are derived out of the objects of the world. They are fleeting in nature and pass away in the course of time. They are impermanent while ananda is permanent. It should be noted, however, that all worldly joys, whether smaller or greater, are but infinitesimally small portions of that very ananda. This latter is an inexhaustible source of all joys that human beings can enjoy through the ephemeral senses and sense-objects. Yet it is much superior to, and quite different from, the ordinary joys of mundane life.

It is true that whenever, wherever, and whatever joys one gets from material things, through the domain of the senses, are but reflections of that supreme bliss of Brahman. The mode of seeking worldly joys is different from that of seeking bliss. Joys are sought with the extroverted mind through the senses and material objects. They are more or less enjoyments of sense-pleasures. On the other hand, bliss is experienced only by withdrawing consciousness from the senses and making the mind introverted. Bliss can be found only within as a ray of atman (spirit). Those human beings who are in a state of ignorance (as is the case with most people), strive to seek petty and impermanent joys from objects and remain ever more caught in the whirlpool of joys and sorrows. But those few, upon whom wisdom dawns, deny all external enjoyments and turn their consciousness inward in order to seek perennial bliss through yogic contemplation. That is the eternal and supreme Brahmic bliss, *ananda,* which everyone should seek.

Joys of Objects

Joys derived out of material objects are said to be of three kinds: (i) *priya* (pleasure), (ii) *moda* (delight), and (iii) *pramoda* (exhilarating joy).

Even when a person feels the prospect of obtaining the desired object, he or she experiences some sort of happiness or pleasure. That is only a preliminary kind of joy and is known as priya (pleasure). When the desired object is actually acquired, a person experiences satisfaction and more happiness. In this case, the pleasure is greater than the first kind and is known as moda (delight). Having acquired the object, when one actually enjoys it, the pleasure and happiness derived from that is still more intensive. Extreme joy arising from such gratification is known as pramoda (exhilarating joy).

Infinite Bliss

But all these joys sought from material objects and sense-enjoyments are inferior in nature as compared to ananda (supreme bliss). When desires for external objects and sense-enjoyments are subdued or quieted, the mind stops being agitated. Subsequently, one renounces all such enjoyments and with a calm and peaceful mind directs his or her consciousness inward. When one's consciousness establishes contact with the higher self, through quiescence of mind, the greatest happiness and extraordinary joy are experienced in his or her being. That is ananda, infinite joy or supreme bliss.

When the mind is there, bliss is not experienced. All mental operations are conditioned and accompanied with desires. The quieter the mind, the lesser are desires and the greater is joy. A completely quiescent mind is attached to consciousness or it merges with consciousness. When the mind is not there, all modifications of chitta (individual consciousness) come to an end. Then only chit (pure consciousness) shines forth and its inseparability from sat (infinite existence) and ananda (supreme bliss) is experienced. That is the state of moksha (liberation).

Sublime Joy of God-realization

At the level of human existence a jiva (embodied soul) has limited consciousness due to the veiling of the true essence of atman, which is otherwise identical with satchidananda Brahman. Therefore, in a human being, the satchidananda aspect of atman is concealed. One experiences only a conditioned state of being, limited awareness, and diluted bliss in the form of worldly joys.

In the case of atman or Brahman, the three aspects: sat, chit, and ananda (existence, consciousness, and bliss) are not separate from each other but are integral aspects predicated by only one essence or reality. Each of these three aspects is inclusive of the other two. At the level of human existence, however, they appear to be three separate characteristics due to the veil of maya (illusion). But the identity of atman and Brahman is never forfeited.

Atman can be reunited with nondual Brahman on the dissolution of all illusory superimpositions causing phenomenal existence. But before such a reunion is realized, an aspirant, through the quest for the real entity of self, reaches at-one-ment with Ishvara (God). This supreme Lord is but a reflex of impersonal satchidananda Brahman in the form of a magnificent, personal, divine being. Ishvara possesses omniscience, omnipotence, universal sovereignty, and sublime bliss, among other virtues. An aspirant, in the course of his or her spiritual progress, attains the state of God-realization and partakes of Ishvara-like virtues. A person rises from the level of the diluted bliss of worldly joys to the level of the higher bliss of sublime joy. But this is merely an inflation of individual joy into universal joy and not the supreme bliss of Brahman. So, leaving it aside, the aspirant should press beyond that level to realize transcendental nondual Brahman, which is the ultimate reality.

Yoga Leads to Supreme Bliss

When an individual is convinced about the unreality and the transitory nature of the world and when he or she comes to appreciate (at least intellectually through discrimination) that the sense-pleasures in themselves do not have any intrinsic value, the person begins to strive for spiritual development. He or she then recognizes all the senses and sense-objects to be ephemeral and does not run after them madly with carping desires. Having recognized the cravings and the weaknesses of the mind and having developed *viveka* (discrimination) through intellectual balance, he or she tries to attune to a greater and more perfect ideal and seeks to regain the lost harmony or oneness of atman (individual spirit) with Brahman (universal spirit). A person attempts to rise from the lower, mundane plane of living to the higher, divine plane of sat-chit-ananda existence. Atman strives to realize perfection by reestablishing its oneness with Brahman.

Satchidananda Brahman is too near in theory but too far in practice. In order to realize it, one should gain pure knowledge that is not mixed up with matter or prakriti (nature). For that, one should remove the veil of maya and come out of avidya (nescience). This, in turn, can be achieved by not identifying one's self with the body, mind, and intellect, but by standing apart and viewing these aspects as a witness. This can be achieved by way of the diligent practice of yoga.

Through yoga, one can transcend the triple bodies with their five-fold sheaths and quiet the fluctuations of the mind and the oscillations of the intellect. When the mind is rendered without any thoughts and all the modifications of consciousness are halted, one achieves the transpersonal experience of Brahman. Here the atman experiences Ishvara (God) or Brahman endowed with the attributes of omniscience, omnipotence, universal sovereignty, etc. But this is still the experience of only the Brahman with saguna (attributes). The ultimate reality is the satchidananda Brahman: impersonal, anonymous, transcendental, and nirguna (attributeless) Brahman. That is known as the advaita (nondual) state of Brahman.

Such a state is experienced only when atman (individual spirit) merges fully into Brahman (universal spirit). It is a state of perfect nondual reunion in which there is no distinction between the experiencer or knower (subject), the experienced or known (object), and the experience or knowledge (the process linking the subject and the object). None of these three exist in that homogenous state of yoga (unison) between atman and Brahman.

The ananda (supreme bliss) experienced in this perfect state of nondual unison between atman and Brahman is indescribable, since the knower, knowledge, and known are indistinguishable during such an experience. It is beyond the grasp of mind and intellect and hence it is not possible to narrate the experience by means of thoughts and words. It can only be conceived to some extent through comparative statements. Ordinary pleasures or joys of earthly life are not even a shadow of this ananda (supreme bliss). Heavenly happiness derived from subtle and constant joys of paradise is also negligible as compared to this ananda. Even the sublime joy of God-realization, bestowing superlative happiness, cannot equal this supreme Brahmic bliss, of which the former is a mere reflection. Ananda experienced by way of complete unison with Brahman is the bliss par excellence. It is the most perfect experience of the absolute Brahman as the triad of sat-chit-ananda. Here, there is perfect unity even in trinity. That is the highest state of liberation.

ॐ

chapter thirteen

Modifications of Consciousness and Yoga

As we have observed in the preceding chapters, the macrocosmic essence of Brahman, and the microcosmic essence of atman are pure, undifferentiated spirit. Brahman is the source of the atman, or free soul, which is known as the jivatma when it is embodied within the microcosm.

The jivatma can at best only partially represent the original reality, because it is essentially only the reflection of the atman. A reflection of the sun can never equal in power and brilliance the sun itself. Likewise, the power and brilliance of a conditioned jivatma can never equal that of Brahman.

Through the limiting power of Brahman's maya the jivatma succumbs to avidya. It then loses awareness of its oneness with Brahman and becomes entangled in the material trappings of prakriti. Its encasement in the three layers of the microcosm creates within it a desire to live and cling to its enveloping bodies. Then, because of the ego-principle and a lack of discriminative knowledge, it takes the unreal to be real. Thus, due to its conditioned consciousness, an embodied jivatma helplessly comes into being again and again, trapped within the cycle of births and deaths.

Brahman, being pure consciousness, is not affected by prakriti. Brahman is the original source and substratum of all phenomena, and cannot be touched by phenomena in any way. It remains only a passive witness to creation. The jivatma, on the other hand, due to its limited consciousness, becomes involved with temporal existence, or samsara, and is entangled in the resulting consequences of reducing the atman to its conditioned consciousness as a jivatma which leads it to forget its own true nature.

Levels of Human Consciousness

As we now know, human consciousness can exist on four distinct levels. This spectrum of consciousness extends from the unlimited Brahman/atman state down through the causal and subtle states to the relatively extreme limitations of the waking state on the physical plane. Almost everyone is limited during their waking hours to this physical, or vishva state of consciousness that is sufficient to enable one to maintain survival and attain various material goals. For attaining knowledge of metaphysical truths, however, and experiencing the true nature of reality, one must transcend the boundary of normal consciousness and rise to higher planes of consciousness. In order to realize our inner self, we need to abolish all intermediate states of consciousness and become established in the final and highest state of super-consciousness. This objective can be achieved by means of the contemplative techniques that are a part of yoga.

Keeping this basic principle in view, sage Patanjali has defined yoga briefly but succinctly in only three Sanskrit words: *"Chitta vritti nirodha"* which literally means cessation of the modifications of consciousness. Yoga is the process of returning limited consciousness to its pure, undiluted state at the level of Brahman/atman by inhibiting or removing the vrittis, or "modifications" inherent in the three lower states of consciousness. When the limitations inherent in the physical, subtle, and causal levels of consciousness are successively transcended, consciousness returns to its original, unmodified state. The classical Indian sages, out of their own experience, have prescribed various yogic techniques for achieving this end.

Each of the three words used by Patanjali, in the above-mentioned definition of yoga have great meaning. In order to clearly grasp the definition of yoga we must first understand these terms and their relation to one another in greater detail.

What is Consciousness (Chitta)?

We have already observed that chit is one of the triple aspects of satchidananda Brahman, the ultimate reality. *Chit* means "pure consciousness" or "absolute awareness." This aspect of Brahman is known as chidatma or paramatma. When this aspect is reflected in samashti avidya (universal nescience), it is known as Ishvara or God. When reflected in vyashti avidya (individual nescience), it is known as the jivatma, or individual soul. Thus, both Ishvara and the jivatma are chidabhasa, or reflections of pure consciousness. The difference between the two is that Ishvara is the creator, dissolver, and maintainer of prakriti (creation) and thus is not bound by its effects, while the jivatma is subject to all the limitations and modifications inherent in phenomenal creation. Ishvara controls not only creation and its manifestations, but also each individual soul. Ishvara regulates the lives of all sentient beings by rewarding them for good deeds and punishing them for evil deeds.

Ishvara, as the first *adhyasa,* or reflection of pure consciousness, is without a beginning or an end. Ishvara is *anadi* (beginningless) and ananta (endless). All subsequent reflections have a beginning and an end. All the forms of phenomenal creation are transient in nature.

The reflection of pure consciousness in an individual being is known as "chitta." This is an originally unlimited atman, or free soul, covered or obscured by the veil of avidya. It is a limited, individual unit of intrinsically pure consciousness functioning within the realm of manifested nature. As we know from our reading in earlier chapters, once a free soul is limited by avidya, all of the other limiting dynamics of creation automatically manifest, trapping an earth-bound soul at the waking or physical level of consciousness, until such time as that soul resorts to the consciousness-elevating techniques of yoga.

Difference Between Consciousness and Mind

Because there is no word in the English language that corresponds to "chitta," it is often translated as "mind." While the mind is limited to the cognition of thoughts, sensations, and images, chitta has a much more comprehensive field of operation. Chitta includes the manas, or thinking mind, as well as having a host of other functions. Chitta not only thinks, but desires, feels, senses, remembers, and intuits. Chitta is thus inclusive of the mind, but the opposite is not true. Therefore, chitta is more suitably translated as "consciousness."

The mind is a purely material medium of expression. It is the product of the finer and subtler matter of prakriti (creation). Chitta, on the other hand, is pure spirit limited by its reflection by and entanglement in the finest matter of prakriti in the form of avidya (nescience). Therefore, it is neither pure consciousness nor pure matter. It is a curious combination of living consciousness of the soul and the lifeless matter of creation. Although basically living consciousness, it is affected and defiled by lifeless matter.

The mind is the medium of cognitive perception while chitta is the medium of perceptions that take place on higher planes beyond the realm of thought, logic, and sensation. Chitta is capable of direct or trans-intellectual cognition, which when filtered down to the level of physical consciousness is usually called "intuition." Because our awareness is so heavily centered around the functioning of our ego-directed logical minds, we are unable to clearly perceive or differentiate the functions of chitta and buddhi, the other two components of our inner, psycho-cognitive instruments. Preoccupied with the endless streams of words, ideas, and concepts that flow across the screens of our ego-minds, we are by nature and preference unable to penetrate the inner recesses of our psyches to experience, understand, and utilize our higher faculties of awareness. This inability to go within and explore the inner dynamics of consciousness perhaps explains the still highly undeveloped state of the science of psychology in comparison to other modern sciences.

Functioning of Consciousness

Chitta or consciousness, by itself, is quite pure and luminous; but it becomes dull and impure due to defilement by matter that limits it to the functional level of psycho-mental consciousness. A limited individual consciousness functions on the physical plane and becomes further defiled through prolonged identification with the internal and external faculties or vehicles (karanas) of the human organism. An individual takes recourse to these instruments in order that his or her senses and faculties of action under the "executive" control of the ego-mind may provide the data needed to develop his or her understanding and mastery of the phenomenal world.

On the physical plane, an individual microcosm cognizes through the working of the antahkarana, or inner instrument of cognition, consisting of consciousness, intellect, ego, and mind. When an individual identifies him or herself with "his or her" body or "his or her" emotions, it is his or her ego, or ahankara, that functions. When an individual ponders the pros and cons of any subject, but still remains undetermined about its nature, it is the mind, or manas, that functions. When he or she determines or "knows" the nature of the subject/object considered by his or her mind, it is the intellect, or buddhi, that operates. When a person tries to remember some information, linked with any subject or object stored in his or her subconscious or conscious memory, he or she is said to function through consciousness, or chitta.

When an individual interacts with the external environment, his or her antahkarana (inner instrument) operates with the aid of the bahyakarana (external instrument) consisting of the senses of perception and faculties of action. In this manner, when the inner and the outer instruments function jointly under the guidance of the ego-mind, information in the form of sense-objects can be ingested and assimilated to construct a comprehensive picture of the external environment. This is how an individual consciousness obeys the inner urgings of its inbuilt evolutionary drive to gain knowledge and experience of samsara, the realm of conditioned existence.

Because chitta functions in close collaboration with mind and intellect, it is customary to identify it with manas (mind). In order to make some distinction between the two, however, chitta is often called "mind-stuff" instead of merely "mind." But it does not make much practical difference, because when the mind-stuff becomes active and undergoes transformation or modification, it virtually assumes the form of mind. To all intents and purposes, chitta acquires the property of mind. In yogic literature, the terms "chitta" and "manas" are often used synonymously.

In the context of yoga, chitta is best described as the contemplative mind, as distinguished from manas which is essentially the perceptive/logical mind. When Patanjali defines yoga as the complete cessation of all the modifications of chitta, he is referring to the contemplative mind rather than the perceptive mind. This is because the realm of the thinking mind is transcended upon completion of the very first, primary stage of yoga sadhana, or practice. When a yogi who has begun the second stage of sadhana returns from his or her daily entry into samadhi (superconsciousness) to the waking state of consciousness, his or her thinking mind still exists, but it no longer has any real relevance to the practice of yoga.

The perceptive/logical mind can, at most, help one to obtain word-based, indirect knowledge of the spirit. But the basic ignorance of the nature of the real self is not destroyed by such knowledge. On the other hand, knowledge obtained by direct contact with the contemplative mind or chitta destroys the hindrances that prevent one from realizing one's true nature as spirit. This is why chitta, the contemplative mind, has a central role in yoga.

How Do Modifications Occur?

In its state of bondage, limited consciousness identifies itself with the various modifications or transformations it undergoes due to its involvement with the external environment. In its original, undifferentiated state as chit, or pure consciousness, there were no modifications or fluctuations because of its complete dissociation with and isolation from matter. But veiled by that first covering of avidya, consciousness became limited, subject to the effects of material phenomena.

An analogy can be used here of a clear spring into which a pebble has been thrown. The pebble has caused ripples which now mar the spring's still surface. The pebble is avidya, which has turned the once still, undifferentiated chit into the limited, oscillating consciousness of chitta. The ripples created by the pebble are the vrittis, or modifications of consciousness.

Once avidya and the other four kleshas (afflictions) set in, they cause consciousness to identify itself with the endless changing fluctuations of matter that occur at the gross, subtle, and causal levels of awareness. These fluctuations of matter are then "felt" by consciousness through a reflex action, causing it to oscillate or fluctuate in direct proportion to the degree to which it has been affected by any given material phenomenon. These oscillations of consciousness are the vrittis, or modifications of chitta.

Although the vrittis have their origin in the reactive fluctuations of chitta, or consciousness, they are for the most part generated by the functioning of the ego, mind, and intellect, the first three hierarchical derivatives of prakriti (creation). The modifications generated at the ego-mind-intellect levels of ordinary human consciousness thus constitute the vast bulk of all vrittis experienced by any individual.

Because the vrittis have their source and root in chitta that is where they must be controlled and eradicated. Due to the diffused and scattered nature of physical consciousness, the control of the vrittis of the physical level is impossible. This is why yogis take recourse to the practice of yoga which gradually enables them to enter the state of samadhi, or superconsciousness, and thus transcend the lower levels of consciousness at which the ego, mind, etc., function, to directly deal with chitta and the vrittis that arise from it. Only by elevating his or her awareness to the highest level at which chitta functions can a yogi be in a position to control or stop the modifications of consciousness.

This means that in order to reexperience pure consciousness, one must first stop all modifications of chitta. When all the fluctuations of consciousness are stilled, the vision of pure consciousness can be attained. Keeping this important principle in view, sage Patanjali aptly defines yoga as the "total cessatian of all modifications of chitta." (Yoga Sutras, I:2)

Types of Modifications of Consciousness

As an individual involves him or herself in the daily activities of life, his or her chitta acts in concert with his or her mind, ego, and intellect to experience and record all of the impressions received through the five jnanendriyas (cognitive senses). Because an individual identifies with these experiences, considering them to be real, they create corresponding modifications, or vrittis, in his or her stream of consciousness. These "chitta-vrittis," as they are called, are theoretically of infinite variety because of the innumerable ways sensory input can be perceived, biased, interpolated, etc., to create inner experience. Sage Patanjali, however, has classified all vrittis into five broad categories of (i) *pramana* (right knowledge), (ii) *viparyaya* (wrong knowledge), (iii) *vikalpa* (imagination), (iv) *nidra* (sleep), and (v) *smriti* (memory).

Pramana, or right knowledge, can be derived through direct cognition, inference, or testimony. It may involve direct contact with an object or it may not.

Viparyaya, or wrong knowledge, is taking to be real what is unreal; the misconception of an object. It is characterized by the distortions of perception produced by the five kleshas, or hindrances. Both pramana and viparyaya are cognitive states resulting from the direct contact of consciousness with external objects through the sense-organs, or by indirect contact with the same or similar objects through memories, from which conclusions can be inferred.

Vikalpa, or imagination, is the creation of fanciful mental impressions that are a mixture of reality and unreality.

Nidra, or sleep, is the temporary suspension of the flow of consciousness. Both vikalpa and nidra are perceptive states caused by the withdrawl of consciousness from the physical senses. In both cases, there is a reduction of consciousness, of course, more so in the case of nidra (sleep) than in that of vikalpa (imagination). In a withdrawn or reduced state of consciousness, images are projected inwardly upon one's mental screen from memory without any direct contact with such objects in the outer world.

The final category of vritti is memory, or smriti. A memory is the unembellished recollection of objects previously experienced. It is the combination of the impressions made by an object as it was perceived and the experience that it produced within the mind at that time. Memories themselves can also be remembered, and the memories of memories (and so on).

Each of these five general types of modification of consciousness may either be pleasurable or painful. All physical, mental, and emotional experiences create either a feeling of pleasure or of pain. If the reaction to an experience is positive, chitta is attracted to it and the modification that occurs is pleasurable. On the other hand, when the reaction to an experience is negative, chitta recoils from it and the resulting modification is painful.

In addition to this five-fold classification of chitta-vrittis, there is another way of classifying them. According to this second method, modifications of consciousness are of three general kinds, depending upon which of the three gunas (qualities) of prakriti (creation) is predominant when a vritti is generated. Vrittis are either sattvic (illuminative), rajasic (passionate), or tamasic (delusive). This three-fold classification of chitta vrittis, with the corresponding gunas is as shown below.

Shanta vrittis are predominantly sattvic and reflect the illuminative, peaceful qualities of that guna. Their arousal generates serenity and mental stability and can give rise to some or all of the following additional qualities: *oudarya* (large-heartedness), *kshama* (tolerance), vairagya (detachment), *dhairya* (patience), *rijutva* (uprightness), viveka (discrimination), *alolupatva* (dispassion), *daya* (compassion), and other virtues.

Ghora vrittis are predominantly rajasic, generating *chapalya* (restlessness), raga (attachment), *trishna* (craving for things), sneha (clinging to people), kama (passion or lust), lobha (greed), and other such inferior qualities.

Mudha vrittis are predominantly tamasic, generating *sammoha* (delusion), krodha (anger), *bhaya* (fear), *darpa* (arrogance), ajnana (ignorance), *parusya* (harshness), *pramada* (negligence), *alasya* (indolence), and such other vices.

Vrittis Reflect Evolutionary Development

Every unliberated being experiences *shanta* (sattvic), *ghora* (rajasic), and *mudha* (tamasic) modifications of consciousness that reflect underlying karmic tendencies. No being within samsara is entirely sattvic, rajasic, or tamasic, but rather possesses these qualities in varying proportions according to its relative level of evolutionary development. Even the basest and most tamasic of people experiences vrittis that are rajasic or sattvic. Likewise, even a genuinely sattvic individual will at times be subject to the arousal of modifications of consciousness that are rajasic or tamasic. The nature of the three gunas is such that they are continually fluctuating, alternately becoming dominant or latent within an individual's mind-stream according to their respective proportional strengths within that individual.

The relative proportions of these three primal qualities within an individual reflect his or her degree of evolutionary maturity. One in whom tamasic tendencies prevail, with only some rajasic and a few sattvic traits, can be considered a "young" soul. Such a soul has not yet spent many incarnations in human form, and thus retains a large proportion of the traits that enabled it to survive in its many incarnations as an animal. An "old" soul, on the other hand, is one who has spent many lifetimes in human form, developing a predominantly sattvic personality. Having spent many, many incarnations tasting of life's bittersweet pleasures and mastering all of life's conventional roles, an "old" soul becomes tired and jaded with the endless cycles of pursuing, attaining, and enjoying rajasic goals. Such an individual has now largely dropped tamasic behavioral tendencies; and while rajasic sense-pleasures still offer some temptation, they are negligible. An "old" soul is now almost exclusively attracted to the knowledge, sweetness, and serenity that derive from sattvic pursuits.

The speed at which a human being evolves through its tamasic and rajasic phases of development depends largely upon the degree to which it decides to consciously or unconsciously adopt the practice of sattvic, dharmic behavior. Dharma, as discussed in earlier chapters, is eternal religion. If even a very tamasic soul consciously adopts the practice of dharmic virtues, like mantra chanting, for example, that practice will generate a powerful flow of sattva within that individual. Having once tasted of the sweetness of sattva, that soul will strive to repeat the experience again and again. Thus its passage into the predominantly sattvic state of human life will be relatively rapid if it develops a strong taste for sattva that causes it to disdain rajasic and tamasic pleasures.

One in whom sattva has become ascendent naturally enjoys an abundance of good qualities. His or her mind is usually bright and clear, has a healthy body, and is good looking. He or she is cheerful, patient, loving; possessed of good memory and sharp intellect. People instinctively trust such an individual. When he or she speaks, people listen. But even in a sattvic individual, the indulgence in rajasic or tamasic behavior can cause a rapid erosion of the subconscious predominance of sattvic karmas from which his or her superior qualities derive. One lifetime's indulgence in sin and pleasure could require three or four subsequent lifetimes of effort to karmically offset it.

This is why the sages teach that one must eschew rajasic and tamasic temptation, which only tarnish the soul and erode positive qualities. In the Bhagavad Gita, Lord Krishna says, "The gate to hell leading the soul to ruin is three-fold: lust, anger, and greed. Therefore one should abandon these three." (XVI:21) Again, when asked by Arjuna as to what impels a man, as if by force to commit sin, Lord Krishna replies, "It is this lust, this anger, born of rajas, a mighty devourer and most sinful. Know that to be the enemy here (in this world)." (III:37)

Therefore, one desirous of evolutionary progress who wants both to improve the conditions of his or her next birth and to develop knowledge, love, and contentment should strive to make the quality of sattva ascendant in his or her nature through the practice of dharma. Mastery of dharma will give rise to the intense, wholehearted longing for liberation, and the other qualities necessary for the practice of yoga, the last great adventure within samsara, that will eventually take him or her beyond samsara itself to establish blissful oneness with his or her very own self. But to accomplish this final aim, the individual will first need to remove from his or her body, mind, and spirit all of the dross accumulated through countless births. Only when all such impurities have been removed from his or her being will he or she be able to completely still all the modifications of consciousness and enter the final state of radiant superconsciousness to which there is no end.

ॐ

chapter fourteen

Superconsciousness Through Yogic Purification

Chitta, or limited consciousness, being the subtle-most and closest element to the self, does not cease to exist as long as the experiencer standing behind it is active. Empirical experiences influence consciousness and bring about changes or modifications (vrittis) in its character, but it never ceases to exist throughout the various levels of awareness, namely the waking state, dream state, and deep-sleep state. This continuous awareness is called *chitta samvit,* which may exist not only in the three states mentioned above, but also throughout a lifetime and even eternity. It ceases to exist only in the state of samadhi (a blissful experience in which there is no duality between the subject and the object), which is beyond the three states of awareness mentioned above. In that state, chitta, or limited consciousness, is transformed into chit or pure and unlimited consciousness, or superconsciousness.

Superconsciousness can be experienced only after the identity of the self is withdrawn from the three states of ordinary consciousness of waking, dreaming, and deep sleep. At any given time, an individual normally identifies himself or herself with one or the other of these three states of consciousness, experienced externally or internally. One undergoes the experiences externally when one's consciousness is identified with the physical body or annamaya kosha. This is the waking state. When in the dream state, one undergoes experiences internally and the consciousness remains identified with the subtle body or the collection of pranamaya kosha (sheath of sensitivity), manomaya kosha, (sheath of thoughts and will) and vijnanamaya kosha (sheath of intellect). But in the deep-sleep state, consciousness remains identified with the causal body or anandamaya kosha (sheath of unique pleasure). In this state, all external as well as internal experiences are absent, but the sense of duality about the subject and object persists. It is only when these three states of consciousness connected with the triple bodies are transcended that the higher mystic experience of samadhi (blissful state) dawns and the superconscious state of real self-awareness is achieved. This is the state of *atma-sakshatkara* or self-realization. There atman (self) shines in its own light, and the world of all empirical experiences vanishes.

Need to Purify the Triple Bodies

Although the atman or self is indestructible and identical with the limitless reality of Brahman, a human being is not able to recognize this because it is hidden within the three bodies of the microcosm. As the waters of a clear spring screened by vegetation cannot be seen, sc also the human soul concealed within the three bodies cannot shine forth, and its real nature remains beyond comprehension. In order to realize the true nature of the self, we have to use these bodies or sheaths as the tools for transcending all of our limitations. When the jiva's bodies, physical, subtle, and causal are purified and perfected, they can no longer hide the luminous brilliance of the immortal self dwelling within.

Most of us recognize the existence of only the physical body, considering the other two as imaginary. This is due to lack of experience. When one transcends the gross body through near-death experiences, or yoga techniques, the subtle body becomes just as real as the physical one. Similarly, the causal body is realized when the subtle body is transcended. The main reason why the subtler bodies are not experienced by most people, is the existence of the antarayas, or hindrances. These antarayas are of three types: (i) *mala* (physical impurity), (ii) vikshepa (mental distraction and unsteadiness), and (iii) *avarana* (subtle/causal obscuration).

Mala connotes obstacles within the material body. Any physical impurity or imbalance that stands in the way of vibrant physical health is known as a mala. In the yogic scriptures there are twelve specific kinds of mala that are primarily concerned with imbalances or disorders that impede the optimal efficiency of the digestive, eliminative, circulatory, and reproductive systems. When the physical body is not pristinely pure by yogic standards, its latent impurities prevent it from withstanding the intensive neuro-physical demands of sustained yoga practice. These impurities then manifest as physical disorders and diseases, which in turn create several types of vikshepa, or mental distractions.

Vikshepas affect the psyche, especially during the purification of the subtle body and its mental instrument, the antahkarana. The vikshepas are nine in number: sickness, lack of energy, doubt, inattentiveness, laziness, pleasure-seeking, delusion, nonattainment of progress, and instability in meditation. The vikshepas cause and reinforce the outward projection of the sense-faculties, creating a distracted condition of mind which disrupts the practice of yoga.

The third and last antaraya or hindrance is avarana, usually defined as "obscuration." Both vikshepa and avarana are the functions of maya (macrocosmic illusion) or avidya (microcosmic nescience). Through vikshepa shakti, the distracting power of maya, an individual considers the unreal universe as really existent, due to the extroversion of his or her mind and senses. Vikshepa shakti binds the individual soul to its mental-emotional conditioning. Through avarana shakti, the obscuring power of maya associated with the causal body, an individual soul is veiled by or enveloped in the primal matter of prakriti, forgetting its true nature as the self. Avarana shakti thus conceals reality behind the causal veil and produces worldly illusion.

Levels of Purification: Bhuta, Sattva, and Chitta Shuddhis

Impurities in the physical body, the malas, prevent the clear experiencing of the subtle body. In the same way, on the level of the subtle body, the vikshepas obstruct the experiencing of the causal body. And the obstacle of avarana at the level of the causal body prevents the realization of the atman. One must strive to purify in turn the gross, subtle, and causal bodies by removing mala, vikshepa, and avarana, respectively. When the gross body is purified and transcended, the subtle body can be experienced clearly; and when the subtle body is purified and mastered, the causal body can be experienced.

An aspirant of yoga begins with the purification of the physical body, because in the beginning of his or her practice, consciousness is usually limited to the waking state on the material plane. The gross body is purified through the adoption of a reduced, simple diet, the practice of celibacy, and through preliminary yogic techniques, such as postures, locks, breath control, rectum control, and egoless karmas. When an aspirant of yoga learns to fully awaken his or her prana, or inner life energy, and release it from the control of the conscious ego-mind, prana itself then automatically and spontaneously moves his or her body through the various purificatory movements. During these practice sessions, after awakening and releasing prana, the aspirant then becomes a delighted but totally passive witness to the often complex and sometimes dangerous techniques and movements that spontaneously manifest without conscious volition or forethought.

This process of purifying the gross body is called *bhuta-shuddhi,* the "purification of the gross elements." As a result of bhuta-shuddhi, the aspirant gradually transcends the level of extroverted consciousness and begins to attain refined experiences of the subtle body. Subsequently, he or she proceeds to purify the subtle body in order to attain still higher experiences. For that purpose the individual allows advanced yoga techniques, such as the withdrawal and concentration of the mind, to spontaneously arise through the release of prana, his or her vital force.

Yogis have found that by releasing prana, the mind is controlled automatically. The mind can also be controlled by learning to completely suppress and consciously regulate prana. But by experience they have found it easier to control the mind indirectly through the release of prana. When prana is allowed to direct the mind, the mind is no longer attracted by desirable or repulsed by undesirable sensory phenomenon, and passes beyond the biases of attachment and aversion. It remains balanced in the awareness of its own inherent equanimity. With this mental equilibrium as a starting point, the purification of the inner psychological components of the subtle body can begin.

This process of purifying the subtle body is called *sattva-shuddhi.* Due to the agitative influence of rajas and the dulling effect of tamas, our personalities retain a negative or undesirable quality that makes the mind restless and tends to reduce our overall level of consciousness. Through the release of prana, when the dross of rajas and tamas is slowly removed, the illuminative awareness of the sattva element shines forth in its complete purity and the mind attains blissful steadiness. Extrasensory perception is developed and the powers of intellect and intuition are dramatically expanded.

When the subtle body is transcended and awareness settles in the causal body, a yogi experiences the distant and serenely blissful reflection of his or her atman, which gradually becomes clearer and closer. But like sunlight reflected in a mirror, no matter how bright or clear it becomes, it remains a reflection. The yogi must pass beyond seeing and knowing the reflection of his or her atman, and transcend the causal body, to become the atman. That is the turiya state of ultimate superconsciousness, the goal of yoga. No matter how sublime and exalted the experiences of the causal or prajna state are, they are still within the reflective realm of asmita, which creates the sense of self-consciousness; of "I see atman," compared to "I am atman."

When the pure consciousness of atman (self) becomes a limited jivatma, embodied into the elements of prakriti through the power of avidya, it loses the knowledge of its true nature and begins to identify itself as an individual entity with ego-sense. This is asmita. The moment the nescient veil of avidya falls on the pure consciousness of the self, asmita begins. Consciousness then becomes conditioned and limited, assuming itself to be a distinct entity possessing a body. Asmita or self-consciousness, and avidya, its direct cause, are weakest in the causal body and strongest in the physical body.

Asmita in the causal body is very subtle and refined. Similarly, the veil of avidya is also very thin and weak in the causal body where they both operate in their subtlest forms beyond the ego-mental thought of manas (lower mind), and eventually even beyond the translogical direct cognitions or "causal consciousness" of buddhi. The causal intellect, or buddhi, is the product or effect of avidya interacting with unmanifest prakriti. Therefore, it is unable to fully comprehend unmanifest prakriti, which is essentially beyond the matter of which buddhi itself is composed. So, unless one transcends even the realm of this intellect, one is not able to grasp the workings of asmita and avidya. For that, one must undergo the process of *chitta-shuddhi*, the purification of consciousness, and thereby attain the purely discriminative knowledge called *viveka-khyati*. This is a trans-intellectual state of consciousness in which one is able to discriminate between the real and the unreal, between spirit and matter. When viveka-khyati dawns, avidya disappears with asmita, as the causal body is transcended.

The attainment of viveka-khyati, however, is not the final step of yoga. Although viveka-khyati brings one closer to the goal, it is not the goal itself. It only imparts the discriminative knowledge of reality, but does not establish union with the pure and transcendent spiritual consciousness. There are seven levels of this discriminative knowledge, or viveka-khyati. When a yogi, through uninterrupted practice of *sabij samadhi* (superconsciousness), attains these levels by gradual transition from one to the next, he or she develops spiritual insight of an unsurpassable caliber that completely purifies his or her mental stream of consciousness. The first four levels of this knowledge can be attained only through the unstinting efforts of years or even lifetimes of practice. Until the fifth level of this knowledge is actually attained, through the mastery of para vairagya (absolute nonattachment), there is even the danger of backsliding to lower states of consciousness. But when the fifth stage is reached, the remaining two levels of knowledge are attained spontaneously without any effort or danger of relapse. When the seventh and final level of knowledge begins to unfold, a yogi is forever freed from the effects of the gunas of prakriti. This final stage of discriminative knowledge is called *kaivalya jnana*, the "knowledge of one reality." This stage of knowledge corresponds to the attainment of *nirvikalpa samadhi*, the highest and final state of ecstatic superconsciousness. Thus, kaivalya jnana is illumination, enlightenment, self-realization, liberation, the final beatitude, and perfection. An individual soul that attains kaivalya, having transcended all the bodies and the sheaths that bind it, is forever freed from limitations and suffering and becomes perpetually established in its own real nature. He or she is called jivanmukta or one liberated while alive.

At this point, if the liberated yogi so wishes, he or she can voluntarily leave his or her microcosmic sheaths and ascend to the highest heaven from which he or she need never return. Or, the yogi can remain on earth, fully liberated, and strive to reach the ultimate perfection by attaining the *divya deha,* or divine body.

In Yogatattvopanishad it is said, "Should there be desire on the part of a jivanmukta yogi to give up his own body, he will himself renounce it and seek repose in Brahman. To him there will be no rebirth. Alternatively, if he is not inclined to give up his body and prefers to retain it, he will roam about the celestial worlds becoming a celestial being possessing all psychic and supernatural powers." (I:07–1:108)

But before the yogi becomes capable of moving in various celestial worlds, he or she should transform his or her mortal body composed of five elements (earth, water, light, air, and ether) into the divya deha (divine body) that is indestructible, or capable of surviving in any atmospheric condition. In Shvetashvatar Upanishad it is said, "One who has conquered the five-fold elements, namely: earth, water, light, air, and ether through the practice of yogic meditations, attains a body purified by the fire of yoga and he is not touched by disease, old age, or death." (II:12)

By attaining a divya deha, a yogi attains the final goal of yoga, and becomes a siddha, a perfected being. The yogi can then express compassion for the sufferings of creation by joining the assembly of other siddhas who watch over the Earth, guiding and protecting with their omniscience, omnipotence, and perfect wisdom, the awakening souls striving and struggling to climb the ladder of spiritual perfection.

appendix one

This book is designed to present only the philosophy of yoga in all its aspects in an intelligible manner. Since the philosophy of yoga is based on the profound mysteries of life, it is inevitably associated with an atmosphere of obscurity. In order to gain real insight into its mysteries one should take up the path of practical yoga. Though this book is not intended to give details about the practical techniques of yoga, an attempt is made in this appendix to give in a nutshell the process of how yoga works, to help the readers who may be willing to attempt it.

At present there exists a vast amount of literature dealing with yoga techniques, and thousands of centers imparting training in the practical aspects of yoga. Different systems and techniques may confuse a student. In order to avoid creating any further confusion, we have chosen here to give an idea about the most effective process that can help an aspirant on the path of yoga. Before explaining the process of yoga, it will be useful to recapitulate, in brief, what is required on the basis of what has been discussed in the book so far.

Recapitulation

Sage Patanjali has defined yoga as "the complete inhibition of modifications of chitta, or consciousness." Some authors identify the word *chitta* with the concept of "mind" in modern psychology, but chitta carries greater import than mind, which is generally expressed through thoughts, feelings, and volition. Chitta consciousness is the basic substratum that creates an individual's mind, intellect, and ego. It is instrumental in materializing an individual's personal world through an evolutionary process.

Unlike the mind, which functions mostly in terms of reactions to its external environment, chitta consciousness has a more comprehensive field of functioning on all planes of consciousness, internal as well as external. The realm of chitta consciousness transcends the limited field of the mind. It is the modifications of chitta consciousness, not just the thoughts of the mind only, that are to be stopped in order to achieve yoga, the union of the individual self with the universal self.

The tendency of chitta consciousness is to run after sense-objects in the outer world through the mind, to react to what others do according to the mood and whim of the ego, and to build up or destroy human relationships using discrimination or indiscrimination as guided by the intellect. This tendency of chitta consciousness drags an individual into worldly life. For leading a higher spiritual life, such tendencies are to be checked, regulated, and diverted toward the inner realm of consciousness. To keep the chitta consciousness directed within the self is a must for the practice of yoga. Thus, to begin, an aspirant must develop the capacity to check the chitta consciousness and divert it within.

It is not possible for a person who is absorbed in worldly life to check the chitta consciousness all at once because he or she is under the influence of the five kleshas (afflictions). The individual has to go through kriyas (various yogic processes) that lead to the attenuation of these afflictions. Only after the afflictions vanish does an aspirant become eligible for the superconsciousness of samadhi.

The five afflictions, as we have discussed in chapter 8, are avidya (nescience or illusion), asmita ("I-am-ness"), raga (attachment), dvesha (repulsion), and abhinivesha (clinging to the body). As an aspirant's chitta consciousness is drawn inward, the afflictions get reduced and finally vanish one by one as progress is made on the spiritual path. When the last of the afflictions vanish, the chitta becomes steady without any modification, and superconsciousness dawns.

Linked with the afflictions are the different planes in which the chitta consciousness functions. Consciousness is linked with the different bodies and their corresponding sheaths. As discussed in chapter 6, the gross body is made up of the sheath sustained by food, annamaya kosha. The subtle body has three sheaths: the sheath through which the vital air functions, pranamaya kosha, the sheath through which mind functions, manomaya kosha, and the sheath through which the intellect functions vijnanamaya kosha.

The causal body is made up of a single sheath called the sheath of blissful joy, anandamaya kosha. This is the innermost sheath covering the soul. The sheaths of intellect, mind, and vital air, in progressive order, form the subtle body, which covers the causal body. The outer sheath is the physical body.

Generally, the functioning of consciousness on this gross physical plane results in kleshas (afflictions) and many other limitations. In order to reduce these afflictions and limitations, one should withdraw consciousness from the gross plane to the subtle plane and then from the subtle to the causal plane. Finally, when consciousness is withdrawn even from the causal body, an aspirant realizes the true self, the atman.

This means that the three bodies have limitations accompanied by specific afflictions. Limitations and afflictions are greatest when consciousness functions on the gross plane identified with the physical body. They are reduced as consciousness is withdrawn into the subtle body, and they are least expressed when the identification of consciousness is with the causal body. Finally, when consciousness is further withdrawn even from the causal body, it is dissociated from all the three bodies, their corresponding five sheaths, and all the five afflictions.

Since the three bodies are constituted by the twenty-four elements of prakriti (nature), it is obvious that the withdrawal of consciousness from different bodies indicates withdrawal from their respective constituents. We have discussed the sequence of evolution of prakriti into twenty-four elements in chapter 5, and the composition of the triple bodies in chapter 6.

Accordingly, when consciousness is withdrawn from the gross body, it is dissociated from the five gross elements, namely ether, air, fire, water, and earth. Subsequently, when it is withdrawn further from the subtle body, it is dissociated from the five subtle primary elements, the five cognitive faculties, the five cognitive sense-faculties, the mind, and the ego—seventeen elements in all. Finally, when consciousness is withdrawn from the causal body, it is dissociated from the buddhi intellect, the first devolute of prakriti. This automatically dissociates consciousness from prakriti itself.

Thus, when consciousness is freed from the bondage of all the elements of prakriti, it is automatically dissociated from prakriti and remains identified with the soul, or atman, only. This is the establishment of consciousness in its own true nature. Then it is no more identified with matter or modified into any other state. It remains in its pristine form. The goal of yoga—the inhibition of the modifications of chitta consciousness—is now achieved. This is the fourth state, called turiya, the state of pure consciousness, beyond the three states of waking, dream, and dreamless deep sleep, as discussed in chapter 6.

In the waking state, consciousness is identified with the physical body, which experiences the external phenomenal world. In the dream state, consciousness is identified with the subtle body, which perceives internal images based on the mental impressions gathered during the waking state. In the deep-sleep state, consciousness is identified with the causal body, which is devoid of perceptions or memories.

Pure consciousness is free from all past impressions, samskaras, and the resulting bondage of karmas as discussed in chapters 8, 9, and 10. A soul remains bound to phenomenal existence, samsara, due to these karmas. It transmigrates endlessly from one existence to another according to the karmas accumulated in each life, reaping the good or bad fruits of those karmas. Such transmigrations are carried on with the two inner bodies, the subtle and the causal, which are not formed afresh with every rebirth as is the physical one.

In order to break the cycle of transmigration, one must not only exhaust his or her entire store of karmas, but also resist the urge to commit new ones. For most, this will sound like a very difficult proposition indeed. However, yoga philosophy offers a solution to this by suggesting an indirect approach to the problem. It says that the underlying basis of all latent karmas are the five afflictions (kleshas). Therefore, one must nullify karmas by removing the afflictions.

Now the task before a yoga aspirant is clear: to attain liberation from the cycle of birth and death, one should make efforts to remove the five afflictions through the practice of yoga.

How to Begin Practice

In order to become free from the afflictions, an aspirant must transcend the three bodies and their corresponding sheaths by gradually withdrawing consciousness from the gross, subtle, and causal planes in turn. This means that one should first withdraw the extroverted consciousness of the gross body and attain introversion, or withdrawal of consciousness from pratyahara (sense-objects).

After that, consciousness should be totally withdrawn from the gross body and identified with the subtle body. When that happens, an aspirant goes through the higher and refined experiences derived from extrasensory perceptions. This stage is called dharana, the focusing of consciousness within.

Next comes dhyana (contemplation), when consciousness becomes concentrated in an uninterrupted flow toward any single concept or object. Subsequently, an aspirant should proceed to transcend the subtle body and establish consciousness in the causal body only. When that is achieved, one's consciousness dwells in a formless and merely reflective realm. This state is called *sabij samadhi* (absorption).

Finally, when the causal body is also transcended, consciousness is established in itself, revealing its true nature of the atman. This is the final stage of yoga, called *nirbij samadhi,* or total absorption, and it marks the attainment of liberation.

Before transcending the gross body, it is necessary to make it steady, which requires it to be purified. An aspirant of yoga should bear in mind one basic tenet: an impure body remains unstable, an impure mind remains restless, and an impure consciousness remains diffused and afflicted. All three must be purified to achieve steadiness. Only then can they be transcended to achieve the higher stages of yoga.

Unless the body remains comfortably steady in a particular posture, it becomes a source of disturbance in meditation. An aspirant who lacks mastery over the physical body cannot obtain control over the mind and subtle body and gain spiritual enlightenment. So the individual should first try to gain control over the physical organism by purifying it through the practice of yogic techniques such as asanas or pranayamas and the six cleansing processes, *shatkriyas.*

These techniques are not merely physical exercises for promoting health. Apart from toning up the physique, they have a remarkable impact on the functioning of the endocrine glands and the pranic currents (flow of the vital airs), which to some extent also affect the subtle body. They help in bringing about greater identification of consciousness with the subtle body. They constitute the first step in withdrawing consciousness to a deeper level, so that in the course of time and after persistent practice, an aspirant, at will, can completely forget the physical body altogether and identify consciousness with the subtle body.

At this juncture it should be pointed out that the real mastery over the body is achieved not by the willful practice of the techniques mentioned above, but by the spontaneous manifestations of those activities in a seeker's body. One does not need to make an effort of will; it happens automatically as the consciousness of the seeker shifts spontaneously from the level of the annamaya kosha (gross body) to the next immediate sheath, the pranamaya kosha (subtle energy body).

No sooner does such a shift of consciousness take place than prana takes over control of the body from the mental will, giving rise to the spontaneous manifestations of various postures, pranayamas (breathing patterns), and different processes aimed at purifying the body. This is a gradual process, but a sure one for finally breaking the connection between consciousness and the gross body.

However, it may be borne in mind that such a transfer of consciousness is not achieved by everyone without assistance. It is advisable to seek the guidance of an experienced teacher in order to avoid wasting time and effort. To a modern seeker this advice may sound meaningless or distasteful, but a genuine aspirant of yoga should not hesitate in accepting the need of a guru.

An expert guru awakens the dormant life-force of the aspirant through a special technique. From then on, yoga becomes a spontaneous practice for the aspirant, leading to the higher realms of supreme consciousness, where the soul is freed from the bondage of all bodies and corresponding afflictions. This marks the real beginning of the practice of yoga.

Once an aspirant is put on the path of spontaneous yoga by the grace of the guru, the seeker has to drop all willful efforts. The watchword should be "surrender." He or she needs to surrender completely and unconditionally to the awakened life-force within. This becomes easier through relaxation and the relinquishing of all willful efforts directed by the trio of ego, mind, and intellect.

Willful efforts keep one bound to the surface of our being, the physical body, while relaxation and surrender to prana lead to the deeper strata of our being, the subtle body, spontaneously. Relaxation and surrender to the vital force ensure gradual but automatic relinquishing of the control arising out of the ego, mind, and intellect. They give to an aspirant the experience of a different kind of existence.

What Is Prana?

The concept of prana should be understood at two levels, universal and individual. Universal or cosmic prana is the creative energy that springs from the *paramatma* (universal spirit). It remains the motionless, unmanifested, and undifferentiated energy called Brahman after the great maha pralaya (deluge) and before *sarga* (creation) begins. When vibrations are caused in it by universal will, it brings forth Brahmanda (the macrocosm).

Similarly, individual prana, or vital force, springs from the atman (individual spirit). It brings forth the microcosm, that is, the human body. Prana in the human body manifests as physical activities at the gross level, and as mental activities at the subtle level. It sets both body and mind in motion and serves as a link between the gross and subtle bodies.

Prana can be called a scientific term for the spiritual energy out of which matter evolves. The whole atmosphere of the universe is filled with this imperceptible energy. When it vibrates and manifests in accordance with universal will, it becomes visible in the form of prakriti, or matter. Prana is the highest form of matter, and matter is the lowest form of prana. It is manifested to a high degree in the causal body, to a medium degree in the subtle body, and to a low degree in the gross body.

A human is composed of spirit, mind, and body, which are nothing but the different degrees of manifestation of the same universal energy called prana. Steam, water, and ice have the same contents, but different degrees of density. As steam, water, and ice can be put to different uses, so also spirit, mind, and body have different functions.

All kinds of energy are derived from universal energy, or prana. We are familiar with energies of the atom, steam, heat, light, magnetism, gravitation, and so on. These can be related to the mahabhutas (five gross elements), the last elements manifesting out of prakriti (nature), prakriti being nothing but the visible form of prana.

Earth, water, fire, air, and ether are the five elements called mahabhutas. The source of atomic energy is the earth element; the source of steam force, the water element; of heat and light, the fire element; of electricity, the air element; and finally, it is ether that establishes the gravitational balance through magnetism, which is prana itself. Prana is the total of all energies existing in prakriti (nature). Nature is the great reservoir of prana energy. It is through the subtle energy of prana that everything in nature comes into existence and functions.

Importance of Prana in Spiritual Upliftment

The human body is the only fit vehicle for seekers who wish to tread the path of conscious spiritual evolution. The first step on this path is to recognize and understand the role of prana (vital force) in the body. When prana is regulated and properly directed, it can charge the various parts of the body like a battery, purifying and rejuvenating them. Finally, when one controls prana, *siddhis* (spiritual powers) are gained, as well as infinite peace and bliss. This is the state of liberation, the goal of yoga.

Vedanta philosophy says, "Prana is Brahman, or absolute reality." The Vedas declare, "He who knows prana, knows the Vedas." In Shiva Svarodaya, an ancient text on yoga, Lord Shiva also says, "Prana is a great friend, companion, and brother to all human beings in this world, because everything can be achieved with its help."

Truly, prana has a great friendship with the soul. When either of them leaves the body, the other immediately follows. In the Yoga Chudamani Upanishad it is said, "So long as prana is restrained in the body, the soul does not leave the body. Then there is no fear of death. Hence one should practice the regulation of prana." (Stanza 90)

In the Gheranda Samhita it is said, "By practicing the restraint of prana, a man becomes like a lesser god." (V:1)

All these statements explain the importance of prana and its regulation for achieving spiritual realization.

The Working of Prana in the Gross and Subtle Bodies

From prakriti's inexhaustible reservoir the human body draws prana for carrying out its biological functions throughout its span of life. Prana is extracted from prakriti as subtle energy. When stored in the human apparatus, it acts as the essential power source for carrying out bodily functions.

Ordinarily we derive prana from prakriti through breathing. In the gross body, breath is drawn through the nostrils and carried to the lungs, which extract oxygen from it. Oxygen is called prana vayu in Sanskrit. Prana vayu is different from the prana called the vital force. Oxygen is capable of sustaining only the gross body, while the vital force nourishes and sustains the subtle body. This vital force flows through the channels of the subtle body and can rejuvenate even the gross body, increasing its longevity.

While breathing through the nostrils one derives not only oxygen for the gross body but also vital force, or prana, which travels through the subtle body by means of subtle channels known as *ida* and pingala. These subtle channels, like the gross air passages, have their upper ends at the openings of the left and right nostrils. But they do not end up in the lungs like the respiratory system of the gross body. Instead they run down to a bulbous subtle structure, *kanda,* situated about three inches below the navel of the gross body.

There are fourteen principal channels or nadis in the subtle body. All of them converge into the subtle bulb or kanda. They branch into 72,000 smaller channels and 350,000 minute tributaries spreading all over the subtle body. However, from the point of view of yoga, only three of these nadis—the ida, pingala, and *sushumna*—are important.

Of the three major nadis, the sushumna is the most important. These subtle channels are located in the subtle body coinciding with the spinal column of the gross body. The sushumna is the middle channel, while ida and pingala are located on its left and right, respectively.

When we breathe in air though the nostrils, we also drive the vital force of prana through the ida and pingala. This prana is utilized for psychological and spiritual functions. On the other hand, the air that we breathe into the lungs gets diffused into the various parts of the body for the performance of different biological and physical functions.

The vital force drawn into the subtle channels assumes different forms, which are known as the vital airs. There are five major vital airs functioning in the subtle body, as discussed in chapter 5. They are called prana, apana, samana, vyana, and udana. It is through these vital airs that the subtle body is linked with the gross body.

The vital air prana works in the chest region making the heart throb and the lungs inhale and exhale. Since this vital air performs the most important functions, it derives its name from its source, the vital force prana.

The vital air apana is just opposite to prana in its functioning. It applies a downward pull while prana applies an upward pull. Apana is responsible for excretion, urination, and orgasm, since it works in the lower abdominal region.

The vital air samana works in the abdominal region, striking a balance between the upward-pulling prana and the downward-pulling apana. The Sanskrit word *sama* means *equal.* Samana is the equalizing vital air. It equalizes the opposite pulls of prana and apana. Its function is to fan the digestive fire in the belly and enhance metabolic activities. In the Bhagavad Gita, Lord Krishna says, "Becoming the fire of life in the bodies of living creatures by mingling and equalizing the prana with apana, I digest the four kinds of food [dry, succulent, raw, and cooked]." (XV:14)

The vital air vyana pervades the whole body and facilitates the working of the autonomic nervous system.

The vital air udana works in the throat as well as all the joints of the body. Its main function is to counteract gravity and to send all the humors of the body upward. It helps in maintaining erect posture, and also in articulation and singing.

Apart from these five major vital airs there are five minor vital airs called *naga, kurma, krikkal, devadatta,* and *dhananjaya.* They also help in performing minor functions, such as blinking of the eyes, yawning, burping, and sneezing. Of these minor vital airs, four belong to the subtle body, while dhananjaya belongs to the gross body and does not leave it even after death.

All ten vital airs help in establishing the contact between the subtle and the gross bodies and in carrying out involuntary psychophysical functions and reflex actions. So, in order to recognize the vital force prana, it becomes inevitable, first, to regulate the various vital airs; then to merge them into their original source, prana. The vital airs can be regulated by practicing a series of scientific steps of yoga, such as asanas (postures), exercises to control the pranayamas (breath), and the shatkriyas (six cleansing processes).

Willful and Spontaneous Practice of Yoga

Various yoga exercises can be practiced either willfully or spontaneously. The latter method is superior to the former, but one requires proper guidance for learning the spontaneous method. That can be available only from an experienced guru (spiritual teacher). On the other hand the willful method can be learned from a less experienced teacher or even by reading books.

It should be borne in mind that such willful practice cannot lead to the higher spiritual experiences. For that, one should adopt the spontaneous method after finding an experienced guru and learning under his or her guidance. This means that one should follow the willful method only until one finds a real guru and receives instructions about spontaneous practice.

It should be made clear, at this point, that one should not make the mistake of avoiding willful practice and thereby losing time until a real guru can be found. Willful practice of yoga exercises has its own importance. Though it cannot produce the higher spiritual experiences, it does strengthen an aspirant's prana (vital force), which plays a key role in spontaneous practice. Those who have done willful practice and strengthened their prana earlier find the spontaneous practice easier and more rewarding than those who have avoided it. Strong prana is an asset for attaining success in spontaneous practice. Willful practice is very important for beginners.

Pranopasana and *pranavidya* are Sanskrit terms used for the spontaneous practice of yoga, in which the vital force of prana plays the key role. Before beginning such spontaneous practice one should cultivate *pranaprabalya* (intensifying the vital force). The next step is *pranasfurana* (release of the vital force). The third step is *pranotthana* (the raising of the vital force) along the path of sushumna (the central subtle channel). The fourth step is *pranastambhana* (stabilization) or *pranajaya* (conquering) of the vital force in the frontal region. The fifth and final step is that of *prananirodha* (annihilation) or *pranalaya* (dissolution) of the prana.

Pranaprabalya (strong vital force) is a must for an aspirant who intends to take up the spontaneous practice of yoga. Pranadaurbalya (weak vital force) cannot take one very far on the path. In order to strengthen the vital force one should observe Brahmacharya (celibacy), eat moderately, sleep for the minimum required hours only, and practice willfully the yogic exercises mentioned earlier. When, through such willful practice, the vital force is intensified, one should lift mental control over the body through the shithilikarana (relaxation of the bodily organs and limbs). If this is done properly, the intensified vital force is released. This is pranasfurana, in which various physical movements occur spontaneously. Thus one gains entry into spontaneous practice.

It is possible to attain the release of the vital force even without guidance from an experienced teacher or guru. But if one fails to comprehend and apply the art of relaxation, shithilikarana, properly, guidance should be sought from a person who has experienced it. Often those who try to learn by themselves are not able to recognize the release of prana even though it occurs.

Sometimes the manifestations are very slow and mild and are not understood properly. In such cases guidance from an experienced person will also prove useful. The best way, however, is to learn the technique of releasing prana, pranasfurana, under the guidance of a yogi guru.

Manifestations Resulting from the Release of the Vital Force

Any of the following manifestations may spontaneously occur in an aspirant's body when the vital force is released:

- Performing various special yogic gestures with hands and fingers, *mudras.*
- Leaning forward, backward, or sideways.
- Rocking or swaying in a circular manner

from the waist, or stretching and twisting the body.

- Shaking of the body or jerking of the limbs.
- Rolling on the floor.
- Spinning around on the buttocks while in a sitting position.
- Crying or laughing.
- Emitting meaningless sounds from the mouth.
- Singing or chanting holy mantras.
- Getting up and beginning to dance.

The above list of manifestations is only illustrative and not exhaustive. In fact, countless manifestations occur as a result of the release of the vital force. Moreover, apart from the gross physical manifestations, certain subtle processes are also experienced as mentioned below.

Visualizing the inner light and various colors with closed eyes.

Visualizing various angelic or demonic forms or fierce animals through the inner vision.

Visualizing pleasant, frightful, or miraculous dreams during the relaxation caused by the release of the vital force.

All these manifestations, being of a subtle nature, are not visible to the external eyes but are perceived through the inner vision.

As a result of the release of the vital force, or prana, an aspirant experiences gross as well as subtle manifestations spontaneously. In the initial stages the gross manifestations may appear to be more interesting, but as a matter of fact, the subtle experiences are more important for attaining the higher spiritual levels.

Purpose behind Spontaneous Manifestations

Gross manifestations are related to the gross body, and the subtle experiences to the subtle body. This statement needs elaborate explanation.

Consciousness is diffused from the soul to the causal body, further to the subtle body, and finally to the gross body. It remains so diffused under the willful control of the mind. But when the vital force is released from the control of the mind, it tends to withdraw from the gross body to the subtle body, and further from the subtle body to the causal body, and finally from the causal body to its source, the soul.

Consciousness is withdrawn along with the vital force in the same order because both of them are closely linked. When one is identified with the gross body, the other also functions on the gross plane. Likewise, when one is withdrawn from the gross body, the other is also withdrawn from that plane. Similarly, when one moves, the other also becomes unstable, and when one becomes steady, the other also becomes steady. In the Hatha Yoga Pradipika it is said, "When the vital force is destabilized, consciousness becomes disturbed. By stabilizing the vital force, a yogi attains steadiness of consciousness." (II:2)

Prana is the driving force behind all the manifestations—physical, mental, and subtle. During willful activities it manifests in outward physical or. mental dynamism. During spontaneous activities resulting from its release from the control of the mind, there is a reverse process of dynamism caused by its withdrawal from the gross external sheath of the body into the subtle internal sheath.

When that happens, the reverse process of dynamism sets in, producing gross as well as subtle manifestations. At that time an aspirant can observe, as a witness, the various actions performed by his or her own body spontaneously. Similarly, on the subtle level, one can witness the mind functioning in a manner as if detached from the external sense-perceptions. It gives a sense of freedom from mental control, rendering all thoughts and sense experiences insignificant.

These spontaneous manifestations are the purificatory activities cleansing the gross body of its various impurities and causing the imaginary desires of the mind to fall off. As one progresses in this spontaneous practice, physical ailments are cured, dispassion prevails, and nonattachment grows, automatically.

Results of Spontaneous Meditation

With the release of the vital force, a continuous process of meditation starts, leading ulti mately to the real awareness of the self through the gradual transformation of an aspirant's consciousness. From that time on one should fully surrender to the released prana that knows well how to lead an aspirant forward on the path of self-realization. The released prana works steadily at gross as well as subtle levels to remove impurities and obstacles and prepares the way for awakening to the higher levels of consciousness.

It is the process of withdrawing consciousness from the physical body to the subtle body, from the subtle to the causal body, and from the causal body to its real source, the self. Aspirants should submit themselves fully to the released vital force that shapes their spiritual destiny.

Initially the vital force is withdrawn from the gross body and is focused into the subtle body. When that happens, all the physical manifestations stop and the body becomes steady. Then an aspirant is able to sit in a single posture comfortably for a long time without feeling fatigue or pain. This is called *asanajaya* or mastery over the posture.

Now an aspirant feels the flow of prana within the subtle body through the left and right subtle channels known as ida and pingala, respectively. When the flow through these channels is brought into equilibrium, it strikes at the root of the sushumna (principal subtle channel), situated in the middle.

Due to the pressure of the vital force, the kundalini, which is the serpentine energy lying dormant at the lower entrance of the sushumna, is aroused. It becomes dynamic and begins to move upward into the central channel along with the flow of the vital force. At this time a strong psychic impulse is generated and the mind becomes introverted and incapable of running outward after sense-objects. This withdrawal of the mind from sense-objects is known as pratyahara, which cuts off the external world.

As the capacity to retain prana in the sushumna is increased through continuous practice, the period of suspension of breath also increases. Finally, when the inhalation and exhalation come to a standstill, it is called ***kevala kumbhaka.*** Such mastery over the flow of the vital force results in the withdrawal of consciousness from the pranamaya kosha (sheath of the vital energy body) to the manomaya kosha (sheath of the mental body).

At this point the yoga of mind begins, and the klesha (affliction) of abhinivesha (clinging to the body) is overcome. Now the mind has the ability to confine itself to a limited range with intense focus. This focusing is called dharana. In dharana, the mind concentrates on a gross or subtle object of meditation, deeply considering all its aspects in a higher reasoning process. Note that dharana is not merely an empirical, scientific analysis conducted by the lower mind, but a spontaneous focus of consciousness and prana on the form, essences, energies, and qualities that make up the gross or subtle object focused upon.

Through dharana, tamas and rajas go on diminishing while sattva increases, revealing knowledge derived from the extrasensory perceptions of the higher mind. Sattva is always linked with knowledge. As sattva increases, the horizon of knowledge also increases and the seeker finds his or her subtle body illuminated from within. The Bhagavad Gita states, "When the light of knowledge streams forth in all gates of the body, then it may be known that Sattva has increased." (XIV:13) With this process, purification of the subtle body or sattva shuddhi, is now underway (see chapter 14).

Dharana is only the first stage of an actually inseparable three-fold process that makes up the last three arms of ashtanga yoga. With ever-increasing concentration, dharana deepens into dhyana (meditation), and dhyana deepens yet further into samadhi (absorption). We will use a story from the Mahabharata to help illustrate the distinction of each stage in this three-fold process.

Drona, the wise guru and archery master of the Pandava and Kaurava princes, was one day instructing his students. Pointing to a bird perched in a nearby tree, he asked them to assume they were going to fire an arrow into the eye of the bird. Then he asked them to tell him what they saw.

One student said he saw the sky, the tree, branches, leaves, and the bird. The next one said he saw the bird only. When Arjuna, the greatest archer in the world, was asked what he saw, he replied, "An eye."

The first student represents the normal seeing of extroverted perception. The second student, whose focus was on the bird only, represents dharana. His focus was confined to a limited area but not solely on the object; in this case, the bird's eye. Arjuna's concentration on the eye alone represents dhyana; that is, fixed focus, without distraction, on one point.

If Arjuna remained in dhyana on the eye long enough, he would eventually feel he was the eye—with no separation of knower and object known. That is samadhi. Through the spontaneous process of dharana, dhyana, and samadhi, all the elements that make up the subtle body, including the sheaths of the manomaya (mind) and vijnanamaya (intellect), are purified.

To clarify, let us trace the path of purification as it relates to the sheaths of the subtle body. When pratyahara (withdrawal of the senses) proceeds, consciousness is identified with pranamaya kosha (the sheath of the vital air). When dharana begins, contact with manomaya kosha (the sheath of the mind) is established. As dharana proceeds, rajas and tamas decrease and sattva automatically increases, purifying the mind at the same time.

As the sheath of mind is purified, raga (attachment) and dvesha (aversion) are attenuated. With the increase of sattva, contact is established with vijnanamaya kosha (the sheath of the intellect). Sattva is always accompanied by jnana (the light of knowledge). Now a higher knowledge is dawning, and thus the name for the sheath of intellect, vijnanamaya.

Also at this stage, many powers of extrasensory perception and superability have been attained. When the sheath of intellect is purified, the affliction of "I-am-ness" or asmita is attenuated, leading to the first stages of samadhi, sabij samadhi, in which there are still seeds of karmas, afflictions, and the mind. Through the experience of sabij samadhi, the causal body is purified of the three gunas, chitta consciousness, and the last remaining affliction: nescience, or illusion.

With the three bodies and all the sheaths transcended, the final, permanent state of samadhi, nirbij samadhi begins. Now the soul is established in turiya (supreme consciousness). The longer the yogi remains in nirbij samadhi, the greater the powers of omnipotence, omniscience, and omnipresence unfold. (See Patanjali's Yoga Sutras, section 3: the "Vibhuti Pada," for a more detailed description of these powers.)

Once the yogi has achieved one month of uninterrupted nirbij samadhi, there is no possibility of the return to lower states. The yogi then remains in nirbij samadhi continually for a twenty-four-year period, which culminates in the highest crowning attainment possible: the divine body (see chapter 14).

The idea of attaining a divine body sounds wonderful to everyone. Somewhere inside all of us, no matter how rational and logical the layers of our conditioning, we experience a resonance of truth whenever we come across the concept of superhumanity in the arts, literature, mythology, or spiritual texts. However much we may skeptically deny such a resonance, a knowing remains nonetheless.

Seeing the possibilities, what if one is open to the truths stated in the scriptures and is genuinely interested in beginning the practice of yoga?

The ancient classical texts stated that four *kripas* (graces) were needed for one to be truly successful in the practice of higher yoga. The first is the grace of God, *Ishvara kripa.* Our karma decides our destiny, but God decides when that destiny is dispensed. In order to receive the blessing of our favorable karma in this life, we need the grace of God.

What happens if our destiny is favorable and we have a sincere desire to practice, but cannot find the right guru, or we find a teacher who is not a true guru, or a true guru who does not choose to give the needed key? Without the grace of a *guru kripa* (true guru), success cannot be assured.

Then again, we may have the needed key through the guru's grace but cannot find the support needed. The *shastra kripa* (scriptures) are there, but we must have the ability to understand them. Thus, the grace of understanding the scriptures is necessary. Even a realized guru needs the support of scriptures to reinforce his or her teachings; as well as to guide, inspire, and quell the doubts of the disciple. Chapter II, Stanza 10, of the Yoga Kundali Upanishad states: "Even Gurus are not able to convey the real significance of this science without referring to the scriptures."

Finally, we may be blessed with all three of the above graces, but do not have the inspiration and energy to begin and sustain our practice. Without the grace of one's self (atman), the final goal cannot be reached.

For those considering embarking upon the path of higher yoga, note that while it takes a very long time to reach the final goal, there is no shortcut to liberation. One should continue on patiently, enjoying the many rewards along the way and remembering the words of Lord Krishna: "In this path, no effort is lost and no obstacle prevails; even a little of this practice saves one from the great fear." (Bhagavad Gita, II:40)

appendix two

As was stated earlier, this book is not intended to be a comprehensive, practical guide to yoga. For those sincere seekers, however, who feel moved to begin preparatory practice, the following practices are given.

Before even beginning the preliminary exercises of yoga, a seeker should build up a strong fortress of physical, moral, emotional, and mental purity. The yogic scriptures prescribe the practice of yamas and niyamas, restraints and observances, to create that fortress. The yamas and niyamas are the first two limbs of ashtanga yoga.

In general it can be said that yamas and niyamas are the basic guidelines that are the indispensable foundation of yoga. Yama means "restraint," or control applied to the behavior, attitudes, and morals of the seeker. The practice of the yamas is designed to bring about in a seeker an internalization of ethical values and self-control.

Niyama means "observance," "discipline," or "rule." The practice of niyamas is designed to reduce and remove impurities in the body and mind, thus creating physical well-being and inner peace.

Both yamas and niyamas forbid any kind of misuse of body or mind. Through their practice an aspirant cultivates unselfish behavior, health, genuine happiness, one-pointedness of mind, and strong willpower. They move an aspirant toward the goal of perfection and self-realization, the ultimate goal of yoga.

The Five Yamas, or Restraints

Ahimsa (nonviolence): ahimsa means causing no harm to any living being, including oneself, in thought, word, or deed. Nonviolence is the basis of all the other yamas and niyamas. True nonviolence is love.

Satya (truth): satya means not only abstaining from falsehood, but also seeing the inherent good in everyone. Whenever possible, practicing periods of silence will greatly support you in this yama. Try, perhaps, to be silent one morning or even one day a week. If that is not possible, create times where social interaction is minimized, in which you speak only when necessary, with truth and sweetness.

Asteya (nonstealing): asteya also means releasing the desire to possess that which belongs to another.

Aparigraha (nonpossessiveness): we all need certain possessions. Many of us, however, not only accumulate more than we need, but continually desire even further luxuries. Thus engaged, we disturb our peace of mind. The more simply we live, the more energy can be devoted to our spiritual practice.

Brahmacharya (continence, celibacy): Volumes could be said about this yama alone. Through brahmacharya in all areas of life, a seeker saves, and thus accumulates, great energy that can be channelled into his or her spiritual unfoldment. This practice is imperative for those wishing to embark upon the path of higher sadhana.

The Five Niyamas, or Observances

Shaucha (purity): an impurity is anything on the physical, mental, emotional, or spiritual level that obstructs our optimal functioning. It is our impurities that stand between us and the highest realization. All the practices of yoga are designed to remove these impurities.

Some simple examples are the various cleansing regimens of hatha yoga that help purify the physical body, and mantras that help cleanse the mind and other subtle vehicles. Again, the more work a practitioner has put into willful cleansing disciplines, the easier, swifter, and more successful is his or her spontaneous practice later on.

Santosha (contentment): santosha is the art of being happy with whatever life brings you. It is learning not to expect or desire more than what you need.

Tapas (transformative spiritual practices or austerities): we heat gold ore to burn off the dross and produce pure gold. Tapas creates the heat that purifies and strengthens our bodies and minds to make them fit vehicles for self-realization.

Svadhyaya (spiritual study): this is not study in the usual sense, but a deep contemplation, digestion, and integration of the deeper and often hidden essences contained in the yogic scriptures. It refers to an intensity of contemplation in which this deeper knowledge is revealed to the seeker from within himself or herself.

Ishvara pranidhan (dedication of all one's thoughts and actions to God): this is the practice of "not my will but thine be done, O Lord." Actual practices can include any type of devotional worship, singing of devotional songs, repetition of mantras (names of God), etc. These practices purify the heart and mind.

The above are the major yamas and niyamas given by Patanjali. Some yogic texts give other minor yamas and niyamas as well.

The Practice of Yamas and Niyamas

As stated above, the practice of yamas and niyamas creates a strong fortress of physical, mental, and emotional purity for the seeker. If this purity is not created as a foundation, many complications can manifest later to obstruct a seeker in his or her practice.

Among other occurrences, as one progresses on the path and more power is accumulated, temptations may arise that can distract a seeker from genuine sadhana, causing the loss of valuable time and energy. There are many examples in the scriptures of great yogis backsliding or abandoning their path altogether because they did not have the requisite purity to respond with equanimity to the temptations they met.

The practice of yamas and niyamas removes the major impurities in a seeker so that the seeker is not seriously obstructed or slowed down once he or she has entered spontaneous yoga discipline. Even the best seekers will fall prey to doubt and discouragement on this difficult path, but one who has attained the requisite purity will move through obstacles successfully while others may fail.

It must be said that all will benefit tremendously from the practice of yamas and niyamas, not just those who aspire to yogic practice. Those specific observances and restraints create for any man or woman a life rich with peace, contentment, integrity, and clarity.

The practice of yamas and niyamas has been likened to picking up a garland of flowers: if you pick up one flower of a garland, the rest will come with it automatically. In the same manner, if you choose just one yama or niyama to practice, you will find the others beginning to manifest in your life as well. Some simple steps for integrating the yamas and niyamas into your life follow.

Be still and pray. This will clear the mind and heart. From that consciousness, choose one yama or niyama you are moved to practice. Do not choose simply from what may seem "comfortable." For a specific period of time, perhaps one month, take time each day to contemplate deeply that yama or niyama. Pray that all its practical as well as subtle aspects be revealed to you.

Each day, consciously put into practice the one you have chosen. Be creative in finding ways to remind and inspire yourself in your practice. In your daily period of contemplation reflect on all that you have learned and realized in your practice.

It is very important to remember that as you practice you will come face to face with all the ways you do not live up to that principle. That is expected; do not be discouraged! Remember that the practice is designed to purify the heart, body, and mind, and discouragement is an inevitable part of the purification process. Keep yourself inspired though uplifting reading and sattvic (inspiring) company.

Keep a daily journal of all your experiences and the insights that come to you in both your daily contemplation as well as your practice.

After working with your chosen yama or niyama for a period of time, you may wish to go even deeper with that one or move to another. Remember that you are working with principles that take lifetimes to perfect; the yamas and niyamas only bloom into the flower of full perfection in a yogi who has attained the highest realization.

In the above as well as in all preliminary practices, surrounding yourself with good, inspiring company is very supportive. Of course, the later stages should be done in solitude and seclusion.

Creating Pranaprabalya: The Strengthening of Prana

As explained earlier, a necessary prerequisite to the higher sadhana is the strengthening of prana, or pranaprabalya, as well as purification of the subtle energy channels, or nadis. The stronger the prana and more purified the nadis, the more successful is the later spontaneous yoga practice.

To effect that strengthening and purification, the preliminary practice should include *anuloma viloma* pranayama (alternate nostril breathing) in addition to yoga postures. The following is instruction in the practice of alternate nostril breathing. This is considered a powerful exercise in creating pranaprabalya, or the strengthening of prana, as well as the purification of the nadis. The more this pranayama is done, the more prana is stored in the kanda, the bulbous subtle structure located about three inches below the navel of the gross body.

The Practice of Anuloma Viloma Pranayama

Your place of practice should be neat, clean, and quiet, with plenty of pure fresh air, if possible. Bathe first, and put on minimal clothing. In a cooler climate, wear loose-fitting clothes. It is best to practice pranayama on an empty stomach. Do not practice after taking food or milk. Success in the practice depends much upon the observance of these two restraints: *mitahar* (moderation in diet) and brahmacharya (continence).

The technique:

Begin by taking a few long, deep, relaxing breaths.

Close off your right nostril with your right thumb and inhale through the left nostril to the count of two.

Close the left nostril with the right fourth finger and hold your breath for eight counts. Both nostrils are now closed off.

Open your right nostril and exhale for four counts.

Inhale through the opened right nostril for two counts.

Close off the right nostril and hold the breath for eight counts.

Open the left nostril and exhale for four counts.

The above constitutes one round. You will note that the ratio of inhalation to holding to exhalation is 1:4:2. You may use a metronome to keep the counts in a consistent rhythm.

Gradually, through practice, your rounds should take at least two full minutes each and your number of counts will increase as well, 6:24:12 or 8:32:16, depending on the length of each count.

A one-hour session in the morning and another in the evening is recommended. Beyond that, it is suggested you practice under the guidance of an experienced teacher. (Note: If you are a beginner with a history of high blood pressure, heart disease, or stroke, see a physician before beginning any practice that involves holding the breath.)

Most important in creating pranaprabalya is the holding part of the pranayama. The longer the holding time, the more prana is stored in the kanda. This powerful strengthening of prana and purification of the nadis greatly contributes to a seeker's fitness for effective spontaneous yoga sadhana.

Beginning Spontaneous Yoga Practice

Once a seeker has created a strong fortress of physical, mental, and emotional purity through sincere practice of the yamas and niyamas, and has attained sufficiently strong prana and purification of the nadis through the willful disciplines of hatha yoga and pranayama, he or she may enter the path of spontaneous yoga. It is not recommended that one begin this meditation until many years of dedicated willful practice have been completed.

This yoga technique involves relaxing and allowing prana to become activated. The activated prana will then generate spontaneous manifestations of asanas, pranayama, and other kriyas (cleansing processes) in the body. This is the intermediate stage of sadhana. Ideally, the prana is initially activated by an experienced guru through a method of energy transference called *shaktipat.* If a seeker, however, has practiced the preliminary disciplines described above, prana may be activated without a guru.

Guidance for Spontaneous Yoga Practice

Environment: A secluded, quiet room or cabin dedicated and used for sadhana alone is ideal. Make it a sacred place that will take on a powerful holiness as you deepen in your practice. Use candles, incense, and divine images as you wish to further create an atmosphere conducive to practice.

Above all, attitude is your best environment. Genuine enthusiasm will help you overcome any shortcomings in your place of practice.

Schedule: Ideally this sadhana is for a seeker who can retire from worldly duties and make it his or her main activity. In that case the seeker would meditate in three sittings per day—early morning, noon, and evening—starting with one to one and one-half hour sittings and adding half an hour to each sitting every two weeks. When a seeker has worked up to three sittings of three hours each, he or she would no longer increase the length of time of the sittings, but would spend the rest of the time in scriptural study and other spiritual pursuits. In actuality, each seeker will find the schedule, personal rhythm, and length of sitting that suits him or her best.

The seeker's energy should be engaged while sitting in sadhana. If sittings are so long that the focus is regularly lost, it is better to tailor the length of time accordingly. This is one area in which guidance from an experienced practitioner-teacher is most valuable.

While the meditation itself is spontaneous, it is most important that regular beginning and ending times are conscientiously and consistently kept. That creates the strong riverbanks in which your sadhana can steadily progress.

Seekers still involved in worldly duties should have at least one hour to one and one-half hour sittings once or twice a day. They should keep a consistent schedule that fits in with their lifestyle.

Preparation: One should be in good health, the more physically fit the better. Ideally one should be eating a light, highly digestible, vegetarian diet. Before sittings the stomach should be empty. The whole point of the meditation is for the activated prana to do its purification work. If it is involved in digestion it is less available to do that. Overeating will create sluggishness and boredom. In addition, one should always bathe before meditation.

Instructions: One should sit on a thick, firm, padded mat, about the size of a small bed. One should choose a position that can be held comfortably for the duration of the sitting. One should then begin with a prayer to God or one's guru.

A traditional Sanskrit prayer is:

Asatoma sadagamaya
Tamasoma jyotir gamaya
Mrityorma amritam gamaya.

(O Lord) Lead me from the unreal
to the real,
Lead me from darkness to light,
Lead me from death to immortality.

Any prayer that awakens your devotion, faith, and inspiration may be chosen.

In the beginning, sit for the full time with your eyes closed to cut down on distractions. If the years of willful practice have been done, the body and mind will be disciplined and purified enough to sit without too much restlessness. Sit with the spine comfortably erect.

Start with twenty long, deep, slow breaths, filling and emptying the lungs completely. Focus the mind by counting each breath. This counting can be combined with a short mantra, such as "aum" on the inhalation and "one" on the exhalation. Continue with "Aum-two, Aum-three," etc. The slowness is important. This breathing exercise will help release tensions in and stabilize the body and mind.

Sitting with the body relaxed and comfortably upright, consciously withdraw the control of the mind over prana. From that point on there is an allowing of the activated energy of prana to have full sway for the entire session. As explained in appendix I, different manifestations—postures, pranayamas, kriyas (cleansing actions)—will occur. Allow them to happen.

Let the mind simply observe as a passive witness, and it will become increasingly introverted or absorbed inward. If the activated prana changes the posture while you are sitting, allow that and witness it. Do not change the posture through an act of will, however.

In this way, the body is consciously relaxed and given up to the protection and purification of prana. In the beginning it is an art to relax constantly the hold of the will over prana.

Do not come out of the meditation quickly, but gradually allow the mind to once again become extroverted.

At the end of each session it is good to sing devotional songs or chants.

It is valuable to keep a daily journal of what is experienced in meditation. These experiences should not be shared with anyone except one's guru or a fellow practitioner. To share with someone who is not practicing and does not understand may be a distraction. Experiences should be shared with a qualified person for the purposes of guidance and the clearing of doubts and confusion. Be aware of sharing to build up self-importance.

While it is possible to do this practice without a teacher, there are certain stages at which a seeker may fumble. At those times guidance from an experienced teacher is invaluable.

One must trust in God and pray that the guidance needed, whether in the form of one's inner wisdom or an external teacher, will always be forthcoming.

glossary

Abhinivesha: Survival instinct; desire to perpetuate existence of one's physical body as well as one's ego identity; the fifth klesha (affliction). Unethical or immoral action that incurs negative karmic debt.

Adharma: Contrary to the principles of dharma (eternal religion).

Adhibhautika: Suffering caused by earthly means, either by one's self (accidents, etc.) or by others (robberies, assaults, etc.).

Adhikarana: Topic, heading; the mode by which topics are addressed in the mimamsa system.

Adhyatmika: Suffering created internally, either consciously or unconsciously to produce stress, disease, etc.

Advaita: Nondual, beyond duality; a description of the nature of Brahman; one of the central tenets of vedantic philosophy.

Agni: Fire; God of fire; macrocosmic force underlying the phenomenon of fire.

Ahankara: Ego; "executive" controller of the antahkarana (internal instrument) that operates within the conditioned parameters represented by the five kleshas (afflictions).

Akarma: Inaction; karma (action) performed by a yogi who has attained liberation and whose ego-mind has been forever transcended.

Akasha: Ether; one of the five mahabhutas (gross generic elements).

Ananda: Supreme bliss; substratum of all happiness and joy; an inseparable aspect of satchidananda Brahman, the ultimate reality.

Anandamaya kosha: Sheath of bliss; first sheath or covering of the atman (individual soul) in vedantic metaphysics; causal body.

Annamaya kosha: Sheath of food; fifth sheath of the atman (individual soul) in vedantic metaphysics, so called because it is sustained by food; physical body.

Antahkarana: Internal instrument of cognition composed of chitta (consciousness), buddhi (intellect), ahankara (ego), and manas (mind); the core of an individual's personality, the psyche.

Antarayas: Obstacles to elevation of consciousness existing at the physical, subtle, and causal states of consciousness as mala, vikshepa, and avarana, respectively.

Antarendriya: Internal sense faculty; property of the lower manas (mind) when used as a receptacle for memories, dream images, and imagination.

Anubhava: Actual process of attaining and experiencing an object of desire.

Apa: Water; one of the five mahabhutas (gross generic elements).

Apana: One of the five pranic energies radiated by the soul, centered in the lower abdomen.

Arjuna: Warrior disciple of Lord Krishna to whom the Bhagavad Gita was expounded by the latter on the battlefield of Kurukshetra in the epic Mahabharata.

Artha: Pursuit of wealth, livelihood, and material abundance; one of the four modes of motivation and activity of beings in samsara (conditioned existence).

Asana: Yogic posture(s) that occur spontaneously during the practice of yoga, or that are performed willfully in the practice of dharma (integral religion); third limb of ashtanga yoga.

Asatkaryavada: Theory of creation propounded by sankhya, yoga, and vedanta philosophies, such that there is no latent existence of an effect in its cause.

Ashtanga yoga: Eight-limbed yoga; the classical form of Yoga, codified by sage Patanjali in his Yoga Sutras, from which all later Indian spiritual systems fully or partly derive.

Asmita: Principle of egoism; artificial self-sense composed of tendencies acquired in many births that confuses itself with the atman (individual soul); second of the five kleshas (afflictions).

Atman: Soul, self, spirit; the divine, animating principle that dwells within every living being, and is imperceivable, inconceivable, and beyond time and space; humankind's divine essence which is part of and identical to Brahman.

Atmasamyama yoga: The yoga of self-control; yoga propounded in mimamsa and early vedantic texts that define yoga in terms of Vedic yajna ceremonies and rituals; obscuration, veil, covering; the final obstacle in yoga practice.

Aum (a-u-m): The pranava mantra, which as a whole represents the integral totality of Brahman, and in part represents the padas (three lower states) of Brahman.

Avarana: That which obscures the atman at the prajna (causal) level of consciousness.

Avatara: Willful incarnation of God (Ishvara) in human form for the purpose of renewing humankind's spiritual knowledge. Lord Krishna was an avatara.

Avidya: Primal nescience at the individual, microcosmic level, which causes the soul's embodiment in matter.

Avyakta: Unmanifest; specifically, prakriti (nature) in its unmanifest state in which its three gunas (qualities) are in perfect equilibrium.

Ayuh: Lifespan; predetermined length of life as determined by one's past karmas.

Ayurveda: Ancient Indian medical science derived from yoga.

Bahyakarana: External instrument of action and perception composed of the five karmendriyas (faculties of action) and the five jnanendriyas (cognitive sense-faculties).

Bahyendriyas: The five karmendriyas (faculties of action) and the five jnanendriyas (cognitive sense-faculties) that function outwardly, as distinct from the manas (mind), a sense-faculty that functions inwardly.

Bhagavad Gita: The "Song of God"; part of the ancient Mahabharata epic in which Lord Krishna teaches yoga to his friend and disciple, Arjuna, on the battlefield of Kurukshetra approximately 5,100 years ago.

Bhoga: Enjoyment; specifically, enjoyment of sense-oriented emotional, physical, and/or mental pleasures; the first of the two reasons for being of an embodied soul, which, when it has had enough of bhoga, takes to yoga.

Bhokta: Aspect of personality that experiences and enjoys through the medium of the five jnanendriyas (cognitive sense-faculties).

Bhuta-shuddhi: Initial stage of yoga practice in which the physical body is purified, allowing awareness to ascend beyond the waking state of consciousness.

Brahma: Aspect of God (Ishvara) as the creator of the universe; one of the sacred trinity of Hindu Gods.

Brahmacharya: Celibacy, continence; an essential prerequisite for yoga practice; first or student phase of an ideal human life.

Brahman: Ultimate reality; the supreme essence from which all creation derives; changeless, eternal, infinite, all-pervading, and all-inclusive, the transcendent substratum of the changing material world.

Brahmana: Priestly caste or class of ancient India.

Brahmanas: Series of commentaries to the Vedas compiled by philosophers in the first millennium B.C.

Brahmanda: Macrocosmic existence; cosmos.

Buddhi: Causal intellect; first hierarchical derivative of prakriti (nature) and an integral component of the antahkarana (inner instrument).

Chidabhasa: Macrocosmic reflection of the pure consciousness of Brahman as maya (illusion).

Chit: Pure consciousness inherent in atman/ Brahman; omniscient consciousness.

Chitta: Chit (pure consciousness) that has become a limited individual consciousness through its reflection in or obscuration by avidya (nescience).

Chitta-shuddhi: Final phase of yoga sadhana in which a yogi's chitta (individual consciousness) is purified, enabling him or her to transcend the prajna (knower) state.

Daiva: Fate, destiny; one of the three macrocosmic determinative forces that represents the functioning of the law of karma.

Desha: Space in a macrocosmic, transcendental (i.e., theory of relativity) context.

Devas: Lesser gods; literally, "bright beings"; angelic beings dwelling in the astral and causal realms due to positive karmas accrued during a former earthly incarnation.

Dharana: Concentration; fixation of the mind on one point; sixth limb of ashtanga yoga.

Dharma: Integral or eternal religion; the generic heart of all religions as expressed through ethical and moral behavior. Also includes willful, spiritual practices such as prayer, energy control, exercises, willful practice of asanas and pranayama, fasting, chanting mantras, generosity, alms giving, proper diet, study of scriptures, etc., all of which have the effect of generating the quality of the sattva guna within an individual; pursuit of sattva or sattvic happiness; the third mode of motivation and activity of any and all beings within samsara (conditioned existence).

Dhatus: In ayurvedic medical science, the seven or ten essential substances of the physical body.

Dhyana: Meditation; extended practice of dharana (concentration); seventh limb of ashtanga yoga.

Divya Deha: Divine body; final fruit of yoga attainable by those yogis who have already attained moksha (liberation).

Dravya: Substance; nine essential ingredients of creation in the vaisheshika philosophical system.

Dvandva: Pairs of opposites inherent in duality; heat vs. cold, pleasure vs. pain, etc.

Dvesha: Aversion; the sequential repulsion, antipathy, dislike felt toward any object that causes pain. Dvesha finds expression mainly through the ahankara ego; the fourth of the five kleshas (afflictions).

Gandha: Smell, odor; one of the five tanmatras (subtle primary elements).

Gunas: The three eternally changing constituent aspects of prakriti (nature), namely sattva, rajas, and tamas.

Guru: Preceptor, teacher; an experienced yogi capable of guiding aspirants on the path of yoga.

Hiranyagarbha: Macrocosmic form of God at the subtle, ethereal level; the aggregate of all subtle bodies within creation.

Hitanadis: Extremely small nadis (energy channels) in the subtle body that transmit subtle karmic substance to the causal, unconscious mind.

Indriyas: The ten faculties of sensation and action.

Ishvara: The first willfully assumed dilution of Brahman at the causal level; God (Ishvara) is Brahman in its form as creator, maintainer, and dissolver of manifest creation.

Jagatkarana: Great cause of creation; that is, God (Ishvara).

Jati: Life-state; the predetermined social, economic, cultural, genetic conditions or circumstances of each lifetime as determined by one's past karma.

Jiva/jivatma: Conditioned, bound soul; an atman conditioned by nescience and embodied in the resultant hierarchical derivatives of prakriti.

Jivanmukta: Liberated soul; yogi who has attained moksha (liberation).

Jnana: Knowledge; specifically, knowledge of the self.

Jnanendriyas: The five cognitive sense-faculties of hearing, sight, smell, taste, and touch.

Kaivalya: Liberation; state of complete isolation from matter; synonymous with moksha.

Kala: Cosmic time; time within a transcendental, relativistic context.

Kali yuga: Iron age; the current aeon or age.

Kama: Lust, desire for sensual enjoyment; the first of four modes of motivation and activity of all beings within samsara (conditioned existence) that finds its ideal expression in a committed, married relationship.

Karana sharira: Causal body; first material covering of the atman, caused by nescience.

Karma: Law of cause and effect operating on the metaphysical level, such that each and every action produces (in time and space) an equal and opposite reaction. Its modus operandi is the doctrine of rebirth.

Karma yoga: yoga of action or selfless service; the practice of pranic nishkama (desireless) karmas, that eventually culminates in liberation from all past karmas.

Karmendriyas: Five faculties of action, namely grasping, moving, speaking, reproduction, and excretion.

Karta: Doer, one who acts; the aspect of personality represented by the antahkarana (internal instrument) functioning through the five karmendriyas (faculties of action).

Kartavya karma: Karmas that produce positive effects and that help uphold social and moral order.

Kleshas: The five afflictions, namely, avidya (nescience), asmita (egoism), raga (attachment), dvesha (aversion), and abhinivesha (survival instinct). The afflictions serve as the substratum and five major categories for all karmas.

Koshas: The five sheaths of the body.

Krishna: Avatara of Lord Vishnu who taught yoga to Arjuna in the Bhagavad Gita.

Kriyas: Purificatory actions; actions one performs commensurate with influence exerted by one's ripening karmas.

Lila: Divine play of God; the harmonious yet inconceivable vast functioning of the macrocosmic determinative forces.

Lokas: Worlds, realms; the fourteen causal, astral, mundane, and demonic realms within samsara (conditioned existence), of which the Earth is one.

Mahabharata: Ancient epic depicting the dynastic struggles in India during the beginning of the fifth millennium B.C. The celebrated Bhagavad Gita makes up a part of it.

Mahabhutas: Gross generic elements; in their quintuplified form as ether, air, fire, water, and earth, these make up the physical, empirical universe.

Maha pralaya: Great dissolution; molecular dissolution of manifest creation that occurs upon the death of every Brahma.

Mahayuga: Complete cycle of yugas (four aeons), beginning with satya, then treta, dvapara, and finally kali yuga.

Mahesha/Maheshvara: God (Ishvara) as the destroyer or dissolver; synonymous with Shiva.

Mala: Physical impurity; one of the three antarayas (obstacles) to the elevation of consciousness.

Manas: Lower mind; the linear, logical, "thinking" mind; an integral component of the antahkarana (internal instrument).

Manomaya kosha: Sheath of the mind; third sheath of microcosm in vedantic metaphysics.

Mantra: Syllable, word, or sentence containing inherent mystical power.

Manu: First man of creation.

Maya: Illusory power of Brahman wielded in its form that has attributes by God (Ishvara) to cause the unfoldment of prakriti. At the microcosmic level, illusion is known as avidya (nescience).

Mimamsa: Classical Indian philosophical system founded by sage Jaimini. It is a polytheistic system that largely deals with Vedic sacrifice (yajna ceremonies).

Moksha: Liberation; indicates attainment by a yogi of turiya, the atman/Brahman level of consciousness, synonymous with the final, permanent state of ecstatic, omniscient nirbij or nirvikalpa samadhi (superconsciousness).

Mumukshutva: Total longing for liberation; one of the prerequisites for the practice of yoga.

Nadis: Energy channels of the subtle body.

Nidra: Sleep; one of the five modifications of vrittis (consciousness).

Nirbij samadhi: Final form of samadhi in which the mind forever dissolves, producing a permanent state of ecstatic, omniscient superconsciousness.

Nirguna Brahman: Brahman in its form devoid of aspects; the highest form of Brahman, which is beyond being or becoming and which is experienced in the turiya state of consciousness.

Nirvikalpa samadhi: Synonymous with nirbij samadhi.

Nishiddha Karma: Unethical or immoral actions.

Nishkama Karma: Desireless karma; karmas not performed by the ego-mind, but spontaneously by the life-force (prana).

Niyama: Observances; rules delineating conduct to observe, specifically, contentment, inner and outer purification, austerity, study of scriptures, and surrender to God; the second limb of Ashtanga Yoga.

Nyaya: Logic; classical philosophical system founded by sage Gautama which primarily uses logical inference as a means of obtaining knowledge.

Padarthas: Categories; the categories of classification used in vaisheshika to analyze and so gain knowledge of an object.

Padas: Four states of being of God as both Brahmanda (macrocosm) and individual pindandas (microcosms), namely Brahman/atman, Ishvara/prajna, hiranyagarbha/taijas, and virat/vishva.

Para vairagya: Highest form of detachment or nonattachment gained in advanced sadhana yoga practice; enables attainment of the highest form of viveka-khyati (supreme knowledge).

Paramanus: Smallest subatomic particles of matter that combine to form the empirical universe.

Parinamavada: Theory of creation, upheld by sankhya and yoga philosophies, that views creation as consisting only of the different forms of prakriti.

Patanjali: Founder sage of yoga system; author of Yoga Sutras; also reputed author of ancient texts on Sanskrit grammar and Ayurvedic medicine; lived around the first century B.C.

Pindanda: Microcosmic existence; an atman covered in its enveloping material sheaths.

Prajna: The "knower"; third microcosmic state of consciousness, wherein a yogi through absorption in the lower stages of samadhi sees and knows the atman, but has not yet realized that he or she is the atman.

Prakriti: Nature, creation; negative primal principle that unfolds into twenty-three hierarchical metaphysical and physical categories when catalyzed by purusha (the positive animating principle).

Pralaya: Deluge; cosmogonic process occurring every 4.32 billion years in which all life on Earth is destroyed.

Prana: Vital air, life-force; subtle life energy existing both macrocosmically and microcosmically. In a human being, prana is the generic life-force, which is divided into five major, specific energies, one of which is also called prana; life energy centered in the chest region; energy radiations of the atman.

Pranamaya Kosha: Sheath of pranas (vital airs); fourth sheath of human microcosm in Vedantic metaphysics.

Pranava: The aum mantra.

Pranayama: Breath control; fourth limb (Anga) of classical ashtanga, or eight-limbed, yoga.

Pratyahara: Sense withdrawal; fifth limb of ashtanga yoga.

Purusha: Soul, self, spirit; term used in sankhya philosophy to indicate the divine, animating principle in all creatures; essentially synonymous with atman; positive primal principle which has a catalytic effect on prakriti.

Raga: Attachment to pleasure; third of the five kleshas (afflictions), raga primarily finds expression through rajasic impulses of the ego.

Rajas: Quality prakriti that indicates restlessness, passion, activity, etc.

Rasa: Chyle; digested food that forms the building blocks of the physical body when metabolically utilized.

Rupa: Form, shape, color; objects in the phenomenal world that possess form, shape, color; one of the five tanmatras (subtle primary elements).

Sabij samadhi: Generic term for the lower stages of samadhi in which the "seeds" of the karmas, kleshas (afflictions), and mind still exist; "samadhi with seed."

Sadhana: Yogic practice, beginning with prana sadhana, continuing with the stages of sabij samadhi, and culminating in moksha (liberation).

Saguna Brahman: Brahman with attributes in its God (Ishvara) form that is willfully assumed for the purpose of creating, maintaining, and dissolving the universe.

Samadhi: State of total introversion; superconsciousness attained through yogic practice.

Samana: Pranic energy centered in the mid-abdominal region. It is primarily concerned with the digestion of food.

Samsara: Conditioned existence; wheel or cycle of births and deaths that ends only with moksha (liberation).

Samskara: Subconscious memory or impression that is created whenever a karma is performed; samskaras remain latent until triggered by circumstances into releasing a subtle desire or motivational impulse into the mindstream.

Samyavastha: Prakriti with its three gunas in equilibrium; unmanifest prakriti.

Sanatana dharma: Eternal religion; religion specifically derived from Yoga.

Sanjna: Deeper personality structure; the general tone of an individual's conscious/subconscious personality as determined by past karmas.

Sankhya: Classical system of Indian philosophy founded by sage Kapila. Sankhya is primarily concerned with the knowledge of the tattva categories of prakriti and the purusha (soul); such knowledge is normally attained through the practice of yoga.

Sannyasa: Renunciation of worldly life to become a mendicant yogi; last phase of an ideal human life.

Santosh: Supreme contentment; happiness derived from giving up all desire for things to be a certain way.

Sat: Ultimate truth; one of the three inherent aspects of atman/Brahman.

Sat-chit-ananda: Truth-consciousness-bliss; the three indivisible aspects of atman/ Brahman.

Satkaryavada: Theory of creation maintained by vaisheshika and nyaya philosophies, such that creation existed potentially in its cause prior to its actual manifestation.

Sattva: Quality of prakriti signifying serenity, illumination, insight, stability, etc.

Sattva shuddhi: Second of three phases of total purification inherent in yoga practice, whereby the subtle body is purged of rajas and tamas, leaving only sattva.

Shabda: Sound; God as sound; one of the five tanmatras (subtle primary elements).

Shad darshana: Six systems of classical Indian philosophy, namely sankhya, yoga, vedanta, mimamsa, vaisheshika, and nyaya.

Shakti: Power; energy; specifically, the energy of maya (illusion).

Shatsampatti: "Garland of six precious virtues," namely shama (dispassion), dama (self-restraint), uparati (detachment from the world), titiksha (endurance), shraddha (perfect faith), and samadhana (mental-emotional composure); the set of six prerequisites to yoga practice in the vedanta system.

Shishya: Disciple; one who practices yoga under the guidance of a guru.

Shiva: God (Ishvara) in form as the universal destroyer or dissolver; one of the sacred trinity of Hindu gods.

Siddha: Perfected being; liberated yogi who has attained the divine body in addition to all the major and minor psychic powers.

Smriti: Memory, remembrance; one of the five types of vritti (modification of consciousness).

Sukshma sharira: Subtle body.

Taijas: "The luminous one"; the second microcosmic state of consciousness corresponding to the subtle body.

Tamas: Inferior-most quality of prakriti, indicating dullness, stupidity, inertia, static resistance, etc.

Tanmatras: Subtle primary elements; subatomic particles in their potential form.

Tattva: Category; the categories of spirit and matter defined and discussed in the sankhya, yoga, and vedanta systems of philosophy especially.

Turiya: The fourth state, beyond the states of waking, dream, and dreamless sleep; corresponds to the atman/Brahman level of consciousness.

Udana: One of the five major life energies. Udana is centered in the throat and head region.

Upadana: Stage of the karma-samskara cycle where an individual mentally conceives a way to attain the object of desire.

Upanishads: Series of nearly two hundred texts composed between 800 and 500 B.C. that address the principal tattva categories in a nondual context.

Vairagya: Nonattachment; detachment especially towards external pleasures, goals, etc.; a prerequisite to yoga practice.

Vaisheshika: System of classical Indian philosophy founded by sage Kanada. Like the nyaya system, vaisheshika places special emphasis on inferential logic as a means of attaining knowledge.

Vanaprastha: Period of gradual withdrawal from worldly activities; retirement; third phase of an ideal human life immediately preceding the sannyasa (renunciation) phase.

Vasanas: Volitionally empowered desires; desires that have acquired motivational momentum.

Vedanta: System of classical Indian philosophy founded by sage Vyasa and based almost entirely upon the nondual philosophy of the Upanishads.

Vedas: Series of four books containing mystical hymns, prayers, and mantras.
Composed in the fifth millenium B.C., they assumed written form by 1200 B.C.

Vidya: Knowledge; specifically, knowledge of Brahman.

Vijnanamaya kosha: Sheath of causal intellect; the causal body in a Vedantic context.

Vikalpa: Imagination; third type of modification of consciousness in which memory and unreality combine to produce images, concepts, etc.

Vikshepa: Distraction; second of the three obstacles to the elevation of consciousness; Vikshepa reflects the mental and emotional distractions that can disrupt yoga practice.

Viparyaya: Wrong knowledge; misperception or misunderstanding of an object or concept, whether directly or inferentially perceived.

Virat: First state of Brahman in the form of the empirical universe; the universal physical form of God.

Vishaya: Sense-object.

Vishesha: Distinguishing or differentiating characteristic of an object.

Vishnu: God (Ishvara) as the preserver of creation; one of the sacred trinity of Hindu gods.

Vishva: First microcosmic state of consciousness; waking, physical consciousness.

Vivartavada: Theory of creation espoused in the vedanta philosophical system, such that creation is only an illusory manifestation caused by maya (Brahman's illusion).

Viveka: Discrimination; ability to differentiate between pairs of opposites; prerequisite for yoga practice.

Viveka khyati: Highest form of supreme knowledge that enables a yogi to enter the turiya state and know himself or herself as atman/Brahman.

Vritti: Modification or oscillation of chitta consciousness. Vrittis are of theoretically unlimited variety, but are classified in five major categories.

Vyana: Pranic energy that pervades the entire body and is associated with the nervous system.

Yajnas: Vedic sacrificial ceremonies that make use of subtle but elementary yogic processes to allow the performer to harness macrocosmic forces or amass positive karmas for the purpose of attaining heaven after death.

Yama: Abstinences; rules delineating conduct to abstain from, specifically, violence, lying, stealing, indulgence in sense-pleasures, and attachment to possessions or relationships; the first limb of ashtanga yoga. Also God of death, Yama has the responsibility of assessing the karma of all souls that have entered the after-death intermediate state, to determine the conditions, etc., of their next birth.

Yoga Sutras: Text written by sage Patanjali codifying the science of yoga in a remarkable series of terse aphorisms.

Yuga: Aeon, age; there are four successive yugas: satya, treta, dvapara, and finally kali yuga. Each yuga is of different duration.

index